Eyes of a Typhoon

From Regional Conflicts to Global Security Crisis

JAYSON PARK

JAYSON PARK

Eyes of a Typhoon

From regional conflict to global security crisis

To. JUNE and JIYEON

"Mankind must put an end to war or

War will put an end to mankind."

- John F. Kennedy

CONTENTS

PREFACE

On a morning in August 2022, I was sitting on the second floor of a Starbucks coffee shop, drinking coffee and reading an article on Nancy Pelosi's visit to Taiwan on my smartphone. I thought it might have a negative impact. The article stated that US House Speaker Nancy Pelosi pushed ahead with her visit to Taiwan despite strong opposition from China. As expected, China soon took retaliatory measures such as conducting military exercises in the form of a blockade of Taiwan. As the US and China continue to fight in the Taiwan Strait in this manner, experts are concerned that an imminent crisis may arise.

The relationship between Taiwan and China has been complicated for decades due to their political differences and the historical context of the civil war that led to the separation of Taiwan from mainland China in 1949.[1] In recent years, tensions have escalated due to a series of events, including the increasing military activities of China near Taiwan, Taiwan's growing independence movement, and China's efforts to diplomatically isolate Taiwan.[2] Experts have described the relationship between Taiwan and China as precarious, with the potential for conflict always present. The Chinese government has long viewed Taiwan as a renegade province and has not ruled out the use of force to bring it back under its control. Taiwan, on the other hand, regards itself as an independent state and has consistently opposed China's attempts to establish influence over it. China has increased its military activity near Taiwan in recent years, including flying fighter aircraft and bombers above the island and conducting naval exercises in the nearby waters. Experts have noted that these activities are meant to intimidate Taiwan and demonstrate China's military capabilities.

At the same time, Taiwan has been expanding its international presence, seeking to establish diplomatic relationships with more countries and participate in international organizations. This has led to increased tensions with China, which has sought to limit Taiwan's international influence. In terms of future prospects, experts are divided. Some believe that the tensions between Taiwan and China will continue to escalate, potentially leading to a military conflict. Others believe that both sides will seek to avoid such a conflict and instead focus on maintaining the status quo.[3] One factor that could play a significant role in the relationship between Taiwan and China is the involvement of the United States. The U.S. has long been a supporter of Taiwan, and recently, it has increased its military presence in the region. Some experts believe that the U.S. could play a role in preventing a conflict between

Taiwan and China by acting as a mediator and providing support to Taiwan. Another aspect that cannot be overlooked is that some experts analyze that if a war breaks out as the regional conflict between China and Taiwan intensifies, the war could escalate to World War III. It is important to note that any prediction about the outbreak of war is highly speculative and should be taken with a grain of salt. However, in the event of a serious conflict between China and Taiwan, there are several factors that could potentially lead to a wider conflict and potentially escalate into a world war.

Firstly, China is a major global power with a large and modern military, and any conflict with Taiwan could draw in other major powers that have interests in the region. The United States, for example, has a longstanding commitment to defend Taiwan, and any escalation of hostilities could prompt the US to get involved, potentially leading to a direct military confrontation with China.

Secondly, China has been increasingly assertive in its territorial claims in the South China Sea and other parts of the region, and any conflict with Taiwan could be seen as part of a larger pattern of aggression that threatens the balance of power in the region.[4] This could prompt other countries in the region, such as Japan and South Korea, to get involved in the conflict, potentially leading to a wider conflict.

Thirdly, any conflict between China and Taiwan could disrupt global trade and destabilize the global economy. Taiwan is a major hub for high-tech manufacturing and a key player in global supply chains, and any disruption to its economy could have ripple effects across the world. This could prompt other countries to get involved in the conflict in order to protect their economic interests. Any conflict involving nuclear powers like China and the US would carry the risk of a nuclear exchange, which would have catastrophic consequences for the entire world.

All of these factors make it possible that a regional conflict between China and Taiwan could potentially escalate into a wider conflict that involves major world powers and threatens global stability. However, it is important to emphasize that this is just one possible scenario and that many other factors could come into play to prevent such an outcome.

The regional dispute between China and Taiwan discussed above is a complex issue that extends beyond the region and can even pose a threat to global security. In addition to the cases of China and Taiwan, regional conflicts have been escalating in many regions in the 21st century. These conflicts are often caused by a variety of factors, including resource scarcity, political instability, and ethnic and religious tensions. While these conflicts may seem isolated, they can have a significant impact on global security.

Although I examined instances of whether the escalating conflict between China and Taiwan could eventually lead to a global security crisis beyond regional conflict, another regional conflict that comes to mind when this author thinks about regional conflict is the regional conflict, the Syrian civil war.

The Syrian civil war, which began in 2011, has been one of the most devastating conflicts in recent times, resulting in the deaths of over 400,000 people, the displacement of millions, and a humanitarian crisis that has affected the entire region.[5] The conflict has its roots in a complex mix of political, economic, and social factors, including the authoritarian rule of President Bashar al-Assad, rising sectarian tensions, and the impact of the Arab Spring. The Syrian civil war can be traced back to the Arab Spring protests that erupted in Tunisia in 2010 and quickly spread to other countries in the Middle East, including Syria. In March 2011, peaceful protests began in Syria, calling for political reform and an end to the Assad regime's authoritarian rule. However, the Syrian government responded with force, and the protests quickly turned violent. The conflict escalated as various opposition groups, including the Free Syrian Army, emerged to fight against the government forces. The situation was further complicated by the involvement of regional and international actors, including Iran, Russia, and the United States, who backed different sides in the conflict. The causes of the Syrian civil war are complex and multifaceted. One key factor was the authoritarian rule of President Assad, who inherited power from his father in 2000 and has since maintained a tight grip on power, suppressing dissent and opposition. The regime's brutality and corruption fueled popular discontent and led to the emergence of opposition groups. Another factor was rising sectarian tensions, with the government dominated by the Alawite minority and the opposition largely Sunni.[6] The conflict also had economic roots, with high unemployment, inflation, and corruption exacerbating social and political grievances.

If so, it is impossible to predict the ripple effect of the potential impact on global security if the Syrian civil war escalates further. The Syrian civil war has had a significant impact on global security, with implications for the Middle East and beyond. The conflict has created a humanitarian crisis, with millions of Syrians displaced and seeking refuge in neighboring countries and Europe. This has led to tensions and political instability in the region, as well as a rise in nationalism and xenophobia in Europe. The conflict has also had implications for regional security, with the involvement of regional and international actors exacerbating tensions and increasing the risk of conflict. The conflict has created a power vacuum that has been exploited by extremist groups, including the Islamic State, who have carried out attacks in Syria and beyond. The Syrian civil war has been a complex and devastating conflict with roots in political, economic, and social factors. The conflict has had significant implications for global security, with a humanitarian crisis, regional instability, and the rise of extremist groups. The Syrian Civil War has had a devastating impact on Syria. Millions of people have been killed or displaced, and the country's infrastructure has been severely damaged. The war has also had a destabilizing effect on the region, and it has contributed to the rise of extremism. When regional conflicts escalate, they can lead to the displacement of millions of people, the spread of violence and extremism, and the disruption of global trade and commerce. In some cases, regional conflicts can even lead to the outbreak of war.

As previously examined, the main factors and reasons that could pose a threat to global security if the border dispute between China and India potentially worsens are quite complicated. Overall, an escalation of the border conflict between China and India has the potential to transcend regional boundaries and pose a significant global security crisis. The involvement of nuclear weapons, the interests of major powers and the broader geopolitical context make it imperative for the international community to actively engage in preventive diplomacy, promote dialogue, and work towards a peaceful resolution to prevent further destabilization and ensure global security.

In terms of international politics and geopolitics, the dispute between China and India could potentially become more aggravated due to their relationships with different countries. Here are a few scenarios that could influence the escalation of the conflict: First, the United States has been strengthening its strategic ties with India as part of its Indo-Pacific strategy to counterbalance China's influence in the region. The U.S. has conducted joint military exercises with India, signed defense agreements, and expressed support for India's territorial integrity. If the conflict escalates, the U.S. could be more inclined to support India diplomatically, economically, or even militarily. This could aggravate the situation, as it would bring a major global power directly into the equation and potentially escalate the conflict. Second, Pakistan has a long-standing territorial dispute with India over the region of Kashmir. China has been a key ally and supporter of Pakistan, both politically and militarily.

If the conflict between China and India escalates, Pakistan could perceive an opportunity to assert itself in the region and potentially provide support to China. This could lead to a proxy conflict between India and Pakistan, further aggravating the situation and increasing the risk of a broader conflict. Third, Russia has maintained a historically close relationship with India and has been a major supplier of defense equipment to the country. While Russia also has economic ties with China, its relations with India could influence its stance in the conflict. If the situation escalates, Russia may be more inclined to support India, potentially exacerbating the tensions between the two countries.

Finally, the Association of Southeast Asian Nations (ASEAN) countries have their own territorial disputes with China in the South China Sea. If the China-India conflict escalates, these countries may see an opportunity to gain support from India or take advantage of China's focus being divided. Their involvement or support for either side could increase tensions and complicate the resolution of the conflict. It is important to note that these scenarios are speculative and depend on various factors, including the nature and intensity of the conflict, the involvement of other countries, and the diplomatic efforts undertaken to de-escalate the situation. The outcome will be influenced by complex geopolitical dynamics and the strategic calculations of each country involved. Efforts to engage in diplomatic negotiations, promote dialogue, and seek peaceful resolutions will be crucial to prevent the situation from aggravating further.

The idea of a new Cold War between Western liberal democracies and socialism centered on China and Russia has been gaining traction in recent years. This phenomenon has its roots in the historical context of the Cold War between the United States and the Soviet Union that lasted from 1947 to 1991. The Cold War was a period of intense geopolitical rivalry and ideological competition between the two superpowers, with the world divided into two opposing blocs, the Western capitalist democracies led by the United States and the Eastern communist bloc led by the Soviet Union. The current phenomenon of a new Cold War has been driven by a combination of factors.

First, the rise of China as an economic and military superpower has challenged the dominance of the United States in the world. China's economic growth has been fueled by its state-controlled capitalist system, which has allowed the government to direct investment and control key industries. This has led to tensions with the United States, which has accused China of engaging in unfair trade practices and stealing intellectual property. Second, Russia under the leadership of President Vladimir Putin has also been challenging the Western liberal democratic order. Russia's annexation of Crimea from Ukraine in 2014 and its military intervention in Syria have raised concerns among Western democracies about Russian aggression and expansionism. Third, the erosion of democracy in some Western countries, including the United States and Europe, has undermined the credibility of the Western liberal democratic model. The rise of populist and nationalist movements in these countries has challenged the values of pluralism, tolerance, and human rights that underpin liberal democracy Experts have different opinions on the future of this phenomenon. Some experts argue that a new Cold War is already underway, with China and Russia working together to challenge the dominance of Western democracies. They believe that this rivalry will intensify in the coming years, leading to greater economic and military competition, as well as cyber warfare and disinformation campaigns.

Others, however, argue that the current situation is not a new Cold War but rather a new era of geopolitical competition between different models of governance. They suggest that this competition is not necessarily a bad thing and that it could lead to greater innovation and experimentation in governance systems. They also argue that there is room for cooperation between Western democracies, China, and Russia on issues such as climate change, nuclear non-proliferation, and global health.[7] Regardless of the opinions of experts, it is clear that the current era is marked by intense geopolitical competition and ideological rivalry. The future will depend on how the different actors navigate these challenges and whether they are able to find common ground on key issues. A more pessimistic view of the current global security crisis is that regional conflicts continue to occur. This is because such a series of regional conflicts can eventually develop into a global security crisis. As readers are well aware, the world is becoming increasingly interconnected with global economies and communication systems that enable instant connectivity across borders. Unfortunately, this connectivity also means that regional conflicts have the potential to escalate and become global security crises.

Experts have provided various explanations regarding global security threats caused by regional conflicts based on theoretical frameworks, geopolitical orientations, and empirical experiences. However, after analyzing some general trends and perspectives, it is evident that Realist scholars argue that regional conflicts pose a significant threat to global security, especially when they involve major powers or strategic regions. Realists emphasize the role of power, national interest, and competition in shaping international relations, and they view regional conflicts as a manifestation of the struggle for influence and resources among states. For example, the ongoing conflict in Syria, which involves multiple regional and global actors, has heightened tensions and generated a refugee crisis that affects neighboring countries and Europe. Realists also point out that regional conflicts can escalate into wider wars or trigger alliances, which could lead to a global conflict. Thus, realists advocate for a balance of power and deterrence strategies to manage regional conflicts and prevent them from spiraling out of control. Liberal scholars tend to view regional conflicts as a symptom of weak institutions, governance, and norms that fail to address the root causes of the conflicts.

Liberals emphasize the role of cooperation, norms, and institutions in promoting peace and security, and they advocate for multilateral diplomacy, conflict resolution, and peacebuilding efforts. For example, the Oslo Accords of 1993, which aimed to resolve the Israeli-Palestinian conflict through a two-state solution, were seen as a significant breakthrough in regional peacebuilding.[8] Liberals also point out that regional conflicts can generate transnational threats, such as terrorism, extremism, and human rights abuses, which require collective action and cooperation among states. Thus, liberals support international institutions and mechanisms, such as the United Nations, regional organizations, and international law, to prevent and resolve regional conflicts.

From the point of view of constructivist scholars, they argue that regional conflicts are socially constructed and shaped by ideas, identities, and norms, which vary across different regions and cultures. Constructivists emphasize the role of discourse, norms, and values in shaping international relations, and they view regional conflicts because of contested narratives and identities. For example, the conflict between India and Pakistan over Kashmir is seen as a clash between competing national identities and narratives of history and religion. Constructivists also point out that regional conflicts can generate opportunities for norm diffusion, dialogue, and reconciliation, which could transform the regional security landscape. Thus, constructivists advocate for intercultural dialogue, people-to-people exchanges, and conflict transformation initiatives to address the underlying causes of regional conflicts and promote regional security. The opinions of experts on the global security threat caused by regional conflicts reflect the diversity of theoretical and empirical perspectives in international politics. While realists emphasize the role of power and balance of power, liberals emphasize the role of institutions and norms, and constructivists emphasize the role of identity and discourse. However, all of these perspectives recognize the complexity and interdependence of regional conflicts and the need for collective action and cooperation to address them.

With due consideration to this background and awareness, this book has been composed in order to present a comprehensive exposition of the perils emanating from regional conflicts. This book conducts an analysis of the causal factors and historical contexts surrounding regional conflicts, examines the ramifications of these conflicts on global security, and delves into the challenges associated with resolving regional conflicts from international political and geopolitical standpoints. Furthermore, the book undertakes a comprehensive examination of regional disputes from diverse perspectives, such as international politics and political philosophy theory, with the aim of comprehending the present state of affairs and conceptual approaches.

This publication is of great significance to individuals who harbor concerns about the future of our world. Its purpose is to offer a lucid and succinct overview of intricate matters while providing insights into the prevention of regional conflicts from escalating into global crises. It is hoped that this work will prove valuable not only to scholars in the corresponding academic domain but also to politicians and policy makers.

Finally, to avoid any misunderstanding, I would like to say something about the choice of title for this book. Above all, I would like to say that I carefully chose the word "Eyes of the Typhoon" after much consideration.

In meteorology, the "eye of the typhoon" refers to a distinct feature at the center of a tropical cyclone, known as a typhoon in the western Pacific or a hurricane in the Atlantic and eastern Pacific. The eye of the typhoon is created through the mechanism of the storm's circulation. From a social and humanities perspective, the "eye of the typhoon" holds symbolic significance and can be used as a metaphor in various contexts. Here are a few implications:

Firstly, the eye of the typhoon can represent a moment of tranquility or stability amidst turbulent circumstances. It can be used to describe a person or situation that remains composed and unaffected by the chaos and challenges surrounding them.

Secondly, just as the eye of the typhoon offers a clear view of the surroundings, it can signify a state of heightened awareness, deep contemplation, or self-reflection. It implies the ability to step back from a situation, gain insight, and make well-considered decisions.

Thirdly, the existence of the eye within a typhoon symbolizes the coexistence of opposing forces. This can be related to societal or personal conflicts, where seemingly contradictory aspects or viewpoints coexist and need to be understood and addressed in order to find resolution or balance.

Fourthly, the eye of the typhoon represents the transition from chaos to order. It can embody the idea that within turmoil and upheaval, there is potential for growth, renewal, and positive change.

These interpretations are not limited to meteorological phenomena but are often used metaphorically to describe human experiences, social dynamics, and philosophical concepts. Accordingly, it also refers to the root cause of an event that has a great impact on the surroundings. Therefore, as a symbolic expression, "typhoon" represents the world security crisis, and the "eyes" in the term "eyes of a typhoon" are used to mean various regional conflicts occurring in various regions around the world. It is considered a term that implicitly contains the message to be conveyed in this book more than any other meaning.

INTRODUCTION

This book has emphasized the possibility for regional conflicts to erupt and threaten global security. Conflicts in the Middle East, Africa, and Asia show that regional conflicts can have terrible consequences, including population displacement, economic ruin, and political instability. To prevent regional disputes from increasing, it is necessary to address them and implement preventative measures and effective conflict resolution procedures. Preventive measures can include investing in regional stability and development, as well as establishing diplomatic channels for conflict resolution. Mediation and negotiation are two effective conflict resolution tactics that can be used to resolve regional problems before they become crises.

In an increasingly interconnected and interdependent world, the impact of regional conflicts on global security cannot be underestimated. The potential of these conflicts to escalate and trigger a crisis with far-reaching consequences has become a pressing concern for the international community. This narrative, supported by numerous cases in the Middle East, Africa, and Asia, serves as a compelling reminder of the devastating effects regional conflicts can have on the stability of nations, the displacement of people, economic prosperity, and political equilibrium.

Regional conflicts possess a unique capability to evolve into global security crises due to their intricate dynamics and multifaceted nature. The Middle East, with its volatile geopolitical landscape, has long been a hotbed of tensions and conflicts that have reverberated far beyond its borders. The protracted conflict in Syria, for instance, has unleashed a myriad of challenges, including the displacement of millions of Syrians, severe economic devastation, and a breeding ground for extremism. These consequences not only affected neighboring countries but also had a ripple effect on the global stage, contributing to a refugee crisis of unprecedented proportions.

Similarly, the African continent has witnessed various conflicts, many of which have attained international dimensions, exacerbating the already complex web of regional security challenges. The long-standing conflict in the Democratic Republic of Congo (DRC) provides a stark illustration of how a regional conflict can escalate, leading to a dire humanitarian crisis and political instability. The DRC conflict's repercussions have spilled across borders, involving multiple neighboring countries and attracting the attention of international actors. Furthermore, the vast and diverse continent of Asia has experienced its fair share of regional conflicts, each with its distinct ramifications for global security. The ongoing tensions in the South China

Sea, involving competing territorial claims among several Asian nations, have the potential to disturb the delicate balance of power in the region and provoke a wider conflict. The aftermath of such a conflict could significantly affect global trade routes, disrupt economic interdependencies, and compromise the stability of nations worldwide.

Given the dire consequences that regional conflicts can unleash upon the international community, it becomes imperative to develop preventative measures and effective conflict resolution strategies. Preventative measures should encompass proactive investments in regional stability and development, aiming to address the root causes of conflicts and alleviate the conditions that fuel them. Simultaneously, the establishment of robust diplomatic channels dedicated to resolving regional conflicts is vital, enabling timely dialogue, negotiation, and mediation. These mechanisms serve as crucial tools in preventing regional conflicts from escalating into full-blown global security crises.

Therefore, the potential of regional conflicts to escalate and engender global security crises necessitates a proactive approach in addressing their root causes and devising effective conflict resolution strategies. The cases of conflict in the Middle East, Africa, and Asia offer tangible evidence of the devastating consequences that regional conflicts can inflict upon nations and regions, reverberating globally. By investing in regional stability, development, and establishing diplomatic channels for conflict resolution, the international community can work towards mitigating the risk of these conflicts spiraling out of control and protect global security in an interconnected world.

The division of the world into two halves, with Western liberal democracies on one side and socialist countries on the other, was a key feature of the international system during the Cold War. There are several theories from the fields of international politics and political philosophy that can be applied to explain this phenomenon.

Realism is a dominant theory in international politics that suggests that states are the main actors in the international system and are driven by their own self-interests. According to realists, the Cold War division of the world into two camps was a result of the balance of power between the US-led Western bloc and the Soviet-led socialist bloc. Each side sought to maintain its own security and expand its influence at the expense of the other, leading to a long period of confrontation and competition.

Liberalism emphasizes the importance of individual liberty, human rights, and democratic institutions in the international system. From a liberal perspective, the Cold War division of the world into two camps can be seen as a clash between two different political systems – liberal democracy and socialism. Liberal theorists argue that liberal democracy is the best system for promoting peace and prosperity, and that the confrontation with socialist countries was a result of their rejection of these values.

Marxism is a political philosophy that emphasizes the importance of class struggle and economic factors in shaping the international system. From a Marxist perspective, the Cold War division of the world can be seen as a result of the contradictions between capitalism and socialism. Marxist theorists argue that the US-led Western bloc was driven by its desire to protect capitalist interests and maintain its dominant position in the global economy, while the Soviet-led socialist bloc sought to challenge this dominance and establish an equal economic system.

Constructivism is a theory in international politics that emphasizes the importance of social norms, identities, and ideas in shaping the behavior of states. From a constructivist perspective, the Cold War division of the world can be seen as a result of the different identities and beliefs held by Western liberal democracies and socialist countries. Constructivist theorists argue that the division of the world was not simply a result of material interests or power politics, but also reflected deeper cultural and ideological differences between the two camps.

Realism, liberalism, Marxism, and constructivism offer different perspectives on the causes and consequences of this phenomenon, highlighting the importance of power, values, economic factors, and social norms in shaping the behavior of states in the international system. When you think of the fierce Cold War and its end, a book comes to mind. It is Francis Fukuyama's "The end of history and the last man". "The End of History and the Last Man" is a book by Francis Fukuyama that was first published in 1992. The central thesis of the book is that the end of the Cold War and the triumph of liberal democracy and capitalism mark the end of human history as a struggle between competing ideologies and the final form of human government.

Fukuyama argues that the end of the Cold War represents the triumph of liberal democracy and capitalism, which he sees as the culmination of the historical evolution of human societies. He contends that liberal democracy provides the best form of government because it protects individual rights and freedoms and provides opportunities for economic growth and development. He also argues that liberal democracy and capitalism are inherently self-correcting, capable of adapting to changing circumstances and addressing their own internal contradictions.[1]

This triumph of liberal democracy and capitalism represents the "end of history" in the sense that there will no longer be any fundamental conflicts between different political systems or ideologies. He contends that all societies will eventually adopt liberal democratic and capitalist principles, and that the world will be characterized by a universal recognition of the value of individual rights and freedoms. Fukuyama introduces the idea of the "last man," which he sees as the ultimate outcome of the historical process. The "last man" is an individual who has achieved all of his or her material needs and desires, but lacks any higher sense of purpose or meaning.

Fukuyama argues that the challenge for liberal democracy and capitalism in the future will be to provide a sense of purpose and meaning for individuals, and to address the potential for nihilism and despair that may arise in a society that has achieved all of its material goals. Fukuyama's book has been both praised and criticized for its bold thesis and sweeping historical narrative. While many have found his argument compelling, others have pointed out the potential limitations and challenges of liberal democracy and capitalism, and questioned whether the end of history is truly at hand.

A New Cold War, the Divided World and Global Security Crisis

The Cold War refers to the antagonistic relationship between the United States and the Soviet Union. This antagonism arose from the opposing political and economic beliefs of the United States and the Soviet Union. In the previous Cold War, the United States was able to contain and defeat the Soviet Union. However, in the current new Cold War, competition between China and the United States is at the center. China has grown into the world's largest economic power and is competing with the United States.[2] This competition is also evident militarily.

In addition, there are conflicts between the United States and Europe. These conflicts have been exacerbated by divisions between the European Union and Britain.

Many analysts and commentators to describe the current state of international relations, particularly between the United States and China, have used the term "New Cold War". This term reflects the growing tension, competition, and mistrust between these two global superpowers, which has led to an increasingly bifurcated world order. One of the key drivers of this new Cold War is the changing balance of power in the international system. China has emerged as a major economic and military power, challenging the traditional dominance of the United States. China's economic growth, technological advancements, and assertive foreign policy have given rise to concerns in the United States and other Western countries about the potential threat posed by China's rise.[3]

In response, the United States has taken a more confrontational approach to China, particularly under the Trump administration. The U.S. has pursued a "maximum pressure" campaign against China, imposing tariffs, export controls, and other economic measures to try to force China to change its trade practices and reduce its economic influence. China, for its part, has responded with its own assertive foreign policy, particularly in the Asia-Pacific region. China has expanded its military capabilities, including its naval and air forces, and has built military bases on artificial islands in the South China Sea. It has also pursued a more aggressive posture in territorial disputes with neighboring countries, such as Japan and the Philippines.

These tensions have led to a security crisis, particularly in the Asia-Pacific region. The U.S. has strengthened its military presence in the region, through increased military exercises, deployments of troops and equipment, and closer security cooperation with allies such as Japan, South Korea, and Australia. China has responded by increasing its own military activities, conducting more frequent and larger-scale military exercises, and increasing its naval and air patrols in disputed areas. The security crisis in the Asia-Pacific region has also been fueled by other factors, such as North Korea's nuclear and missile programs, which have led to increased tensions between the U.S. and China. The U.S. has called on China to do more to rein in North Korea's nuclear ambitions, while China has accused the U.S. of exacerbating the crisis through its military presence in the region.

The new Cold War between the United States and China reflects a fundamental shift in the balance of power in the international system. The growing competition and mistrust between these two global superpowers has led to a more bifurcated world order, with implications for security and stability in the Asia-Pacific region and beyond.

The Emergence of Global Security Threats

The 21st century presents unprecedented challenges to global security, with climate change, cybersecurity threats, terrorism, nuclear weapons proliferation, and regional conflicts among the major causes driving the world to the brink of crisis. Adding to this complexity are the emerging nations that pose a significant threat to global security, necessitating a deeper understanding of the current situation and the urgent need for international cooperation to address these threats. In this book, we will delve into the intricate details of these global security threats, with a particular focus on regional conflicts, and explore the ways in which international cooperation, both bilateral and multilateral, can be utilized to promote peace and stability in the world. Through a comprehensive analysis of these critical issues, we hope to contribute to the ongoing dialogue on global security and inspire action to safeguard our future.

There are several global security crises that are currently escalating or have the potential to do so. Here are some examples:

Climate Change: The effects of climate change, such as extreme weather events and rising sea levels, pose a significant threat to global security. These impacts can lead to food and water scarcity, displacement of populations, and conflicts over resources.

Cybersecurity Threats: Cybersecurity threats continue to escalate globally, with state-sponsored actors and non-state actors targeting critical infrastructure, governments, and businesses. The increasing sophistication of cyber-attacks poses a significant risk to global security.

Terrorism: The threat of terrorism remains a global concern, with groups such as the Islamic State, Al-Qaeda, and their affiliates continuing to operate in various regions of the world. These groups can carry out attacks that cause significant harm to people and infrastructure, and their ideology can fuel social and political unrest.

Nuclear Proliferation: The proliferation of nuclear weapons and the potential for their use pose a significant threat to global security. Countries such as North Korea and Iran have been actively pursuing nuclear programs, which could lead to an arms race and increased tensions.

Regional Conflicts: Conflicts in regions such as the Middle East, Africa, and Asia continue to escalate, causing human suffering, displacement, and destabilization. These conflicts can also have global implications, such as the displacement of refugees and the spread of extremist ideology.

These and other global security crises require international cooperation and coordinated action to mitigate their impacts and prevent further escalation.

Which Countries, if any, are Triggering a Global Security Crisis?

It would be difficult to pinpoint specific countries that are triggering a global security crisis, as there are multiple factors and actors involved in the various crises that exist today. However, some countries have been identified as contributing to or exacerbating specific security challenges. Here are some examples:

China: China's rise as a global power has been a source of concern for many countries, particularly in the Indo-Pacific region. China's territorial claims in the South China Sea and its increasing military capabilities have led to tensions and conflicts with neighboring countries. China has also been accused of engaging in economic espionage and intellectual property theft, and has been criticized for human rights abuses in Xinjiang and Hong Kong.

North Korea: North Korea's nuclear and missile programs pose a significant threat to global security, with its frequent missile tests and provocative rhetoric raising tensions in the region. The country's human rights record has also been widely condemned.

Russia: Russia has been accused of interfering in elections and engaging in cyber-attacks, leading to concerns about its intentions and actions in the international community. Its actions in Ukraine and annexation of Crimea have also raised tensions with NATO and the EU.

Iran: Iran's nuclear program and its support for terrorist organizations have led to tensions with the US and other countries. The country's involvement in conflicts in the Middle East, including in Syria and Yemen, has also contributed to regional instability.

It is important to note that global security crises are complex issues that involve multiple factors and actors, and it is often not helpful to single out specific countries as the sole cause of these challenges. Addressing these crises requires a coordinated and cooperative international effort.

To overcome this immediate global security crisis, it is necessary to establish an international cooperation system above all else. In order to do so, it is important to first understand meaningful phrases related to international cooperation for global security. These words and phrases highlight the importance of international cooperation and dialogue in addressing common security challenges and promoting peace and stability around the world. They emphasize the need for countries to work together to prevent conflicts, protect human rights, and address global security threats.

Collaborative security: This term refers to a security concept that emphasizes the importance of countries working together to address common security challenges. It emphasizes the need for cooperation, dialogue, and coordination among nations to prevent conflicts, promote stability, and combat threats such as terrorism, cyber-attacks, and nuclear proliferation.

Multilateral security cooperation: This phrase refers to cooperation among three or more countries or organizations in addressing common security challenges. It emphasizes the importance of working together to pool resources, expertise, and information in order to achieve common security goals.

Joint security operations: This phrase refers to military operations conducted by two or more countries to achieve a common security objective. Examples of joint security operations include peacekeeping missions, counterterrorism operations, and humanitarian assistance and disaster relief efforts.

Intelligence sharing: This phrase refers to the sharing of intelligence information among countries to combat common security threats. It emphasizes the importance of working together to gather and share information on issues such as terrorism, organized crime, and cyber-attacks.

Counterterrorism cooperation: This phrase refers to cooperation among countries to combat terrorism. It emphasizes the importance of sharing intelligence, coordinating law enforcement efforts, and developing common strategies to prevent terrorist attacks and disrupt terrorist networks.

Nuclear nonproliferation: This phrase refers to efforts to prevent the spread of nuclear weapons and technology. It emphasizes the importance of international agreements, such as the Nuclear Non-Proliferation Treaty, to prevent countries from acquiring nuclear weapons and to promote disarmament.

Arms control agreements: This phrase refers to agreements among countries to limit the production, possession, and use of conventional weapons, including nuclear weapons. It emphasizes the importance of international cooperation and dialogue in reducing the risk of conflict and promoting disarmament.

Humanitarian intervention: This phrase refers to military intervention by one or more countries to protect civilians from mass atrocities or humanitarian crises, such as genocide or ethnic cleansing. It emphasizes the importance of international norms and values, such as the Responsibility to Protect, in promoting human rights and preventing mass atrocities.

Peacekeeping operations: This phrase refers to military or civilian missions conducted by international organizations or coalitions to promote peace and stability in conflict-affected areas. It emphasizes the importance of international cooperation in resolving conflicts, protecting civilians, and building peace.

Security sector reform: This phrase refers to efforts to reform the security sector in countries affected by conflict or instability, in order to promote good governance, accountability, and respect for human rights. It emphasizes the importance of international assistance and cooperation in building sustainable peace and stability.[4]

Approach to Global Security Crisis

Global security is a complex issue that requires a comprehensive and collaborative approach to address. The need for international cooperation is especially critical in the face of emerging security challenges such as cyber-attacks, terrorism, nuclear proliferation, and climate change. Here is a detailed discussion on what kind of international cooperation approach is needed to resolve the global security crisis from an expert's point of view:

Multilateralism is an important approach to address security challenges as it enables states to work together towards common goals.[5] It promotes the principles of cooperation, dialogue, and compromise, and encourages countries to seek peaceful and inclusive solutions to security problems. Multilateral institutions such as the United Nations provide a platform for countries to discuss and coordinate on security issues. Collective security is a framework that emphasizes the shared responsibility of all countries to maintain international peace and security. It involves the use of collective action by states to prevent and respond to threats to global security. The United Nations Security Council is the primary body responsible for maintaining international peace and security through collective security. Intelligence sharing is critical for effective security cooperation between countries. It involves the exchange of information between intelligence agencies of different countries to prevent and respond to security threats. The sharing of intelligence enables countries to identify and disrupt terrorist plots, track the movements of criminals and smugglers, and prevent cyber-attacks. Terrorism is a major security threat that requires international cooperation to combat effectively. Countries need to work together to disrupt the financing of terrorist groups, prevent the movement of terrorists across borders, and prosecute those who support or participate in terrorist activities. The sharing of intelligence and joint operations are critical in counterterrorism cooperation. Arms control and disarmament are essential for reducing the risk of conflict and promoting international peace and security.

International treaties such as the Nuclear Non-Proliferation Treaty and the Chemical Weapons Convention have been instrumental in reducing the proliferation of weapons of mass destruction. Arms control and disarmament require international cooperation and the willingness of states to work towards a common goal.[6] Climate change is increasingly recognized as a security threat that requires international cooperation to address. Countries need to work together to reduce greenhouse gas emissions, promote clean energy, and adapt to the impacts of climate change. The Paris Agreement provides a framework for international cooperation on climate change.

As discussed above, resolving global security crises requires a multifaceted approach that involves international cooperation on multiple fronts. Multilateralism, collective security, intelligence sharing, counterterrorism cooperation, arms control and disarmament, and climate change cooperation are all critical components of an effective security cooperation approach. Countries need to work together towards common goals, respect each other's sovereignty, and seek peaceful and inclusive solutions to security challenges.

In an increasingly interconnected and globalized world, the preservation of international security is of paramount importance. As conflicts intensify and tensions rise on various fronts, the potential for a crisis in international security looms ominously. While numerous factors contribute to this complex equation, this book aims to shed light on the significance of regional conflicts as a critical catalyst for such a crisis. By examining their historical context and potential ramifications, we can better understand the urgency to address and mitigate the escalating threat they pose.

Regional conflicts, characterized by disputes between neighboring nations or factions within a particular geographic area, possess the potential to exert far-reaching consequences on international security. Traditionally, regional conflicts have been contained within their respective borders, with limited global impact. However, the changing dynamics of the modern world, characterized by interconnectedness, resource scarcity, and ideological polarization, have magnified the significance of such conflicts. In the current geopolitical landscape, regional conflicts have become ticking time bombs, threatening to unravel global stability.

Throughout history, regional conflicts have been responsible for triggering devastating international security crises. One need not look far back to find examples that underline this precarious reality. The Balkan conflicts of the 1990s, for instance, erupted into a full-scale humanitarian catastrophe, drawing in major powers and reshaping the political landscape of Europe. Similarly, the ongoing strife in the Middle East, fueled by a multitude of factors, has led to a surge in terrorism, waves of refugees, and prolonged instability, with reverberations felt globally. One of the primary reasons for highlighting regional conflicts as a significant factor in an international security crisis lies in the concept of the domino effect.

Regional conflicts have a tendency to spread and escalate, dragging neighboring countries into the fray and fanning the flames of tension. The ripple effects of such conflicts are not confined to a specific region; rather, they have the potential to cascade into a wider conflagration, drawing in international powers, exacerbating existing fault lines, and destabilizing the delicate balance of power on a global scale. While it is crucial to recognize the multifaceted nature of global security challenges, regional conflicts possess a unique ability to amplify and exacerbate other threats. Climate change, for instance, when coupled with regional conflicts, can lead to resource scarcity, mass displacement, and increased competition for limited supplies. Likewise, cybersecurity threats can proliferate in the chaos of ongoing conflicts, compromising critical infrastructure, and escalating tensions between nations. Nuclear weapons, already a cause for concern, become even more perilous in regions teetering on the edge of conflict.

Accordingly, as we delve deeper into the complexities of the modern world, it becomes increasingly evident that regional conflicts hold the potential to ignite an international security crisis of unprecedented proportions. The historical context, the domino effect, and the interplay with other global threats all converge to emphasize the urgency of addressing and resolving these conflicts. In writing this book, we aim to shed light on the interwoven nature of regional conflicts and their impact on international security, urging policymakers, diplomats, and concerned citizens to act collaboratively and decisively to avert the looming crisis and foster a more peaceful and secure world for generations to come.

PART I
THE SOURCES OF GLOBAL SECURITY CRISIS

"The best way to predict your future is to create it."

- Abraham Lincoln

CHAPTER 1.

The Uninhabitable Earth: Climate Change

Climate change, a complex phenomenon driven by human activities, has emerged as one of the most significant challenges of our time. Beyond its environmental implications, climate change poses a considerable threat to global security, encompassing political, economic, social, and humanitarian dimensions. This chapter aims to explore the multifaceted nature of climate change as a global security threat, emphasizing the urgent need for global cooperation and concerted efforts to address this issue.

From an international political perspective, the ramifications of climate change are far-reaching, capable of destabilizing nations, exacerbating conflicts, and amplifying existing security risks. The changing climate affects vital resources such as water, food, and energy, creating competition and potential conflicts among nations. Rising sea levels, extreme weather events, and shifting agricultural patterns can lead to mass migrations, internal displacement, and the spread of infectious diseases, thereby straining social cohesion and triggering regional tensions. Moreover, climate change amplifies existing vulnerabilities and inequalities, disproportionately affecting developing countries that often lack the resources and capacity to adapt to its impacts. This disparity can breed social unrest, political instability, and even lead to interstate disputes over limited resources. Therefore, it is crucial to recognize that climate change is not solely an environmental problem but also a global security challenge demanding immediate attention.

Analyzing climate change through the lens of international political theory unveils several important dynamics. Realism, for instance, highlights how competition over scarce resources can intensify, potentially leading to conflicts among states. Liberalism underscores the need for collective action, emphasizing those cooperative efforts, international institutions, and multilateral agreements are essential for addressing the global challenge of climate change. Additionally, constructivism sheds light on the power of norms, values, and shared perceptions in shaping states' behavior towards climate change. By fostering a global normative framework that prioritizes sustainability and climate action, we can influence state behavior and encourage the adoption of responsible policies.

Climate change poses an array of threats to global security that cannot be ignored. It affects the stability of nations, exacerbates existing conflicts, and compromises the livelihoods of millions of people worldwide. Failure to address climate change effectively can lead to increased geopolitical tensions, displacement of populations, and economic disruptions on a global scale. Furthermore, climate change necessitates global cooperation, transcending national boundaries and requiring concerted efforts from all countries. Collaborative endeavors in areas such as reducing greenhouse gas emissions, promoting renewable energy, and implementing adaptation measures are imperative to mitigate the security risks associated with climate change.

This chapter has highlighted the significance of climate change as a global security threat, emphasizing the need for urgent and comprehensive action. By understanding the multi-dimensional impacts of climate change, applying international political theory to its analysis, and recognizing its potential to disrupt global stability, we can foster a greater sense of awareness and urgency in addressing this pressing challenge. It is paramount that humanity acknowledges the gravity of the situation and commits to sustainable practices and international cooperation to safeguard our shared future.

As an academic researcher, I hold the belief that climate change gives rise to intricate ethical and philosophical inquiries. To some extent, it may be due to this factor that discussions on climate change in public and political spheres often oversimplify the issue, mislead the audience, and exhibit conceptual ambiguity. Nevertheless, comprehending the multifaceted ramifications of climate change mandates an examination of the subject matter within the theoretical framework of humanities and political philosophy, at the very least. Climate change can be analyzed through various ethical theories that emphasize the value of human beings and their relationship to the natural world. Some of these theories include environmental ethics, virtue ethics, and existentialism.

Environmental ethics, which is concerned with the moral obligations that human beings have towards the natural world, can be applied to climate change in several ways.[1] Environmental ethics recognizes the intrinsic value of nature and advocates for the protection of natural systems, including the atmosphere. This approach emphasizes the importance of treating nature as an end in itself, rather than just a means to human ends. From this perspective, addressing climate change involves recognizing the importance of the natural world and taking action to preserve it for future generations. Subsequently, let us contemplate how to comprehend the climate change predicament from the standpoint of virtue ethics. Virtue ethics, which emphasizes the cultivation of moral character, can also be applied to climate change. This approach focuses on the virtues that are necessary for addressing the problem of climate change, such as wisdom, courage, and justice. Virtue ethics emphasizes the importance of cultivating a sense of responsibility and caring for the natural world. From this perspective, addressing climate change involves developing the virtues necessary to address the problem and taking action to mitigate its impacts. Finally, Existentialism, which is concerned with the nature of human existence and the meaning of life, can also be applied to climate change. This approach emphasizes the importance of individual responsibility and the need to take action in the face of overwhelming challenges. From this perspective, addressing climate change involves recognizing the gravity of the situation and taking action to preserve the natural world for future generations.

From a political philosophical perspective, climate change can be analyzed through various theories that focus on the role of the state, the distribution of resources, and the ethics of collective action. Some of these theories include liberalism, socialism, and cosmopolitanism.

Firstly, liberalism, which emphasizes individual freedom and the protection of individual rights, can be applied to climate change in several ways. This approach emphasizes the importance of market-based solutions and the role of the state in providing incentives for individuals and businesses to reduce their carbon emissions. From this perspective, addressing climate change involves creating a regulatory framework that promotes sustainable practices and encourages individuals to take action to reduce their carbon footprint. Secondly, socialism, which emphasizes collective ownership and the redistribution of resources, can also be applied to climate change. This approach focuses on the importance of addressing the root causes of climate change, such as economic inequality and the concentration of wealth and power in the hands of a few. From this perspective, addressing climate change involves creating a more equitable society that prioritizes the needs of the environment and the well-being of all its citizens. Finally, cosmopolitanism, which emphasizes the global nature of human society and the importance of ethical responsibility towards all people, can also be applied to climate change. This approach recognizes that the impacts of climate change are not limited to any one country or region and that addressing the problem requires international cooperation and collective action. From this perspective, addressing climate change involves recognizing the interconnectedness of all human beings and taking action to address the problem at a global scale.[2]

Climate change is a global issue that affects everyone on the planet. The United Nations Sustainable Development Goals (SDGs) aim to address climate change by reducing greenhouse gas emissions and promoting sustainable development. Developed countries have pledged to provide climate finance to developing countries to help them transition to low-carbon economies[3]. The Intergovernmental Panel on Climate Change (IPCC) is the leading international body for the assessment of climate change. The IPCC assesses the science related to climate change, its impacts and risks, and options for adaptation and mitigation.[4] According to the latest IPCC report, climate change is widespread, rapid, and intensifying. Many of the changes observed in the climate are unprecedented in thousands of years.[5]

In fact, climate change is a complex and multi-faceted issue that involves a range of actors, including nation-states, international organizations, corporations, and civil society. There are several theoretical perspectives that can be applied to understand climate change and its governance from an international political perspective. I will discuss four of these theories below: Realism is a dominant theory in international relations that emphasizes the role of power and self-interest in shaping the behavior of nation-states. From a realist perspective, addressing climate change is difficult because it requires collective action among nation-states, and there is no overarching authority to enforce compliance.

In addition, realists argue that states are unlikely to prioritize the environment over their own economic interests, which may conflict with the goals of reducing greenhouse gas emissions. Liberalism is another influential theory in international relations that emphasizes the role of institutions and cooperation in promoting peace and prosperity. From a liberal perspective, addressing climate change requires the creation of international institutions and agreements that can coordinate action among nation-states. Liberals also stress the importance of market mechanisms, such as carbon pricing, to incentivize the reduction of greenhouse gas emissions. Constructivism is a relatively newer theory in international relations that emphasizes the role of ideas and norms in shaping behavior. From a constructivist perspective, addressing climate change requires the creation of new norms and ideas about the importance of sustainability and environmental protection. Constructivists argue that new norms can be created through international dialogue and cooperation, as well as through domestic movements and civil society activism. Critical theory is a broad approach to social analysis that emphasizes the role of power and inequality in shaping social relations. From a critical perspective, addressing climate change requires addressing the underlying structural causes of environmental degradation, such as the global economic system and patterns of consumption and production. Critical theorists argue that climate change is not simply a technical problem that can be solved through technological innovation or policy reform, but rather a deeply political issue that requires a radical rethinking of social relations and power structures. In practice, these theoretical perspectives are often used in combination to understand climate change and its governance from an international political perspective. For example, many scholars and policymakers advocate for a combination of institutional cooperation, market mechanisms, and normative change to address climate change, while also recognizing the need for deeper structural change to address underlying causes of environmental degradation. The years 2015 to 2019 were the five warmest years on record. The average global temperature for 2015–2019 was 1.1 ± 0.1 °C warmer than pre-industrial (1850–1900) and is therefore the warmest of any equivalent period on record. It is 0.21 ± 0.08 °C warmer than the average for 2011–2015. The year 2016 is the warmest on record, and 2019 is likely to be the second warmest. Continental-average temperatures typically show greater variability than the global mean. Even so, five-year average temperatures for 2015–2019 were nominally warmer than any five-year period prior to 2015 for each of the inhabited continents. The average temperature of the Earth's land surface from 2015 to 2019 was approximately 1.7 °C higher than pre-industrial levels, and 0.3 °C warmer than the period from 2011 to 2015. With the exception of certain regions such as small areas of Canada, central Asia, and a specific part of the Antarctic in the Indian Ocean sector, almost all land areas experienced above-average temperatures. The average temperatures over the course of five years were the highest ever recorded in significant portions of the United States, including Alaska, the eastern parts of South America, most of Europe and the Middle East, northern Eurasia, Australia, as well as certain areas of southern and eastern Africa.

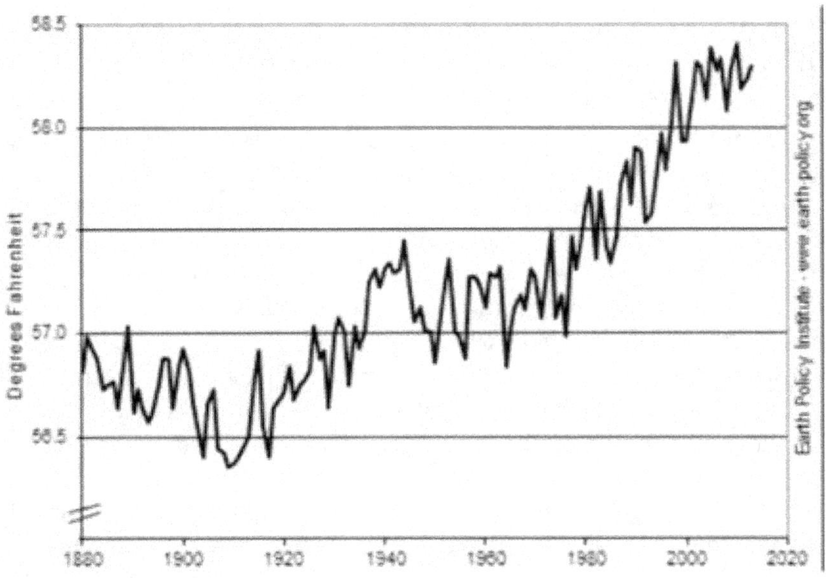

Figure 1. Average Global Temperature[6]   Source: NASA GISS

As for the global average temperature of the sea surface from 2015 to 2019, it was approximately 0.83 °C higher than pre-industrial levels and 0.13 °C warmer than the period from 2011 to 2015. In terms of the oceans, regions with below-average sea surface temperatures were observed to the south of Greenland (one of the few areas globally to have experienced long-term cooling), an area off the coast of West Africa, and certain areas of the Southern Ocean. Other areas were mostly warmer than average. Record warmth was recorded over areas of the northeast Pacific, the western North Atlantic, the western Indian Ocean, and the Tasman Sea, which has seen a number of severe marine heatwaves in the past five years. Climate change is a serious and pressing global issue that is already having significant impacts on people and ecosystems around the world. Climate change is causing an increase in the frequency and intensity of extreme weather events like heatwaves, droughts, floods, and hurricanes.[7]

For example, the heatwave in Europe in 2019, which caused record-breaking temperatures, was made at least five times more likely by climate change. Similarly, the flooding in Southeast Asia in 2020, which affected millions of people, was exacerbated by climate change.[8]

An accompanying WMO report on greenhouse gas concentrations shows that 2015-2019 has seen a continued increase in carbon dioxide (CO_2) levels and other key greenhouse gases in the atmosphere to new records, with CO_2 growth rates nearly 20% higher than the previous five years. CO_2 remains in the atmosphere for centuries and in the ocean for even longer. Preliminary data from a subset of greenhouse gas observational sites for 2019 indicate that CO_2 global concentrations are on track to reach or even exceed 410 ppm by the end of 2019.

Climate change is causing sea levels to rise, which threatens coastal communities and infrastructure around the world. According to the United Nations, sea levels have risen by around 15 cm since the beginning of the 20th century, and they are projected to rise by up to a meter by the end of the century. This could lead to the displacement of millions of people and the loss of valuable land and property. Climate change is causing glaciers to melt at an accelerating rate, which is contributing to sea-level rise and threatening the availability of freshwater in many regions. For example, the Himalayan glaciers, which provide water to over a billion people, are melting at an alarming rate due to climate change, posing a significant risk to regional water security. Climate change is causing significant losses in biodiversity, as many species struggle to adapt to changing environmental conditions. This can lead to the extinction of species and the collapse of ecosystems, with far-reaching consequences for human well-being. For example, warming ocean temperatures and ocean acidification are destroying coral reefs, which provide critical habitat for marine species and protect coastlines from storms. Climate change is contributing to food insecurity, as extreme weather events and changing environmental conditions can reduce crop yields and disrupt food production systems. This can lead to malnutrition and hunger, particularly in developing countries that are heavily reliant on agriculture. For example, in sub-Saharan Africa, climate change is expected to reduce maize yields by up to 40% by 2050, which could lead to a significant increase in food insecurity.[9] Climate change is a serious and pressing issue that is already having significant impacts on people and ecosystems around the world. Addressing climate change is essential to ensure a sustainable future for all.

Climate change poses a significant threat to global security as it can exacerbate existing security challenges and create new ones. Climate change-related impacts, such as sea-level rise, extreme weather events, food and water shortages, and displacement of people, can lead to increased competition for resources, social unrest, and conflict. For instance, sea-level rise can lead to the loss of coastal land and infrastructure, displacement of people, and competition for resources in the affected regions. This can cause tensions between neighboring countries, particularly in regions where maritime boundaries are contested, such as the South China Sea.

The melting of the Arctic sea ice due to climate change has opened up new shipping routes, which could potentially lead to territorial disputes and conflict. Furthermore, extreme weather events like droughts, floods, and heatwaves can lead to crop failures and food shortages, which can trigger social unrest and even civil wars. For example, in Syria, a prolonged drought from 2007 to 2010, exacerbated by climate change, led to the displacement of millions of people and contributed to the country's civil war.[10] Similarly, in Sudan, climate change-related droughts have contributed to food insecurity, displacement, and conflict. Additionally, climate change-related impacts can increase the likelihood of terrorism and political instability, particularly in countries with weak governance and high poverty rates.

For instance, the impacts of climate change, such as water scarcity and crop failure, can create conditions that drive young people into extremist groups like Boko Haram in Nigeria. Climate change poses a significant threat to global security. Its impacts can exacerbate existing security challenges and create new ones, including territorial disputes, resource competition, social unrest, and conflict. Addressing climate change is, therefore, critical to promoting global security and stability. Climate change is a complex and multifaceted problem that requires a range of solutions at different levels, from individual actions to global policy changes. The most effective way to tackle climate change is to reduce greenhouse gas emissions, particularly carbon dioxide emissions from burning fossil fuels.

This can be done by transitioning to clean energy sources like wind and solar power, improving energy efficiency, and investing in low-carbon transportation options. Adaptation measures can help communities and ecosystems cope with the impacts of climate change that are already happening or are unavoidable in the future. This can include building seawalls to protect against sea-level rise, developing drought-resistant crops, and improving water management practices. Forests are essential for absorbing carbon dioxide from the atmosphere and reducing greenhouse gas emissions.

Protecting existing forests and reforesting degraded land can help to mitigate climate change and provide additional benefits, such as improved air and water quality. Carbon capture and storage technologies can capture carbon dioxide emissions from industrial processes and store them underground, preventing them from entering the atmosphere. This can help to reduce greenhouse gas emissions from some hard-to-decarbonize sectors like steel and cement. Developing countries, in particular, may lack the resources to implement climate change mitigation and adaptation measures.

Climate finance can provide financial support to help countries transition to low-carbon economies and adapt to the impacts of climate change. Addressing climate change is a global problem that requires international cooperation and collaboration. This can involve negotiating and implementing global agreements like the Paris Agreement, sharing technology and knowledge, and supporting developing countries to transition to low-carbon economies. Addressing climate change requires a range of solutions, including reducing greenhouse gas emissions, adapting to the impacts of climate change, protecting and restoring forests, developing carbon capture and storage technologies, providing climate finance, and promoting international cooperation. Implementing these solutions will require collective action from individuals, governments, and the private sector to achieve a sustainable future.

CHAPTER 2.

Ghost in the Wires: Cybersecurity Threats

In today's interconnected world, the rapid advancement of technology has brought about tremendous benefits, transforming the way we live, work, and communicate. However, this progress has also introduced new challenges, particularly in the realm of cybersecurity. As our societies become increasingly reliant on digital systems and networks, the threat landscape has expanded to include cyberattacks, data breaches, and other malicious activities that can have far-reaching consequences.

Understanding and effectively addressing cybersecurity threats require a multidimensional approach that goes beyond technological solutions. International political theories provide valuable frameworks for comprehending the complexities of these challenges and formulating strategies to mitigate them. In this chapter, I delve into the intersection of international politics and cybersecurity, exploring how political theories can be applied to understand, analyze, and resolve cybersecurity threats from an international perspective. One of the fundamental aspects I will explore is the concept of global security. Traditional security studies have primarily focused on military threats, but the rise of cyberspace has broadened the definition of security. Cybersecurity has emerged as an integral component of national and global security, as cyberattacks can disrupt critical infrastructure, compromise sensitive information, and undermine the stability of nations. By examining cybersecurity through the lens of global security theories, I aim to provide readers with a comprehensive understanding of the importance of safeguarding digital networks and systems in today's interconnected world. Throughout this chapter, I will explore various international political theories and their applicability to cybersecurity.

By combining insights from these international political theories with concrete examples and case studies, this chapter aims to equip readers with the knowledge and analytical tools necessary to navigate the complex landscape of cybersecurity threats. Furthermore, it seeks to highlight the interconnected nature of cyber threats, emphasizing the importance of international cooperation, information sharing, and collaboration in addressing these challenges. In the future, it may be necessary for us to comprehend and investigate various aspects of the issue of cyber security, which poses a threat to global security. These aspects include the roles of nation-states and non-state actors, the impact on global economy and trade, the evolving legal and ethical considerations, and the future implications of emerging technologies such as artificial intelligence and the Internet of Things (IoT).

By illuminating the diverse facets of cybersecurity from an international political perspective, wherever possible, it is the idea that those involved in cybersecurity need to be empowered to engage critically in this important area and contribute to a concerted effort to ensure a safer and more secure digital future.

Firstly, Realism, also known as political realism, is a view of international politics that stresses its competitive and conflictual side. In the context of cybersecurity, realism suggests that states are primarily concerned with their own security and will prioritize their own interests over those of other actors. Therefore, states may engage in cyber espionage, cyberattacks, or other forms of cyber activity to advance their own interests and gain strategic advantage.[1] Secondly, liberalism emphasizes the importance of international institutions, cooperation, and interdependence in promoting peace and security. In the context of cybersecurity, liberalism suggests that international cooperation and coordination can help to address cybersecurity threats through the establishment of norms, standards, and regulations that promote cybersecurity and protect critical infrastructure. Additionally, liberalism emphasizes the role of non-state actors, such as civil society organizations and private companies, in promoting cybersecurity and reducing cyber threats. Finally, constructivism views international relations as being shaped by shared ideas and norms, rather than just material interests. In the context of cybersecurity, constructivism suggests that states' perceptions of cybersecurity threats are shaped by their own cultural and ideological values, as well as by international norms and standards. Therefore, international cooperation and the establishment of shared norms and standards can help to reduce cybersecurity threats.

If that is the case, I can explore theoretical aspects that may be applied to cybersecurity from a humanistic and political philosophical perspective to facilitate a more fundamental comprehension. These theories focus on the human dimension of cyber security, as opposed to the technological or engineering aspects. One such theory is the social contract theory, which argues that individuals form a social contract with the state in which they give up some of their rights and freedoms in exchange for protection and security. In the context of cyber security, this theory can be used to justify the government's role in protecting individuals and organizations from cyber threats. This could involve the government setting standards for cyber security, enforcing laws and regulations related to cyber security, and investing in research and development to improve cyber security. Another theory that can be applied to cyber security is the theory of justice. This theory holds that justice requires that individuals and groups be treated fairly and equitably. In the context of cyber security, this theory could be used to argue for equal access to cyber security protections and resources, regardless of an individual or organization's size or wealth. It could also be used to argue for the fair distribution of the costs associated with cyber security, such as the cost of implementing security measures or recovering from a cyber-attack. A third theory that can be applied to cyber security is the theory of human rights. This theory holds that all individuals are entitled to certain fundamental rights, such as the right to privacy, freedom of expression, and freedom from discrimination. In the context of cyber security, this theory could be used to argue for the protection of these rights in the online world. For example, it could be used to argue against the collection and use of personal data without an individual's consent, or against censorship or surveillance by governments or other entities. A fourth theory that can be applied to cyber security is the theory of ethics. This theory holds that individuals and organizations have ethical responsibilities to act in ways that are morally right and just. In the context of cyber security, this theory could be used to argue for ethical behavior by individuals and organizations when it comes to cyber security. This could involve promoting transparency, honesty, and integrity in the development and implementation of cyber security measures, as well as a commitment to protecting the privacy and security of users. These theories provide a framework for thinking about cyber security from a humanistic and political philosophical perspective, and can help guide policy and decision-making in this important area

The application of these theories can help to provide a framework for understanding the cybersecurity threat from an international political point of view and developing effective strategies for addressing this threat. However, it is important to note that these theories are not mutually exclusive and can be used in combination to provide a more nuanced understanding of the issue.

Cybersecurity Threats Pose a Serious Threat to Global Security

Cybersecurity threats are becoming an increasingly serious threat to global security, as more and more of our lives are being conducted online. From financial transactions to sensitive government communications, our dependence on digital technology has created new vulnerabilities that can be exploited by malicious actors. It is imperative that we acknowledge the multifarious ways in which cybersecurity threats can pose significant risks to global security, as delineated below. Firstly, cyber-attacks can cause substantial economic damage, resulting in financial losses for individuals, businesses, and governments. Apart from the immediate costs associated with responding to and recovering from an attack, there can also be long-term consequences, such as a decline in investor confidence and adverse effects on the overall economy. Secondly, cyber-attacks have the potential to destabilize political systems. They can be employed as a tool to disrupt political processes, including elections and the normal functioning of government agencies. Additionally, they can be utilized to disseminate disinformation or propaganda, eroding public trust in institutions and leading to social unrest.[2] Moreover, governments possess sensitive information ranging from military secrets to intelligence data, which is susceptible to compromise through cyber-attacks. If foreign governments gain access to such information, it could pose a significant threat to national security. Furthermore, as critical infrastructure systems like power grids, transportation networks, and water supplies become increasingly interconnected with the internet, they become vulnerable to attacks. Compromising these systems could have catastrophic consequences for public safety and the economy. Additionally, cyber-attacks can be exploited by terrorist organizations to carry out acts of violence or propagate their messages online. This instills fear and panic among the public, creating a sense of insecurity and fostering mistrust. Considering the aforementioned points, the threat of cyber-attacks is a complex and multifaceted problem that necessitates a coordinated response from governments, businesses, and individuals. As our world becomes more interconnected, it is imperative that we take measures to safeguard ourselves and our systems against these threats in order to ensure global security.

Several High-Profile Cases

By examining certain cases where cybersecurity threats pose a significant risk to global security, we could gain a comprehensive understanding of the risks associated with cybersecurity. There have been several high-profile cases where cybersecurity threats posed serious threats to global security.

Russian interference in the 2016 US election: The US intelligence community concluded that Russia interfered in the 2016 presidential election through a combination of hacking and disinformation campaigns. The goal was to undermine public confidence in the democratic process and promote the election of Donald Trump.[3]

WannaCry ransomware attack: In May 2017, a global ransomware attack called WannaCry infected hundreds of thousands of computers in over 150 countries. The attack disrupted hospitals, transportation systems, and businesses around the world, causing widespread panic and economic damage.[4]

Iranian cyber-attacks on US infrastructure: In 2013 and 2014, Iranian hackers carried out a series of attacks on US infrastructure, including a cyber-attack on a dam in New York State. While no damage was done in these attacks, they demonstrated the potential for cyber-attacks to cause physical harm and disruption.

Chinese hacking of US government agencies: In 2015, it was discovered that Chinese hackers had breached the US Office of Personnel Management, compromising the personal information of millions of government employees. This information could be used for espionage or blackmail purposes, posing a serious threat to national security.

North Korean cyber-attacks on banks and businesses: North Korea has been linked to several high-profile cyber-attacks, including the 2016 theft of $81 million from the Bangladesh Bank and the 2014 hack of Sony Pictures.[5] These attacks have been carried out to fund the regime and disrupt its enemies, posing a threat to both economic and political stability.

These cases demonstrate the potential for cyber-attacks to cause serious harm to global security, from disrupting democratic processes to causing economic damage and physical harm. It is essential that we continue to invest in cybersecurity measures and work together on a global level to prevent and respond to these threats.

The Solutions for Cyber Security Threats?

In the realm of international politics, addressing cyber security threats necessitates a comprehensive and coordinated approach to safeguarding digital infrastructure and mitigating potential risks. A viable solution to these threats involves adopting a multilateral framework that fosters collaboration among nations, promotes information sharing, and establishes norms and standards in cyberspace.[6] Primarily, international cooperation is essential to effectively tackle cyber security challenges. Governments must engage in dialogue and establish partnerships to share intelligence, best practices, and technological advancements.

By forging alliances, states can collectively enhance their capabilities in detecting, preventing, and responding to cyber-attacks, thereby strengthening the resilience of their digital networks. Furthermore, the establishment of international norms and standards serves as a critical foundation for addressing cyber security threats. Through diplomatic efforts and negotiations, states can work towards developing a common understanding of acceptable behaviors in cyberspace. This entails delineating the boundaries of state-sponsored cyber activities, promoting responsible behavior, and holding accountable those who engage in malicious cyber operations. Such norms provide a framework for establishing trust among nations and reducing the risk of escalating cyber conflicts. Moreover, robust cyber defense mechanisms are imperative in protecting critical infrastructure and sensitive data. States should invest in developing advanced technologies, such as artificial intelligence and machine learning, to bolster their defensive capabilities. Concurrently, it is crucial to enhance the capacity of states with limited resources, ensuring that all nations have the means to effectively combat cyber threats. International assistance programs and knowledge-sharing initiatives can play a vital role in bridging the cyber security gap between developed and developing nations.

In addition, addressing the root causes of cyber security threats necessitates addressing the issue of cybercrime. Strengthening international legal frameworks and enhancing law enforcement cooperation are pivotal in combating cybercriminal networks that exploit vulnerabilities for financial gain. This entails extraditing offenders, harmonizing legislation, and facilitating the exchange of evidence and intelligence across borders. Lastly, public-private partnerships are instrumental in bolstering cyber security efforts. Collaboration between governments, the private sector, and civil society can leverage the expertise and resources of each sector to foster innovation and improve cyber resilience.

Encouraging the establishment of sector-specific information-sharing platforms and facilitating public-private cooperation in research and development initiatives can effectively enhance cyber defenses. Accordingly, the solution to cyber security threats in the realm of international politics lies in fostering collaboration, establishing norms, strengthening defenses, combating cybercrime, and promoting public-private partnerships. By implementing these measures, nations can work, together to safeguard their digital landscapes and protect the security and integrity of the global cyber domain.

The US and China are both developing strategies to defend against cybersecurity threats. Here are some of the strategies each country is pursuing. The US government is currently taking various strategic measures to prevent and respond to cyber security threats. Firstly, the US government has formed public-private partnerships with private companies to facilitate the exchange of information and collaboratively develop strategies to counter cybersecurity threats. Secondly, the US government has implemented robust cybersecurity standards for critical infrastructure, such as power plants and financial systems, in order to enhance their resilience against cyber-attacks.

Additionally, the US government has allocated increased funding for cybersecurity initiatives, including research and development efforts aimed at advancing technologies to bolster cybersecurity measures. Moreover, the US military has adopted an active defense strategy, focusing on proactive identification and disruption of cyber-attacks before they can inflict harm or damage. Furthermore, the US government has established information-sharing programs, allowing for the exchange of threat intelligence with other countries and private companies. This cooperative approach aims to enhance overall cybersecurity by facilitating a collective response to cyber threats. These measures demonstrate the US government's commitment to addressing cybersecurity challenges and safeguarding critical systems through collaboration, strengthened standards, increased funding, proactive defense strategies, and improved information sharing.[7]

Meanwhile, the Chinese government is also gradually seeking diversified strategies to prevent and respond to current cyber security threats. China has enacted a new cybersecurity law, known as the National Cybersecurity Law, which mandates that companies operating within its borders adhere to specific security standards and store their data domestically. In order to enhance cybersecurity, China, with its robust centralized government, has strengthened its oversight over internet and technology companies, aiming to bolster control and safeguard against potential threats.

China has also implemented more stringent data privacy regulations, requiring companies to seek consent before collecting personal data and mandating the deletion of unnecessary data. Furthermore, China has formulated a comprehensive national cybersecurity strategy focused on safeguarding national security and thwarting cyber-attacks targeting critical infrastructure. To further fortify their cybersecurity defenses, China has allocated increased funds towards research and development initiatives, aiming to cultivate new technologies and train cybersecurity professionals.[8]

In conclusion, the escalating threat of cyber terrorism demands urgent attention and concerted action from the international community. Both the

United States and China have recognized the gravity of this challenge and have made substantial investments in cybersecurity to counter cyber threats. However, concerns regarding China's cybersecurity laws, their potential impact on privacy and free speech, as well as the government's control over tech companies, raise legitimate apprehensions. To effectively address cyber terrorism while safeguarding privacy and human rights, it is imperative for both countries to collaborate and engage with the international community in developing robust cybersecurity strategies.

Privacy and free speech concerns stemming from China's cybersecurity laws are well-documented. These laws, including the National Intelligence Law and the Cybersecurity Law, grant the Chinese government broad powers to monitor and control online activities.[9] This has raised significant concerns regarding the potential infringement of privacy rights and the stifling of free expression.[10] The absence of transparent oversight mechanisms and the extensive authority granted to the government over tech companies exacerbate these concerns, necessitating a careful balance between national security imperatives and individual liberties.

Collaboration between the United States and China, both of which possess considerable cybersecurity expertise and resources, is vital in combating cyber terrorism effectively. The synergistic outcomes of joint efforts, such as information sharing, joint research and development, and capacity building, can significantly bolster cyber defenses on a global scale.[11] Establishing platforms for constructive dialogue and fostering trust between the two countries is essential to establish a solid foundation for cooperation in countering cyber threats.

Respecting privacy and human rights should remain a core principle in the formulation of cybersecurity strategies. While protecting national security is crucial, it should not come at the expense of civil liberties. Transparency, accountability, and the inclusion of independent oversight mechanisms are crucial to ensure that cybersecurity efforts align with privacy rights and human rights standards.[12] Striking the right balance between security and individual freedoms requires a nuanced approach that incorporates international best practices.

Engaging the international community is pivotal in effectively combating cyber terrorism. Given the transnational nature of the threat, collaboration on a global scale is indispensable. The United Nations and other regional organizations can serve as platforms for establishing norms, protocols, and legal frameworks governing responsible behavior in cyberspace.[13] By actively engaging with the international community, both the United States and China can contribute to the development of a shared understanding and collective response to cyber threats, fostering trust, enhancing transparency, and promoting global cybersecurity.

In conclusion, the threat of cyber terrorism is an urgent concern that calls for collaborative and comprehensive cybersecurity strategies. Addressing this challenge requires the active participation of both the United States and China, in coordination with the international community. By prioritizing privacy rights, human rights, and international norms, we can forge a secure and resilient cyberspace that protects individuals, societies, and global security.

CHAPTER 3.

Generation Kill[1]: Terrorism

Terrorism and International Politics

Terrorism is a persistent global threat that knows no border, nationality or religion, and is a challenge that the international community must tackle together. It poses a direct threat to the security of the citizens of NATO countries, and to international stability and prosperity. The international development of terrorism means that the impact of terrorism on national security has spread outside the country, affecting the political stability of countries in the region and leading to tension and deterioration of relations between countries.[2]

Terrorism represents an enduring and pervasive global threat that transcends borders, nationalities, and religions, necessitating a collective response from the international community. This menace directly jeopardizes the security of NATO member states, as well as international stability and prosperity. The evolution of terrorism on an international scale has extended its impact beyond national boundaries, resulting in political instability within affected regions and strained relations between countries. Regrettably, the threat of terrorism is projected to persist and potentially worsen in the coming decade, with Islamist extremists from numerous nations operating in diverse locations like never before. Fragile and violence-prone states, particularly in Southeast Asia, continue to be exploited by extremists for establishing safe havens and enhancing their capabilities (Global Terrorism Index, 2021).

The implications of terrorism reach far and wide, contributing to global instability and necessitating international security interventions, notably in the Middle East and Africa. Although the so-called Islamic State (ISIL) has experienced territorial setbacks in Iraq and Syria, extremist narratives continue to inspire violence on a global scale.[3] Additionally, Al Qa'ida maintains its intent to orchestrate attacks against Western interests, while the emergence of other terrorist groups remains a distinct possibility. It is vital to underscore the significance of Afghanistan's security and stability in containing the threat posed by international terrorism.[4]

The complex and multifaceted nature of the terrorism threat necessitates unified and coordinated efforts among nations. It is no longer sufficient for individual states to tackle this challenge in isolation. The transnational reach of terrorism demands collective action, comprehensive strategies, and enhanced international cooperation to effectively mitigate and combat this threat. By fostering collaboration, information sharing, and joint counterterrorism operations, the international community can maximize its capacity to prevent terrorist attacks, dismantle terrorist networks, and disrupt the recruitment and financing of terrorist organizations.[5]

Furthermore, addressing the underlying conditions that fuel terrorism is equally imperative. Socio-economic inequalities, political grievances, and marginalization provide fertile ground for radicalization and the spread of extremist ideologies. By investing in education, social development, and the promotion of inclusive governance, nations can tackle the root causes of terrorism and mitigate the allure of violent extremism.[6]

In this context, terrorism represents a persistent and far-reaching global threat that necessitates a unified and comprehensive response from the international community. Its impact extends beyond national borders, disrupting political stability and straining relations between nations. As terrorism continues to evolve, with a growing number of Islamist extremists operating in various regions, international collaboration is vital in countering this menace. By enhancing cooperation, sharing intelligence, and implementing joint counterterrorism measures, nations can effectively prevent terrorist attacks, dismantle terrorist networks, and address the underlying conditions that fuel extremism. Only through collective action can the international community strive towards a safer and more secure world, resilient against the threats posed by terrorism.

Terrorism is a complex phenomenon that can be analyzed and understood from various philosophical perspectives, including humanistic and political philosophical perspectives. Humanistic philosophy emphasizes the importance of individual freedom, dignity, and autonomy. From this perspective, terrorism can be seen as a violation of these values, as it involves the use of violence to coerce and intimidate people into conforming to a particular ideology or political agenda. Some humanistic theorists argue that terrorism is the result of a lack of empathy, compassion, and moral reasoning, and that terrorists are often motivated by a sense of grievance or injustice that they believe justifies their actions.

Political philosophy is concerned with the nature of power, authority, and the organization of society. From this perspective, terrorism can be seen as a political act that aims to challenge or undermine the existing power structures and social norms. Some political philosophers argue that terrorism is a form of resistance against oppressive regimes or unjust policies, and that it can be justified as a means of achieving political change. However, others argue that terrorism is inherently immoral and illegitimate, as it involves the deliberate targeting of innocent civilians and the use of violence as a tool of coercion.

Major Terrorist Incidents

Since the 9/11 terrorist attacks in the United States in 2001, there have been numerous major terrorist incidents around the world. Here are some of the most significant incidents:

Madrid train bombings (2004): On March 11, 2004, a series of coordinated bombings were carried out on commuter trains in Madrid, Spain, killing 191 people and injuring over 2,000 others. An Islamic extremist group affiliated with al-Qaeda carried out the attacks.[7]

London bombings (2005): On July 7, 2005, four suicide bombers carried out coordinated attacks on London's public transportation system, killing 52 people and injuring over 700 others. The attackers were British nationals inspired by Islamic extremist ideology.[8]

Mumbai attacks (2008): In November 2008, a group of terrorists carried out a series of coordinated attacks in Mumbai, India, targeting multiple locations including a hotel, train station, and Jewish community center. The attacks killed 166 people and injured over 300 others. The attackers were members of a Pakistan-based militant group.[9]

Paris attacks (2015): On November 13, 2015, a group of terrorists carried out a series of coordinated attacks in Paris, France, targeting multiple locations including a concert hall, restaurants, and a sports stadium. The attacks killed 130 people and injured over 400 others. The attackers were affiliated with the Islamic State (ISIS) terrorist group.[10]

Brussels bombings (2016): On March 22, 2016, a group of terrorists carried out coordinated bombings at the Brussels airport and a metro station, killing 32 people and injuring over 300 others. The attackers were affiliated with the ISIS terrorist group.[11]

Manchester Arena bombing (2017): On May 22, 2017, a suicide bomber targeted a concert at the Manchester Arena in Manchester, England, killing

22 people and injuring over 800 others. The attacker was a British national affiliated with the ISIS terrorist group.[12]

Barcelona attacks (2017): On August 17, 2017, a group of terrorists carried out a series of coordinated attacks in Barcelona, Spain, targeting pedestrians with a van and later a car. The attacks killed 16 people and injured over 100 others. The attackers were affiliated with an ISIS-inspired cell.

Christchurch mosque shootings (2019): On March 15, 2019, a white supremacist terrorist attacked two mosques in Christchurch, New Zealand, killing 51 people and injuring over 50 others. The attacker was a 28-year-old Australian man who had published a manifesto expressing anti-Muslim and white supremacist views.

Sri Lanka Easter bombings (2019): On April 21, 2019, a series of coordinated bombings targeted churches and hotels in Sri Lanka, killing 259 people and injuring over 500 others. The attackers were affiliated with a local Islamist extremist group.

Kabul airport attack (2021): On August 26, 2021, a suicide bombing carried out by an ISIS-K terrorist killed 13 U.S. service members and over 170 Afghan civilians at the Kabul airport in Afghanistan.

These are just a few examples of major terrorist incidents that have occurred since the 9/11 attacks. Unfortunately, terrorism continues to be a major threat to global security.

How Terrorism Affects Global security.

Terrorism is a phenomenon that affects global security in multiple ways. The following are some detailed examples of how terrorism can affect global security:

Destabilization of states and regions: Terrorism often targets countries or regions that are already politically or socially unstable. Terrorist attacks can further destabilize these regions by causing panic, fear, and social unrest, leading to an increase in violence and extremism. For instance, the Taliban in Afghanistan, al-Qaeda in the Middle East, and ISIS in Iraq and Syria have been responsible for significant acts of terrorism that have destabilized these regions and caused widespread violence and social unrest.[13]

Damage to critical infrastructure: Terrorist attacks can also cause significant damage to critical infrastructure, such as transportation networks, communication systems, and energy facilities. This damage can lead to disruptions in the economy, affect supply chains, and cause significant social and economic damage. For example, the 9/11 attacks in the United States led to the destruction of the World Trade Center, which caused significant economic and social damage and disrupted the global financial system.[14]

Increase in global military spending: In response to the threat of terrorism, many countries have increased their military spending and implemented security measures to protect their citizens and critical infrastructure. This increase in military spending can strain national budgets, divert resources away from other important programs, and potentially destabilize the global balance of power.

Increase in surveillance and erosion of civil liberties: The threat of terrorism has led many governments to implement surveillance measures and restrict civil liberties in the name of national security. These measures can be controversial and may violate individual rights and freedoms. For example, the Patriot Act in the United States was implemented in the aftermath of the 9/11 attacks to give law enforcement and intelligence agencies greater powers to investigate and prevent terrorism. However, some have criticized these measures as an erosion of civil liberties and a violation of privacy rights.

Increase in international cooperation: The threat of terrorism has also led to an increase in international cooperation between countries in the areas of intelligence sharing, law enforcement, and military operations. This cooperation can be beneficial for preventing terrorism, but it can also be controversial and lead to tensions between countries. For example, the United States has often collaborated with countries in the Middle East to combat terrorism, but this cooperation has also been criticized for supporting repressive regimes and violating human rights. Overall, terrorism has significant impacts on global security, including the destabilization of regions, damage to critical infrastructure, increase in military spending and surveillance, erosion of civil liberties, and increase in international cooperation.[15]

Diplomatic Security Strategies to Prevent Terrorism

Major developed countries, including the United States, have implemented a range of diplomatic and security strategies to prevent terrorism. The following are some examples of these strategies. A crucial strategy is to foster cooperation among countries in countering terrorism. This involves the sharing of intelligence, coordination of law enforcement efforts, and joint implementation of military operations aimed at preventing terrorist attacks.

For instance, the United States has established partnerships with numerous nations worldwide to combat terrorism. These partnerships encompass intelligence sharing, joint military operations, as well as training and support for local law enforcement agencies. Another strategy involves strengthening border security measures to prevent the entry of terrorists into the country. This includes implementing stricter screening procedures at airports and other points of entry as well as enhancing cooperation among border security agencies. As an illustration, the United States has enacted the Visa Waiver Program Improvement and Terrorist Travel Prevention Act, which mandates individuals from certain countries to obtain a visa before entering the United States.

Furthermore, the United States collaborates with other nations to implement similar border security measures. An additional strategy is to counter violent extremism by addressing the root causes of terrorism, such as social and economic inequality, political instability, and religious extremism. This entails implementing programs aimed at promoting education, economic development, and social integration to prevent individuals from being radicalized.

For example, the United States has established programs to counter violent extremism, such as the Global Engagement Center, which focuses on countering extremist propaganda online through messaging and digital engagement. Another strategy involves enhancing intelligence and surveillance capabilities to detect and prevent terrorist attacks. This includes leveraging advanced technologies like drones, artificial intelligence, and big data analytics to identify potential threats. As an example, the United States has implemented the Terrorist Screening Database, which serves as a consolidated repository of known or suspected terrorists.

Additionally, surveillance technologies are utilized by the United States to monitor potential threats and prevent terrorist attacks. Lastly, another strategy is to conduct targeted military operations against terrorist organizations. This entails using military force to disrupt terrorist operations, eliminate or capture key leaders, and degrade the capabilities of these groups. For instance, the United States has carried out targeted military operations against terrorist organizations like al-Qaeda and ISIS in Iraq, Syria, and other regions. Furthermore, the United States provides military support to countries such as Afghanistan and Iraq to combat terrorism.

These strategies aim to prevent terrorist attacks by strengthening security measures, promoting counterterrorism cooperation, addressing the root causes of terrorism, enhancing intelligence and surveillance, and conducting targeted military operations against terrorist organizations.

Experts suggest a range of measures to counter both large and small-scale terrorism occurring around the world. The following are some of the countermeasures that are often recommended. One of the most important measures to prevent terrorism is intelligence sharing and cooperation between countries. This includes sharing information on potential threats, cooperating on investigations, and working together to disrupt terrorist operations. Another important measure is to strengthen border security to prevent terrorists from entering a country.

Countering violent extremism: To prevent individuals from becoming radicalized and joining terrorist groups, it is essential to address the root causes of terrorism. This includes promoting education, economic development, and social integration to prevent individuals from becoming vulnerable to extremist propaganda.

Enhanced surveillance: To detect and prevent terrorist attacks, experts recommend the use of advanced surveillance technologies, such as drones, artificial intelligence, and big data analytics. These technologies can help identify potential threats and prevent attacks before they occur.

Targeted military operations: To disrupt the operations of terrorist organizations, experts suggest conducting targeted military operations, such as drone strikes or Special Forces raids, to kill or capture key leaders and degrade their capabilities. Improving international cooperation: It is important to improve international cooperation on counterterrorism measures, including sharing best practices and coordinating efforts to prevent terrorist attacks. Protecting critical infrastructure: Terrorists often target critical infrastructure, such as transportation networks, communication systems, and energy facilities. To prevent such attacks, experts suggest implementing measures to protect critical infrastructure, such as improving cybersecurity and physical security. Strengthening emergency response: In the event of a terrorist attack, it is important to have a strong emergency response system in place to minimize the damage and prevent further attacks. This includes training law enforcement and emergency responders, as well as conducting regular drills and simulations. A comprehensive approach is needed to counter terrorism, including intelligence sharing, border security measures, countering violent extremism, enhanced surveillance, targeted military operations, improving international cooperation, protecting critical infrastructure, and strengthening emergency response.[16]

Terrorism, an alarming threat with no regard for borders, looms over the entire world. It poses a complex challenge that demands a comprehensive approach to combat and prevent its destructive influence. Internationally, there exist several strategies that can be employed to tackle terrorism effectively. One crucial aspect is enhancing international cooperation among nations. Collaboration is vital for sharing intelligence, coordinating law enforcement efforts, and disrupting terrorist networks. Esteemed organizations like the United Nations, NATO, and the G20 can facilitate this cooperation.

Another imperative is the promotion of good governance. To address the root causes of terrorism, nations must confront issues such as poverty, inequality, and limited opportunities. Economic development, social programs, and political reforms can play a significant role in this endeavor. Upholding human rights and the rule of law is equally crucial. By safeguarding human rights, nations can prevent individuals from falling prey to radicalization and joining terrorist groups.

At the governmental level, several strategies can be implemented to combat and prevent terrorism. Firstly, governments must invest in strengthening law enforcement and intelligence gathering capabilities. The utilization of cutting-edge technologies, including facial recognition software and big data analytics, can aid in identifying and disrupting terrorist plots. Creating a culture of security is another important aspect. Governments must educate the public about the terrorism threat and empower them to protect themselves. Public awareness campaigns and educational programs can play a significant role in achieving this goal. Building resilience within communities is also crucial. Governments can support victims of terrorism, promote community cohesion, and back initiatives that foster tolerance and understanding.

While terrorism poses a complex challenge, it is not insurmountable. By joining forces and working in unison, nations can develop and implement effective strategies to combat and prevent terrorism. In addition to the aforementioned strategies, there are other measures that can be taken to combat and prevent terrorism. Investing in education and economic development stands out as two pivotal tools in the fight against terrorism. By providing individuals with access to education and economic opportunities, the allure of extremism can be diminished. Promoting tolerance and understanding is yet another significant avenue to pursue. Terrorism often thrives in environments of intolerance and ignorance. By fostering tolerance and understanding, a more peaceful world can be cultivated.

Furthermore, it is vital for all individuals to speak out against extremism whenever and wherever it occurs. By voicing opposition to extremist ideologies, we contribute to the creation of a more tolerant and peaceful global community. While terrorism remains a pressing global issue, it is not insurmountable. Through collective effort and collaboration, we can forge a world where everyone can live free from the specter of terrorism.

CHAPTER 4.

Humanity's Unfortunate Journey: the Nuclear Age

The war in Ukraine has led to an escalation of Russia's nuclear threat, which has created a crisis in international security. Before we begin this chapter, I would like to briefly review why Russia openly threatened nuclear weapons during the Ukraine war and why the international security threat could not rule out the possibility of an international security crisis.

The international security landscape has been significantly impacted by Russia's assertive actions and its open threats of nuclear weapon use, particularly evident in the context of the Ukraine war. The escalation of tensions between Russia and Ukraine, coupled with the explicit nuclear threats made by Russian officials, has raised grave concerns about the potential for a crisis in international security. This article examines the reasons why Russia's nuclear weapons threats cannot be dismissed and highlights the implications they have on global stability and security.

The ongoing conflict in Ukraine has witnessed a worrying display of Russian aggression, marked by territorial annexations, support for separatist movements, and a heightened military presence. What sets this conflict apart is the explicit nuclear posturing exhibited by Russian officials. Statements from Russian leaders, including veiled threats to use nuclear weapons, serve to escalate tensions and create an atmosphere of fear and uncertainty. Such rhetoric not only undermines the prospects for peaceful resolution but also intensifies the risk of a crisis in international security.

Russia's nuclear threats have significant implications for regional stability, particularly in Eastern Europe. The Ukraine war, coupled with the explicit mention of nuclear weapons, creates a dangerous environment where the balance of power is undermined. Neighboring countries, already concerned about Russia's assertiveness, must grapple with the possibility of an escalation to the nuclear level. This not only destabilizes the region but also triggers a potential arms race as neighboring states seek to bolster their own security through military build-ups and alliances.

Russia's nuclear threats also have far-reaching implications for global arms control efforts. By openly considering the use of nuclear weapons, Russia undermines the norms and agreements established by the international community to prevent nuclear proliferation and maintain strategic stability. This raises questions about the credibility and effectiveness of existing arms control regimes, such as the Treaty on the Non-Proliferation of Nuclear Weapons, and creates an environment conducive to the erosion of established norms.

The overt nuclear threats from Russia reverberate beyond the immediate region, impacting the broader global security architecture. The potential for a crisis in international security arises from the interconnectedness of global power dynamics. A breakdown in regional stability can trigger a chain reaction of responses, potentially leading to unintended escalations and conflicts. The presence of nuclear weapons further exacerbates the potential for miscalculations and accidents, heightening the risks to international security.

Russia's nuclear threats erode trust among nations and undermine the foundations of cooperative security. Confidence-building measures and diplomatic efforts are essential for maintaining stability and preventing conflicts. However, the explicit mention of nuclear weapons undermines these efforts, fueling mistrust and exacerbating tensions. In turn, this hampers the prospects for meaningful dialogue and negotiation, making it increasingly challenging to find peaceful resolutions to conflicts.

Russia's nuclear threats in the context of the Ukraine war represent a significant crisis for global security. The explicit mention of nuclear weapons, coupled with Russia's assertive actions, threatens regional stability, undermines arms control efforts, and erodes the global security architecture. The potential for unintended escalation and the impact on trust and cooperative security cannot be dismissed. It is imperative for the international community to address these threats through diplomatic engagement, reaffirmation of arms control commitments, and a collective commitment to maintaining global stability. Only through concerted efforts can the crisis posed by Russia's nuclear threats be effectively managed, ensuring a safer and more secure international order.

Nuclear Proliferation and international politics

Nuclear proliferation refers to the spread of nuclear weapons, technology, and information to countries that do not already possess them. It is a significant threat to global security today.[1] The international community has been grappling with the challenge of discouraging countries from developing nuclear weapons while promoting the use of nuclear technology for peaceful purposes such as energy generation and medical research. The International Atomic Energy Agency (IAEA) has been strengthening its safeguards system to address these challenges.

The proliferation and use of nuclear weapons is a critical issue in international politics that requires an understanding of various theoretical perspectives. According to realism, states are rational actors that seek to maximize their power and security. Therefore, the proliferation of nuclear weapons is a rational strategy for states to enhance their security by deterring other states from attacking them.[2] Realists argue that nuclear weapons have prevented major wars between nuclear-armed states, as no state wants to risk the catastrophic consequences of a nuclear war. However, the downside of nuclear proliferation is the risk of nuclear accidents, miscalculations, and escalation of conflicts, which can lead to catastrophic consequences. Liberalism is another theoretical perspective that emphasizes cooperation, interdependence, and international institutions. From a liberal perspective, the proliferation of nuclear weapons is a threat to international peace and security, as it increases the risk of nuclear war and undermines the credibility of international institutions. Liberals advocate for disarmament, non-proliferation, and peaceful conflict resolution through international institutions such as the United Nations and the International Atomic Energy Agency (IAEA). They argue that the long-term benefits of disarmament and non-proliferation outweigh the short-term benefits of deterrence.[3] Constructivism is a theoretical perspective that emphasizes the role of norms, ideas, and identities in shaping international politics. From a constructivist perspective, the proliferation of nuclear weapons is a result of social norms and identities that define the role of nuclear weapons in national security strategies. States acquire nuclear weapons not only for security reasons but also for prestige, status, and identity. Therefore, to reduce the proliferation of nuclear weapons, it is necessary to change the social norms and identities that support nuclear weapons. Constructivists advocate for norms of disarmament, non-proliferation, and peaceful conflict resolution through dialogue and cooperation. Marxism is a theoretical perspective that emphasizes the role of economic and social factors in shaping international politics. From a Marxist perspective, the proliferation of nuclear weapons is a result of the capitalist system that prioritizes profits over human security. The military-industrial complex, which profits from the production and sale of nuclear weapons, has a stake in perpetuating the arms race and preventing disarmament. Therefore, to reduce the proliferation of nuclear weapons, it is necessary to challenge the capitalist system and the military-industrial complex.

The issue of nuclear proliferation and use can be analyzed from various theoretical perspectives, each offering unique insights into the motivations, causes, and consequences of nuclear weapons. Understanding these perspectives can help policymakers develop effective strategies for reducing the risk of nuclear war and promoting international peace and security. The use and proliferation of nuclear weapons are complex issues that involve a range of philosophical, ethical, and political considerations. From a humanistic and political philosophical point of view, there are several theories that can be applied to these issues. One of the most relevant theories in this context is just war theory. This theory provides a framework for evaluating the moral and ethical considerations of war, including the use of nuclear weapons. According to just war theory, for a war to be just, it must meet several criteria, including having a just cause, being declared by a legitimate authority, and being conducted with proportionality and discrimination.

Either formally or informally, countries that now universally recognize themselves, as nuclear powers exist here. According to the BBC, nine countries currently have nuclear weapons: the US, UK, Russia, France, China, India, Pakistan, Israel and North Korea. In this regard, an overview of the estimated nuclear warhead inventories of real nuclear powers worldwide on their status is provided. It is important to note that the information I will provide is based on the most recent available data up until my knowledge cutoff in September 2021. Therefore, the numbers may have changed by the current date of June 2023, and it is always advisable to refer to up-to-date sources for the most accurate information.[4]

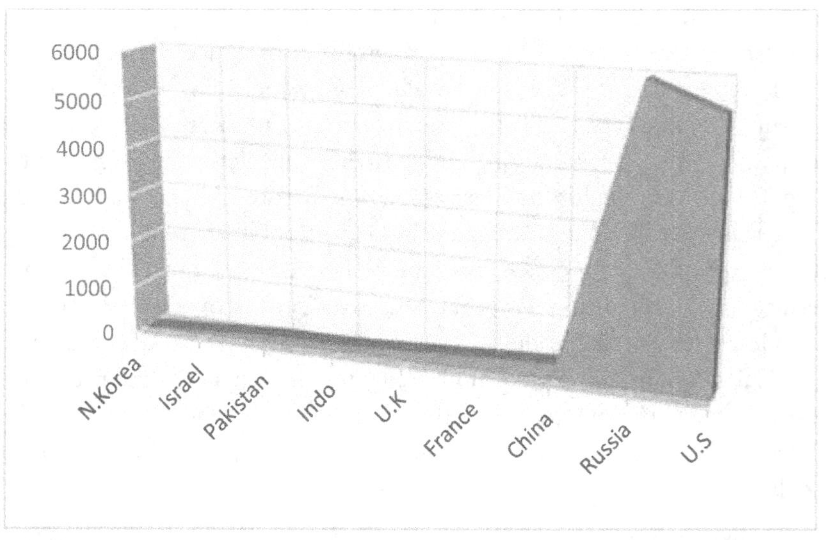

Table 1. Estimated Global Nuclear Warhead Inventories (2022)[5]

Despite making progress in reducing the number of nuclear weapons since the end of the Cold War, the world still maintains a significant stockpile of nuclear warheads. As of early 2022, nine countries collectively possess approximately 12,700 warheads.

Different countries hold nuclear weapons for various reasons. Some nations view them as crucial for their security and defense, while others consider them symbols of power and prestige. Some countries may also develop nuclear weapons as a deterrent against other states with similar capabilities.

As depicted in Table 1, the majority-around 90 percent-of all nuclear warheads are owned by Russia and the United States. Each of these countries possesses roughly 4,000 warheads in their respective military stockpiles. In contrast, no other nuclear-armed nation believes it necessary to have more than a few hundred nuclear weapons for national security purposes.

On a global scale, the overall inventory of nuclear weapons is decreasing, albeit at a slower pace compared to the past three decades. Furthermore, these reductions primarily occur due to ongoing efforts by the United States and Russia to dismantle previously retired warheads.

In contrast to the overall inventory of nuclear weapons, the number of warheads in global military stockpiles – which comprises warheads assigned to operational forces – is increasing once again. The United States is still reducing its nuclear stockpile slowly. France and Israel have relatively stable inventories. However, China, India, North Korea, Pakistan, and the United Kingdom, as well as possibly Russia, are all thought to be increasing their stockpiles[6]

To help readers understand, the following briefly presented the status of nuclear warheads in nuclear countries, officially or unofficially.

United States:
The United States possesses the largest estimated nuclear warhead inventory among all nuclear powers. As of September 2021, it was estimated to have approximately 3,800 nuclear warheads in its arsenal. The United States has been committed to maintaining a nuclear triad, which includes land-based intercontinental ballistic missiles (ICBMs), submarine-launched ballistic missiles (SLBMs), and strategic bombers. It also has a policy of strategic deterrence, aiming to deter potential adversaries through the threat of overwhelming nuclear retaliation if attacked.

Russia:

Russia, as the successor state to the Soviet Union, also maintains a significant nuclear arsenal. It is estimated to have around 4,310 nuclear warheads as of September 2021. Similar to the United States, Russia follows a nuclear triad approach and has modernized its strategic forces in recent years. It is important to note that the New START Treaty, a bilateral arms control agreement between the United States and Russia, limits the number of deployed strategic nuclear warheads to 1,550 for each country.

China:

China possesses a smaller nuclear arsenal compared to the United States and Russia. While the exact number is uncertain due to China's secrecy surrounding its nuclear program, estimates suggest that China had around 350 nuclear warheads as of September 2021. China maintains a policy of minimum deterrence, aiming to have a credible nuclear deterrent capability sufficient to withstand a first strike and to retaliate effectively. It primarily relies on a nuclear force consisting of land-based missiles and submarines.

France:

France is the only nuclear-armed country in Europe and possesses a relatively smaller nuclear arsenal. As of September 2021, it was estimated to have around 290 nuclear warheads. France's nuclear forces are designed to provide deterrence against potential threats to its vital interests and are primarily composed of submarine-launched ballistic missiles, land-based missiles, and strategic bombers.

United Kingdom:

The United Kingdom, another European nuclear-armed state, maintains a nuclear arsenal primarily composed of submarine-launched ballistic missiles. As of September 2021, the UK was estimated to have around 195 nuclear warheads. The UK's nuclear forces are integrated with those of the United States, and it shares some technology and information with the US as part of the Special Relationship between the two countries.

India and Pakistan:

India and Pakistan are both nuclear-armed neighbors in South Asia. As of September 2021, India was estimated to possess around 156 nuclear warheads, while Pakistan was estimated to have around 165 nuclear warheads. Both countries maintain a policy of minimum deterrence, with their nuclear forces being land-based missiles and aircraft-delivered weapons. It is important to note that tensions between India and Pakistan have historically posed risks of nuclear escalation in the region.

North Korea:
North Korea is the only country to have conducted nuclear tests in the 21st century. Its nuclear program has raised significant concerns among the international community. As of September 2021, North Korea's estimated nuclear warhead inventory remained uncertain, with estimates ranging from 30 to 40 warheads. North Korea's nuclear program has been the subject of numerous international diplomatic efforts aimed at denuclearization and non-proliferation.

Israel
Israel is widely believed to possess a nuclear arsenal, although the country has not officially acknowledged it. Israel maintains a policy of nuclear ambiguity, neither confirming nor denying the existence of its nuclear weapons program. As a result, estimating Israel's nuclear warhead inventory is challenging, and the information available is speculative in nature.

According to various assessments by experts and intelligence agencies, it is estimated that Israel possesses a relatively small nuclear arsenal. The stockpile is estimated to range from approximately 80 to 90 nuclear warheads as of September 2021. It is important to note that these numbers are subject to uncertainty and should be treated as rough estimates. Israel's nuclear program is believed to have started in the 1950s and 1960s, and it reportedly possesses a variety of delivery systems, including aircraft and potentially submarines. The country's nuclear doctrine is often described as one of "nuclear ambiguity" or "strategic ambiguity." This means that Israel's nuclear capabilities are intended to serve as a deterrent against potential adversaries, but the country maintains a deliberate ambiguity regarding the specific conditions under which it would employ nuclear weapons.

Israel's nuclear program has been a subject of regional and international concerns, particularly in the context of regional stability and non-proliferation efforts. The country has not signed the Treaty on the Non-Proliferation of Nuclear Weapons (NPT), which is the principal international treaty aimed at preventing the spread of nuclear weapons. However, Israel has expressed support for the treaty's goals and has participated in non-proliferation initiatives.

The status and evolution of Israel's nuclear arsenal remain closely monitored by regional and international actors. The existence of Israel's nuclear weapons program and its policy of ambiguity contribute to a complex security dynamic in the Middle East region, influencing regional rivalries and potential arms races. As with any covert nuclear program, the lack of transparency surrounding Israel's nuclear arsenal poses challenges for arms control and non-proliferation efforts in the region.

These estimates provide an overview of the nuclear warhead inventories of real nuclear powers as of September 2021. It is important to approach nuclear statistics with caution due to the inherent secrecy surrounding these arsenals. Additionally, the numbers presented here may have changed since then, as states continue to adjust their nuclear postures and engage in arms control negotiations. Monitoring and understanding these inventories are essential for assessing the global nuclear landscape and maintaining strategic stability.

When it comes to the use of nuclear weapons, just war theory provides some clear guidance. For instance, the principle of proportionality requires that the damage caused by the use of nuclear weapons should not be disproportionate to the military objective being pursued. Additionally, the principle of discrimination requires that nuclear weapons should not be used against civilian populations, as doing so would be a violation of the principles of justice and human rights. Another relevant theory is the concept of nuclear deterrence. [7] This theory argues that the possession of nuclear weapons by a state can deter other states from attacking it, thereby promoting stability and security in international relations. However, this theory has been criticized for its reliance on the threat of massive destruction and for its failure to address the potential catastrophic consequences of a nuclear exchange.

From a political philosophical point of view, there are also several relevant theories that can be applied to the issue of nuclear weapons. One such theory is realism, which emphasizes the importance of power and security in international relations. According to this theory, states are primarily concerned with maintaining their own security and advancing their own interests, often at the expense of others. In the context of nuclear weapons, realism would suggest that states would seek to acquire nuclear weapons as a means of increasing their power and deter potential adversaries. Another relevant theory is liberalism, which emphasizes the importance of cooperation, democracy, and human rights in international relations. From a liberal perspective, the possession and use of nuclear weapons are seen as a threat to international stability and security, as they promote a culture of fear and mistrust. [8] Instead, liberals would argue for disarmament and non-proliferation, as well as greater cooperation and dialogue between states. The use and proliferation of nuclear weapons raise complex philosophical and political questions. From a humanistic and political philosophical point of view, several theories can be applied to these issues, including just war theory, nuclear deterrence, realism, and liberalism. Ultimately, the challenge is to balance the need for security and stability with the promotion of justice, human rights, and peace.

Nuclear Weapons Proliferation and Global Security Threats

The global proliferation of nuclear weapons is becoming a reality, and how does this situation eventually pose a serious threat to global security?

The global proliferation of nuclear weapons is a serious threat to global security as it increases the risk of nuclear war and the use of nuclear weapons, which could result in catastrophic consequences. The possession of nuclear weapons by more countries increases the chances of accidental or intentional use, as well as the risk of nuclear terrorism.[9] Nuclear weapons are capable of causing immense destruction and loss of life on an unprecedented scale. A nuclear war could result in the deaths of millions of people and cause long-lasting environmental damage that could affect generations to come. Moreover, the use of nuclear weapons by any country could lead to retaliation from other countries with nuclear capabilities, which could result in a devastating nuclear arms race and escalate into a global conflict.

In addition to the risk of direct use, the proliferation of nuclear weapons also increases the risk of nuclear materials falling into the hands of non-state actors, such as terrorist groups. This could lead to the creation of "dirty bombs" or other improvised nuclear devices, which could cause significant damage and loss of life. The global proliferation of nuclear weapons poses a serious threat to global security, and efforts must be made to prevent further spread of these weapons and work towards disarmament. It is essential that countries work together to reduce tensions and promote peaceful solutions to conflict in order to prevent the use of nuclear weapons.

Thoughts of Nuclear Weapons Scientists

The opinions and maxims of relevant scientists regarding nuclear weapons vary depending on their area of expertise and personal beliefs. However, many scientists who have studied nuclear weapons have expressed concerns about their potential for catastrophic consequences and have advocated for disarmament. One of the most famous scientists to speak out against nuclear weapons was Albert Einstein, who co-signed a letter to President Franklin Roosevelt in 1939[10] warning him of the potential of nuclear weapons and urging him to establish a research program to investigate their feasibility.

Einstein later became an outspoken advocate for nuclear disarmament, famously stating, "I know not with what weapons World War III will be fought, but World War IV will be fought with sticks and stones." Another prominent scientist who spoke out against nuclear weapons was Carl Sagan, a renowned astronomer and astrophysicist. Sagan was a strong proponent of disarmament and believed that nuclear war posed an existential threat to humanity. He famously said, "The nuclear arms race is like two people sitting in a pool of gasoline, one with three matches, and the other with five." Other scientists, such as physicist and Nobel laureate Richard Feynman, have emphasized the importance of maintaining a balance of power between nations to prevent the use of nuclear weapons. Feynman argued that the possession of nuclear weapons by multiple nations could act as a deterrent to their use, as each nation would fear retaliation from other nuclear powers. Many scientists have expressed concerns about the potential consequences of nuclear weapons and have called for disarmament and international cooperation to prevent their use.

Strategies of the Nuclear-Armed States

According to public sources, the countries that are currently known to possess nuclear weapons are the United States, Russia, China, France, the United Kingdom, India, Pakistan, Israel, and North Korea. Together, these states have 12,700 nuclear warheads, of which 9,400 are in active military stockpiles. While this is a significant decline from the approximately 70,000 warheads owned by the nuclear-armed states during the Cold War, nuclear arsenals are expected to grow over the coming decade and today's forces are vastly more capable.[11]

Each of these countries has their own motivations and strategies for pursuing nuclear weapons. The United States, Russia, and China developed nuclear weapons during the Cold War as a means of deterrence and as a tool of national security. France and the United Kingdom also developed nuclear weapons during this time, primarily as a means of maintaining their global influence. India and Pakistan both developed nuclear weapons because of their long-standing conflict over the disputed territory of Kashmir. The development of nuclear weapons by both countries has further escalated tensions between them, leading to concerns about the possibility of a nuclear war in the region. Israel is widely believed to possess nuclear weapons, although the country has not officially acknowledged this. Israel is thought to have developed nuclear weapons as a means of maintaining its security in a region where it perceives itself to be surrounded by hostile nations. North Korea is the most recent country to develop nuclear weapons, and its program has been a source of significant international concern. North Korea's pursuit of nuclear weapons is believed to be motivated by its desire to deter an attack from the United States and its allies, as well as to assert its power and influence in the region.

In general, countries pursue nuclear weapons as a means of achieving strategic objectives such as deterrence, enhancing their regional influence, or bolstering their national security. However, the possession of nuclear weapons also comes with significant risks and responsibilities, including the possibility of accidental use, the risk of proliferation, and the potential for a catastrophic nuclear war. Therefore, it is important that countries work together to prevent further proliferation and promote disarmament.

Treaties and Agreements to Prevent the Proliferation of Nuclear Weapons

There have been several historical examples of efforts to prevent nuclear weapons proliferation through treaties and agreements. Here are a few of the most significant examples:

Nuclear Non-Proliferation Treaty (NPT)

The Nuclear Non-Proliferation Treaty (NPT) was signed in 1968 and is the cornerstone of global efforts to prevent the spread of nuclear weapons. The NPT has 190 signatories and aims to achieve nuclear disarmament while allowing countries to access nuclear technology for peaceful purposes. The treaty divides countries into two categories: Nuclear Weapon States (NWS) and Non-Nuclear Weapon States (NNWS). The NWS are the countries that had nuclear weapons at the time the treaty was signed, and they have committed to working towards disarmament. The NNWS have agreed not to develop nuclear weapons and are subject to inspections by the International Atomic Energy Agency (IAEA) to ensure that they are complying with the treaty.

Strategic Arms Limitation Talks (SALT)

The Strategic Arms Limitation Talks (SALT) were a series of negotiations between the United States and the Soviet Union during the Cold War aimed at limiting the number of nuclear weapons possessed by both countries. The first round of talks resulted in the signing of the SALT I Treaty in 1972, which limited the number of strategic ballistic missile launchers and placed restrictions on the development of new missile systems. The second round of talks resulted in the signing of the SALT II Treaty in 1979, which further limited the number of nuclear weapons possessed by both countries.

However, the SALT II Treaty was never ratified by the United States due to political tensions between the two countries.

Comprehensive Nuclear-Test-Ban Treaty (CTBT)

The Comprehensive Nuclear-Test-Ban Treaty (CTBT) was signed in 1996 and aims to ban nuclear weapons tests. The treaty has been signed by 185 countries and ratified by 170, but it has not yet entered into force, as some of the countries with nuclear weapons have not ratified it. The treaty establishes an international monitoring system to detect and verify compliance with the ban on nuclear tests and provides for on-site inspections to investigate suspected violations.

Joint Comprehensive Plan of Action (JCPOA)

The Joint Comprehensive Plan of Action (JCPOA) was signed in 2015 between Iran and the P5+one countries (United States, United Kingdom, France, Russia, China, and Germany) and aimed to limit Iran's nuclear program in exchange for lifting economic sanctions. The JCPOA placed strict limits on Iran's uranium enrichment and stockpiling, as well as requiring extensive inspections by the IAEA to ensure compliance. However, in 2018, the United States withdrew from the JCPOA, leading to increased tensions between Iran and the remaining signatories.

While these agreements and treaties have been successful in preventing some countries from acquiring nuclear weapons, they have not been able to prevent all proliferation. However, these agreements remain crucial in maintaining global efforts to prevent nuclear war and promoting disarmament. Experts generally agree that preventing the proliferation of nuclear weapons is crucial for maintaining global security and reducing the risk of a catastrophic nuclear war. Here are some common opinions among experts on the topic: Multilateral Diplomacy: Many experts believe that multilateral diplomacy is essential for preventing nuclear weapons proliferation. This involves cooperation and negotiations between countries to create and uphold agreements and treaties that limit the spread of nuclear weapons. Multilateral diplomacy can also help to build trust between countries and promote disarmament.[12]

Arms Control: Experts also highlight the importance of arms control measures in preventing the proliferation of nuclear weapons. Arms control can involve agreements and treaties that limit the number and types of nuclear weapons that countries possess, as well as measures that enhance transparency and verification. Addressing Regional Conflicts: Several experts emphasize the need to address underlying regional conflicts that can lead to nuclear weapons proliferation. For example, the conflict between India and Pakistan over Kashmir has been a major driver of nuclear weapons development in both countries. [13] Addressing these conflicts through diplomacy and negotiation can help to reduce tensions and prevent further proliferation. Strengthening International Institutions: Experts also suggest that strengthening international institutions, such as the International Atomic Energy Agency (IAEA), can help to prevent nuclear weapons proliferation. These institutions can provide oversight and verification to ensure that countries are complying with international agreements and can assist countries in developing peaceful nuclear technology. Experts agree that preventing nuclear weapons proliferation is a complex and challenging task that requires cooperation and coordination at the international level. While progress has been made through treaties and agreements, continued efforts are needed to reduce the risk of a catastrophic nuclear war. There were several landmarks in nuclear diplomacy during the past year. These included the entry into force of the Treaty on the Prohibition of Nuclear Weapons (TPNW) in January 2021, having received the required 50 state ratifications; the extension for five years of New START, the last remaining bilateral arms control agreement between the world's two leading nuclear powers; and the start of talks on the USA rejoining, and Iran returning to compliance with, the Iran nuclear deal, the Joint Comprehensive Plan of Action (JCPOA). During 2021, the nuclear-armed permanent members (P5) of the United Nations Security Council—China, France, Russia, the UK and the USA—worked on a joint statement that they issued on 3 January 2022, affirming that 'nuclear war cannot be won and must never be fought.[14]

CHAPTER 5.

Catalyst for a Global Security Architecture: Regional Conflicts

Regional Conflicts and International Politics

In the realm of international politics, regional disputes refer to conflicts or disagreements between countries or groups within a specific geographic region. These disputes typically involve a range of issues such as territorial claims, border disputes, access to resources, historical grievances, ethnic or religious tensions, and political differences. Understanding regional disputes requires analyzing them in the broader context of international politics and considering the various factors at play.

Here are several significant considerations to bear in mind. The dynamics and characteristics specific to the region in question shape regional disputes. Various factors, including proximity, shared history, cultural affinities, economic interdependence, and geopolitical interests, contribute to the complexities of these disputes. Regional organizations and alliances can also play a role in either addressing or exacerbating tensions. Disputes frequently revolve around matters of sovereignty and territorial integrity, with different actors asserting ownership or control over specific territories. The intensity of these disputes can be influenced by historical events, colonial legacies, and competing national narratives. International norms, treaties, and legal frameworks, such as the United Nations Charter and international law, establish the basis for resolving territorial conflicts. Power imbalances among regional actors can significantly affect the nature and resolution of disputes. Stronger countries often assert their influence and leverage their military, economic, or political power to pursue their interests. Weaker countries or non-state actors may resort to diplomatic maneuvers, coalition-building, or asymmetric tactics to counterbalance the power differential. Regional disputes frequently require multilateral diplomacy involving neighboring countries, regional organizations, and international mediators. Diplomatic efforts aim to facilitate dialogue, negotiate settlements, and find compromises that satisfy the interests of all parties involved. These processes can be time-consuming and complex, necessitating sustained engagement and political will from all stakeholders.

Regional disputes can have broader implications for international politics. Powerful countries may become involved due to strategic considerations, economic interests, or alliances with the parties involved. International organizations, such as the United Nations, regional blocs as if the European Union or the African Union, and influential states, can exert pressure, offer mediation, or impose sanctions to help resolve disputes or mitigate their impact. If left unresolved or mishandled, regional disputes have the potential to escalate into larger conflicts. They may involve proxy wars, transnational terrorism, or the spillover of violence, thereby destabilizing not only the region but also the broader international system. Managing regional disputes and preventing escalation is crucial for maintaining peace and stability. Non-state actors, such as insurgent groups, ethnic or religious organizations, or separatist movements, can be involved in regional disputes. These actors often pursue their own agendas, thereby making conflict resolution more challenging. Understanding the motivations and grievances of non-state actors is essential for effectively addressing regional disputes."

In particular, it is important to approach the understanding of regional disputes in international politics with a nuanced perspective, considering the historical, cultural, geopolitical, and power dynamics that shape these conflicts. Analyzing these factors helps policymakers, diplomats, and scholars develop strategies for conflict resolution, peacebuilding, and regional cooperation. Regional conflicts are conflicts that occur within a specific geographical region, often involving multiple countries or groups within the region. These conflicts may have a range of causes, including territorial disputes, ethnic or religious tensions, economic competition, and political power struggles.

Political and Philosophical Perspective.

To gain a comprehensive understanding of regional conflicts and wars occurring locally in many parts of the world, such as the 2022 Russia-Ukraine war, China-Taiwan relations, inter-Korean issues, Israel-Palestinian issues, Pakistan-India border issues, etc., it is necessary to examine these issues from a political and philosophical perspective. Regional conflicts are complex events that involve a variety of social, cultural, economic, and political factors.

From a humanistic and political philosophical perspective, several theories can be applied to understand these conflicts. One approach is to analyze the root causes of regional conflicts, which often involve issues related to power, resources, and identity. Humanistic philosophers emphasize the importance of recognizing the dignity and worth of all individuals, and this perspective can be applied to the political realm by examining how regional conflicts can arise when certain groups feel marginalized or oppressed. For example, conflicts in regions such as the Middle East or Africa often stem from historical and cultural tensions between different groups or nations, which can be further exacerbated by competition for resources or political power.[1] Another approach is to focus on the dynamics of conflict itself, and how it can be perpetuated or resolved through political and social mechanisms. Political philosophers often examine the role of institutions and governance in preventing or managing conflicts, and this perspective can be applied to regional conflicts by analyzing the effectiveness of international organizations such as the United Nations or regional alliances in resolving conflicts. Humanistic philosophers also emphasize the importance of empathy and dialogue in conflict resolution, and this perspective can be applied to regional conflicts by examining the role of civil society and community organizations in promoting peaceful communication and understanding between different groups.

Finally, a third approach is to consider the ethical dimensions of regional conflicts and the responsibility of individuals and governments to uphold certain values such as human rights and justice. Humanistic philosophers emphasize the importance of compassion and respect for human dignity, and this perspective can be applied to regional conflicts by examining the ways in which human rights violations and injustice can fuel conflict and how they can be addressed through political and social mechanisms. A humanistic and political philosophical approach to regional conflicts involves analyzing the complex factors that contribute to conflicts, examining the role of institutions and governance in managing them, and considering the ethical dimensions of conflict and its impact on human well-being.

How to Prevent Regional Conflicts

The prevention of regional conflicts is of paramount importance in safeguarding international security as such conflicts possess the potential to escalate into broader crises with far-reaching consequences. This article delves into the significance of preventing regional conflicts and explores a range of strategies that can effectively mitigate the risk of escalation. Drawing upon scholarly research and expert analysis, it emphasizes the need to address root causes, employ diplomacy and mediation, strengthen regional cooperation, and utilize early warning systems and peacebuilding mechanisms. By adopting these strategies, the international community can proactively address regional conflicts, prevent their transformation into international security crises, and foster a more peaceful and secure world.

Regional conflicts, if left unchecked, possess a significant risk of escalating into international security crises, amplifying the consequences for global stability and peace. Historical precedents, such as the Balkan conflicts of the 1990s and the ongoing Syrian civil war, demonstrate how regional conflicts can attract external actors, strain international relations, and pose formidable challenges to international security.[2] The potential for conflicts to spread beyond their immediate geographic boundaries necessitates the adoption of preventive strategies to curtail their escalation.

Effectively preventing regional conflicts requires a comprehensive approach that addresses the underlying root causes fueling tensions and grievances. Socio-economic disparities, political marginalization, ethnic and religious divisions, and territorial disputes often serve as catalysts for conflicts. By promoting inclusive governance, fostering economic development, and facilitating dialogue, states can proactively tackle these underlying issues and reduce the likelihood of violent conflict. Addressing root causes is essential for sustainable conflict prevention.

Diplomatic efforts and mediation play pivotal roles in preventing regional conflicts and averting their transformation into international security crises. Constructive dialogue, confidence-building measures, and facilitated negotiations can help de-escalate tensions and foster peaceful resolutions.[3] Mediation efforts by regional organizations, international actors, or impartial third parties have proven effective in defusing conflicts, building trust, and facilitating lasting solutions. Robust diplomatic engagement and mediation are indispensable tools for conflict prevention.

Enhancing regional cooperation is critical for preventing and managing regional conflicts. Regional organizations, such as the African Union, the Association of Southeast Asian Nations (ASEAN), and the Organization of American States, play significant roles in conflict prevention and resolution by providing platforms for dialogue, confidence-building, and cooperation.[4] Strengthening these organizations and fostering regional solidarity can contribute to stability, prevent conflicts from spilling over borders, and promote collaboration in addressing shared challenges. Regional cooperation forms a crucial pillar of effective conflict prevention.

The utilization of early warning systems and robust peacebuilding mechanisms are invaluable for preventing regional conflicts and mitigating the risks of international security crises. Timely identification of early warning signs, such as escalating tensions, human rights abuses, or militarization, enables prompt preventive action (United Nations, 2015).

Investing in peacebuilding initiatives, including conflict resolution training, institution-building, and post-conflict reconstruction, can address the root causes of conflicts and foster sustainable peace.[5] Early warning systems and peacebuilding efforts are integral components of proactive conflict prevention.

Preventing regional conflicts is a fundamental imperative for safeguarding international security and maintaining global stability. By understanding the potential for escalation and implementing strategies that address root causes, employ diplomacy and mediation, strengthen regional cooperation, and utilize early warning systems and peacebuilding mechanisms, the international community can proactively prevent regional conflicts from transforming into international security crises. It is through these concerted efforts that a more peaceful and secure world can be fostered.

As mentioned above, preventing regional conflicts that could lead to the global security crisis is a complex issue that requires a range of strategies and actions. Although some of my opinions on the strategic aspect may overlap with those presented above, I would like to present some opinions as an international political scientist to help resolve and prevent regional conflicts. Firstly, diplomacy and dialogue are widely recognized as essential elements in the prevention of regional conflicts. It is imperative for countries to engage in constructive and peaceful dialogues to resolve conflicts and prevent their escalation. Such dialogues foster trust and confidence between nations, thereby reducing the likelihood of conflict. Secondly, robust conflict resolution mechanisms are also recommended by experts to effectively address regional conflicts.

These mechanisms encompass mediation, arbitration, and other dispute resolution processes. Regional organizations, including the African Union and the Association of Southeast Asian Nations, can contribute significantly to the resolution of regional conflicts.[6] Thirdly, many experts contend that providing economic and development assistance can effectively deter regional conflicts. Economic assistance plays a crucial role in addressing the underlying causes of conflicts, such as poverty and inequality, while also providing incentives for peaceful conflict resolution among nations. Fourthly, experts also emphasize the importance of implementing arms control measures to prevent regional conflicts. These measures involve agreements aimed at limiting the quantity and types of weapons possessed by countries. Additionally, measures to enhance transparency and verification are necessary to ensure the effectiveness of such control mechanisms. Lastly, experts underscore the necessity of establishing international norms and standards to prevent regional conflicts. These norms and standards should align with the principles outlined in the United Nations Charter, emphasizing the peaceful resolution of disputes, respect for territorial integrity and sovereignty, and the prohibition of the use of force.[7] Overall, experts agree that preventing regional conflicts is a critical component of preventing the proliferation of nuclear weapons. Diplomacy, conflict resolution mechanisms, economic assistance, arms control measures, and international norms and standards can all play a role in preventing regional conflicts and reducing the risk of nuclear war.

The conflict between Russia and Ukraine has a complex and multi-faceted history. While there are many factors that have contributed to the conflict, some of the key issues that have been discussed include historical and cultural ties, economic interests, and territorial disputes. Historically, Ukraine has been a part of Russia and the Soviet Union for centuries. Ukraine became an independent state in 1991 after the collapse of the Soviet Union. However, Russia has continued to see Ukraine as within its sphere of influence and has sought to maintain close ties with the country. Ukraine, on the other hand, has sought to establish its independence and sovereignty.

Economic interests have also played a role in the conflict. Ukraine is a significant transit route for Russian gas exports to Europe, and Russia has used its control of energy supplies as a political tool in the past. In 2014, Ukraine sought closer economic ties with the European Union, which Russia saw as a threat to its economic interests in the region.[8] Territorial disputes have also been a major issue in the conflict. In 2014, Russia annexed Crimea from Ukraine, which was a significant escalation of the conflict. Russia claimed that the annexation was necessary to protect the rights of ethnic Russians living in Crimea, but the international community largely viewed it as an illegal violation of Ukraine's sovereignty and territorial integrity.[9] The conflict also involves separatist movements in eastern Ukraine, which have received support from Russia. The conflict has also been fueled by cultural and linguistic differences between Ukraine and Russia. Ukraine has a significant Ukrainian-speaking population, while Russian is the dominant language in many parts of eastern Ukraine. These differences have contributed to a sense of division and distrust between the two countries.

Ripple Effects from Russia-Ukraine War

The Russia-Ukraine war is having an outsized impact on the global supply chain, impeding the flow of goods, fueling dramatic cost increases and product shortages, and creating catastrophic food shortages around the world, according to experts at a virtual symposium hosted by the MIT Center for Transportation and Logistics. The upheaval to the supply and demand of goods is exacerbating the already untenable human toll of the conflict, which shows no signs of abating. The February 2022 Russian invasion of Ukraine may have been the straw that broke the camel's back, but it was hardly the only contributing factor to the current global supply chain crisis, panelists at the symposium said. Significant supply chain disruptions started bubbling up during the heat of the trade wars in 2018 and 2019 and were pushed into new territory over the course of the COVID-19 pandemic, continuing to this day. While the focus remains, as it should on the tragedy of human loss and the destruction of Ukrainian territory, the Russian invasion has triggered sanctions and other obstacles that have hampered critical logistics and trade route operations.

The resulting ripple effects are threatening the supply of key food resources like wheat and raising the possibility of a global famine. Simultaneously, disruption to the flow of electronics, raw materials, and parts supplies emanating out of China and other locales has seriously impeded global trade positions, forcing companies to recalibrate and in some cases, wholly reconsider their long-standing supply chain and partner ecosystems. "Supply chain managers need to think carefully about opportunities and risk when looking for new sources while considering how to coordinate the change from one source or mode to another," said Joachim Arts, a CTL research affiliate and associate professor at the Luxembourg Center for Logistics and Supply Chain Management. "If it isn't coordinated carefully, it could lead to all kinds of bullwhip effects throughout global supply chains."[10]

One of the most concerning supply chain challenges arising from the conflict between Russia and Ukraine is the occurrence of food shortages, particularly severe in low-income countries in Africa. Ukraine and Russia collectively contribute to approximately one-third of global wheat production and one-quarter of barley production, not to mention around 75% of the supply of sunflower oil – all of which are essential commodities for sustaining human nutrition. The convergence of Russian sanctions, the blockage of Ukrainian ports, and the inability of Ukrainian farmers to cultivate their fields is generating a highly problematic situation that necessitates governments and businesses to engage in novel forms of collaboration to avert a humanitarian crisis.

This paradigm shift involves establishing alternative suppliers, fostering public-private partnerships, and harnessing advanced analytics to predict food waste and identify opportunities to redirect resources for bolstering global food reserves.

Food supply in crisis

One of the most alarming supply chain issues resulting from the Russia-Ukraine war is food shortages, particularly acute in low-income countries in Africa. Ukraine and Russia account for about a third of the world's wheat and a quarter of barley production, not to mention some 75% of the sunflower oil supply — all critical commodities for keeping humans fed. The combination of Russian sanctions, blocked Ukrainian ports, and the inability of Ukrainian farmers to work the fields is creating a perfect storm that requires governments and businesses to find new ways to collaborate to head off a humanitarian crisis, said Chris Mejía Argueta, director of the MIT SCALE Network in Latin America. In fact, Russia's blockade of Ukrainian ports is considered so damaging that EU Foreign Policy Chief Josep Borrell recently dubbed it a war crime.

"If we have a scarcity of the most common commodities around the world, coupled with climate change issues, that's when we need to start changing our mindset and find ways to collaborate with each other to make a difference," Mejía Argueta said.

That reset entails establishing alternative suppliers, forging public-private partnerships, and leveraging advanced analytics to forecast food waste and identify opportunities to divert resources to shore up global food supplies, he added.

China – Europe routes disrupted

The state of transportation routes connecting China with Europe is another casualty of the Russian invasion. Surging gas prices are increasing freight costs for all modes of transportation. The train route connecting the regions, which became highly competitive during the height of COVID-19, especially for industries valuing shorter lead times such as automotive and electronics, is now stalled. This is especially true for the primary corridor that traverses Russia, Belarus, and Poland before continuing on to Germany, France, and other European countries. "If you shifted your product allocation [during the pandemic], you can't just reverse that decision, [which has] caused a lot of trouble in the automotive industry," said Pascal Wolff, an assistant professor at the SCALE Network's Ningbo China Institute for Supply Chain Innovation. While some companies are redirecting product traffic to an alternative train route, most are shifting back to ocean freight mode, he said, which takes more time to get goods to market.

On 24 February 2022, the world witnessed a significant escalation in the ongoing conflict between Russia and Ukraine, as Russian troops crossed the borders of Ukraine. The subsequent events have sparked a broad outcry and raised concerns about the implications for global politics and security. While Western states have strongly condemned Russia's actions and provided political, military, and moral support to Ukraine, it is essential to critically examine the extent to which this war is transforming global politics and security. This article aims to explore the implications of the Russia-Ukraine War on global security from an academic perspective, backed by citations and sources to support the information presented.

The Russia-Ukraine War has had a significant impact on regional stability, particularly in Eastern Europe. The conflict has highlighted the fragility of the post-Cold War security order, with Russia's military intervention challenging the sovereignty and territorial integrity of Ukraine. This has created a sense of insecurity among neighboring countries, who fear potential Russian aggression. The ongoing hostilities have the potential to escalate further, leading to a broader regional conflict and triggering a new arms race. According to Sergey Lavrov, Russia's Minister of Foreign Affairs, the conflict serves as a "red line" for Russia, which implies that any external intervention might be met with strong military responses.[11]

The Russia-Ukraine War has strained relations between Russia and NATO, exacerbating an already tense situation. The conflict has further eroded trust between the two sides and highlighted the diverging security perspectives. NATO perceives Russia's actions as a violation of international law and an attempt to redraw borders through force, while Russia argues it is protecting ethnic Russians and Russian speakers in Ukraine. This deepening rift between Russia and NATO has implications for global security, as it heightens the risk of miscalculation, miscommunication, and potential military confrontations.[12]

The Russia-Ukraine War has displayed the prominence of cyber warfare and hybrid tactics in modern conflicts. Both sides have engaged in cyberattacks, disinformation campaigns, and the weaponization of social media platforms. These tactics, aimed at destabilizing governments and sowing societal divisions, have far-reaching implications for global security. The proliferation of cyber capabilities and the increasing reliance on information warfare pose challenges to traditional notions of state security and deterrence. As states become more interconnected and dependent on technology, the threat of cyberattacks and hybrid warfare is likely to intensify.[13]

The Russia-Ukraine War has underscored the geopolitical dimensions of energy security. Ukraine serves as a critical transit country for Russian gas exports to Europe, and the conflict has raised concerns about the reliability of energy supplies. This has prompted European states to reassess their energy strategies and diversify their sources of energy, reducing their dependence on Russian gas. The shift towards renewable energy and the development of alternative pipelines has become a priority, with implications for global energy markets and the broader geopolitical competition between Russia and the West.[14]

In fact, the Russia-Ukraine War has far-reaching implications for global security. The conflict has created regional instability, strained relations between Russia and NATO, highlighted the significance of cyber and hybrid warfare, and reshaped energy security dynamics. It is essential for the international community to closely monitor and address these implications to prevent further escalation and ensure global stability. Efforts to promote diplomatic dialogue, enhance cybersecurity measures, and diversify energy sources will be crucial in mitigating the long-term consequences of the Russia-Ukraine War on global security.

Mechanisms of Regional Conflicts and Global Security Crisis

The border dispute between India and China is another regional conflict that has potential to escalate into a global crisis. In 2020, military tensions between the two countries escalated in the Galwan Valley, leading to a violent confrontation that resulted in the deaths of several soldiers from both sides. The dispute remains unresolved, and both countries continue to maintain a heavy military presence in the region, raising concerns about the potential for a more significant conflict. From an international political point of view, the potential escalation of the border conflict between China and India carries significant implications and has the potential to develop into a global security crisis. Here are the key factors and reasons behind this assessment:

Nuclear Powers: Both China and India are nuclear-armed states, which adds a dimension of extreme concern. In case of an escalation, the possibility of nuclear weapons being deployed or the conflict inadvertently escalating to a nuclear level becomes a critical threat not just to the region but also to global security. The involvement of nuclear weapons could lead to catastrophic consequences and trigger a wider arms race or even accidental nuclear conflict.

Regional and Global Interests: The conflict between China and India holds substantial strategic and economic importance for various regional and global powers. The region where the conflict occurs, specifically the Himalayan region, is home to several vital water resources and serves as a gateway to important trade routes. Any escalation could disrupt these routes and affect the global economy. Additionally, neighboring countries with close ties to China or India, such as Pakistan, Nepal, and Bhutan, may become involved, potentially escalating the conflict beyond the China-India border.

Geostrategic Competition: The border conflict between China and India is not occurring in isolation but within the broader context of their ongoing geopolitical rivalry. Both countries seek to expand their influence and assert dominance in the region. The conflict can be seen as an extension of their competition for regional supremacy, as well as control over resources, markets, and strategic military positions. Other major powers, such as the United States and Russia, also have interests in the region and may be drawn into the conflict due to their alliances or strategic partnerships.

International Alliances: The involvement of other countries through alliances and partnerships could further internationalize the conflict. India has strong ties with countries like the United States, Japan, and Australia through initiatives such as the Quad (Quadrilateral Security Dialogue). These countries may be compelled to support India in the event of a conflict with China, potentially leading to a broader confrontation. Conversely, China's close relationships with countries like Pakistan and Russia could also influence the dynamics of the conflict.

Proxy Conflicts: The China-India border conflict could also provide an opportunity for other regional or global powers to pursue their own interests indirectly by supporting one side or the other. This could involve providing military assistance, economic aid, or diplomatic backing. Such involvement by external actors could intensify the conflict, prolong its duration, and complicate efforts to reach a peaceful resolution.

Impact on International Institutions: The escalation of the border conflict could strain international institutions, particularly those involved in conflict resolution and global governance. Institutions like the United Nations and regional bodies may face challenges in mediating the conflict and preventing its spillover into a larger crisis. The international community's ability to maintain peace and security may be tested, and there could be pressure to take sides or intervene in the conflict, leading to further complications.

As previously examined, the main factors and reasons that could pose a threat to global security if the border dispute between China and India potentially worsens are quite complicated. Overall, an escalation of the border conflict between China and India has the potential to transcend regional boundaries and pose a significant global security crisis. The involvement of nuclear weapons, the interests of major powers and the broader geopolitical context make it imperative for the international community to actively engage in preventive diplomacy, promote dialogue, and work towards a peaceful resolution to prevent further destabilization and ensure global security.

Exploring another aspect of regional conflicts can help us better understand the mechanisms between regional conflicts and global security crises. The military confrontation between South Korea and North Korea on the Korean Peninsula is yet another example of a regional conflict that has the potential to become a global crisis. The two countries have been technically at war since the Korean War, which ended in 1953, with occasional flare-ups of violence. North Korea's nuclear weapons program and the potential for the country to use them or transfer them to other states make the situation more precarious. The international community, including the United States, China, and Russia, has tried to mediate the situation, but tensions remain high. From an international political perspective, a military conflict between South Korea and North Korea has the potential to escalate into a global security crisis due to several factors. Let us explore these factors in detail:

Regional Tensions and Alliances: The Korean Peninsula is a region of significant geopolitical importance, surrounded by major powers such as China, Russia, Japan, and the United States. Any military conflict in the region would have a direct impact on these countries' interests and alliances. For example, South Korea is a close ally of the United States, and any aggression against South Korea could prompt the US to intervene militarily, triggering a wider conflict involving its allies and partners.

Nuclear Weapons and Weapons of Mass Destruction (WMDs): Both North Korea and South Korea possess military capabilities that include nuclear weapons and other WMDs. If a military conflict were to escalate, there is a real risk of the use or accidental deployment of such weapons. This could lead to catastrophic consequences not only for the Korean Peninsula but also for neighboring countries and beyond. The international community would be compelled to respond, potentially triggering a chain reaction of military actions and counteractions.

Proxy Conflicts and Great Power Rivalries: The Korean Peninsula has historically been a site of proxy conflicts between major powers. In the event of a military conflict, it is likely that these powers would be drawn into the situation due to their strategic interests in the region. This could exacerbate existing rivalries between the United States and China, for example, or reignite tensions between Russia and the West. Such rivalries have the potential to escalate the conflict beyond the immediate region and affect global security dynamics.

Economic Impact: The Korean Peninsula is a major economic hub, with significant global trade connections. A military conflict would disrupt regional and global supply chains, impact trade flows, and potentially trigger economic downturns. The economic consequences would not be limited to the immediate region but could have far-reaching effects, leading to a global economic crisis and destabilizing financial markets.

Refugee Crisis and Humanitarian Concerns: A military conflict on the Korean Peninsula would likely result in a massive refugee crisis, as civilians from both North and South Korea flee the conflict zone. The neighboring countries, such as China and Japan, would withstand the worst of this influx of refugees. This could strain resources, create social unrest, and potentially lead to further conflicts or tensions in the region. The international community would face immense challenges in managing and resolving such a humanitarian crisis.

Accordingly, a military conflict between South Korea and North Korea has the potential to escalate into a global security crisis due to the complex regional dynamics, the presence of nuclear weapons and WMDs, the involvement of major powers, the economic impact, and the potential for a refugee crisis. Preventing such a conflict and promoting peaceful resolutions through diplomatic efforts and dialogue becomes crucial to avoiding a wider crisis with far-reaching consequences.

The examples of regional conflicts mentioned above demonstrate how regional tensions can have global consequences. If these conflicts are not resolved, they have the potential to escalate and become global security crises. It is essential to understand the underlying causes of these conflicts and work towards peaceful resolutions to prevent them from threatening global security.

PART II

THE CAUSES OF REGIONAL CONFLICTS

"They who can give up essential liberty to obtain a little temporary safety deserve neither liberty nor safety."

- Benjamin Franklin

CHAPTER 6.

Resource Scarcity

The world is facing a growing number of resource challenges, including shortages of water, energy, food, and raw materials. These resource challenges are increasingly becoming a source of conflict at the regional and international levels, as countries compete for access to scarce resources. One of the most pressing resource challenges facing the world today is the shortage of water. According to the United Nations, water scarcity affects more than 40% of the world's population, and this is projected to increase in the coming decades due to climate change and population growth. In some regions, such as the Middle East and North Africa, water scarcity has already led to conflicts over access to water resources. Another critical resource challenge is energy. The world's dependence on fossil fuels has led to environmental degradation and climate change, and many countries are seeking to transition to cleaner sources of energy, such as wind, solar, and hydropower. However, this transition is not happening fast enough, and there are growing concerns about energy security as countries compete for access to oil, gas, and other fossil fuels. Food security is also becoming an increasingly pressing issue, as the world's population continues to grow and climate change affects agricultural productivity. In some regions, such as sub-Saharan Africa and South Asia, food shortages have led to conflicts over access to food and agricultural land.[1] There is a growing concern about the scarcity of raw materials, such as metals, minerals, and rare earth elements. These materials are critical for the production of high-tech products such as smartphones, electric vehicles, and renewable energy technologies. However, many of these materials are concentrated in a few countries, such as China, which has led to concerns about supply chain vulnerabilities and geopolitical competition over access to these resources.

The situation is worsening due to a combination of factors, including climate change, population growth, environmental degradation, and geopolitical competition. As resources become scarcer, there is a growing risk of conflict and instability at the regional and international levels. To address these challenges, there is a need for greater cooperation and collaboration among countries to ensure that resources are managed in a sustainable and equitable manner. This will require new policies and investments to promote resource efficiency, renewable energy, and sustainable agriculture, as well as greater efforts to address climate change and environmental degradation. Global resource scarcity is a complex issue that affects various resources, such as food, water, energy, minerals, and land.[2] Here are a few statistics that highlight the extent of global resource scarcity:

According to a report by Bank of America, over the next several decades, skill scarcity will cost the world $8.5 trillion, more than the current combined GDP of Germany and Japan. Four billion people — almost two thirds of the world's population — experience severe water scarcity for at least one month each year. Half of the world's population could be living in areas facing water scarcity by as early as 2025. By the end of this century, worsening droughts are projected to affect about 700 million people. 87% of global greenhouse gas emissions are caused by energy production.[3]

These are just a few examples of global resource scarcity statistics. You can find more information on these and other related issues on the websites of various international organizations such as the United Nations, World Bank, and International Energy Agency.

Water Scarcity: According to the United Nations, 2.2 billion people lack access to safely managed drinking water, and by 2025, half of the world's population will be living in water-stressed areas.[4]

Food Scarcity: The Food and Agriculture Organization of the United Nations estimates that 811 million people in the world suffered from chronic undernourishment between 2019 and 2021.[5]

Energy Scarcity: The International Energy Agency estimates that over 789 million people still lack access to electricity and the majority of them live in sub-Saharan Africa.[6]

Mineral Scarcity: The World Bank estimates that 3 billion tons of minerals and metals will be needed by 2050 to meet the demand for clean energy technologies. However, many of these minerals are in short supply, leading to concerns about their availability.[7]

Land Scarcity: The Food and Agriculture Organization of the United Nations estimates that around 25% of the world's land is highly degraded, and the rate of land degradation is increasing.[8]

Threats to Global security Caused by Resource Shortage Examples

There are many examples of conflicts in certain regions that have been aggravated or are likely to escalate to global security crises due to resource scarcity. Here are a few:

The conflict in Darfur, Sudan: The conflict in Darfur began in 2003 when rebel groups launched an insurgency against the Sudanese government. The conflict was fueled by competition over land and water resources, as well as political and economic marginalization of the region's population.[9] The conflict escalated into a humanitarian crisis, with hundreds of thousands of people killed and millions displaced.

The conflict in Syria: The conflict in Syria began in 2011 as a peaceful protest movement against the government, but it quickly escalated into a civil war. The conflict has been fueled by competition over water resources, as well as political and economic grievances.[10] The conflict has escalated into a humanitarian crisis, with millions of people displaced and hundreds of thousands killed.

The conflict in the South China Sea: The South China Sea is a critical shipping route and a rich fishing ground, but it is also believed to be rich in oil and gas reserves. China, Vietnam, the Philippines, and other countries have competing territorial claims in the region, and there have been a number of incidents of conflict, including the building of artificial islands, the deployment of military assets, and the harassment of fishermen.

The conflict in the East China Sea: The East China Sea is also a critical shipping route and is believed to be rich in oil and gas reserves. China and Japan have competing territorial claims in the region, and there have been a number of incidents of conflict, including the deployment of military assets, the harassment of fishermen, and the establishment of an air defense identification zone.

The conflict between Israel and Palestine: The conflict between Israel and Palestine has been ongoing for decades and is fueled by a number of factors, including competition over land and water resources. The conflict has escalated into a humanitarian crisis, with millions of people displaced and thousands killed.

These conflicts are just a few examples of the many challenges that arise when resources become scarce. In each case, the conflict has been fueled by competition over resources, and the escalation of these conflicts has the potential to destabilize entire regions and even threaten global security. To address these challenges, there is a need for greater cooperation and collaboration among countries to ensure that resources are managed in a sustainable and equitable manner. Resource scarcity is a critical issue that has often led to regional conflicts and wars, causing global security crises. The competition for limited resources such as water, land, and energy has created tensions and disputes between countries, leading to insecurity and instability. In this article, we will explore how resource scarcity has contributed to regional conflicts and wars and examine some examples.

One of the primary causes of conflict is the competition for water resources. As the population grows, water scarcity becomes a major issue, leading to disputes and tensions between countries. In the Middle East, the lack of water has led to tensions between Israel and its neighbors, including Jordan, Syria, and Lebanon. For instance, the construction of the Israeli West Bank Barrier has been a major source of conflict, as it restricts the flow of water to Palestinians. Similarly, the dispute over the Nile River between Egypt, Ethiopia, and Sudan is another example of how resource scarcity can lead to conflict.

The Nile River is a critical water resource for all three countries, but Ethiopia's construction of the Grand Ethiopian Renaissance Dam has led to tensions with Egypt and Sudan. Egypt is highly dependent on the Nile for its water supply, and the construction of the dam could threaten its water security, leading to potential conflict. Another critical issue related to resource scarcity is the competition for energy resources. As countries become more dependent on fossil fuels, competition for access to these resources increases. This can lead to conflict and instability, as we have seen in the Middle East. The 1990 Gulf War was largely about control of oil resources, with Iraq invading Kuwait to gain control of its oil fields. Similarly, the ongoing conflict in Syria has been fueled by the competition for energy resources, with Russia and Iran backing the Syrian government to secure their access to energy resources.

Lastly, the competition for land resources is another significant issue that has led to regional conflicts and wars. Land scarcity is becoming increasingly problematic as populations grow, leading to the competition for fertile land for agriculture and other uses. In Africa, land disputes have led to conflict, such as the ongoing conflict in Darfur, Sudan. The conflict is fueled by competition for land and resources between ethnic groups. Resource scarcity is a major cause of regional conflicts and wars that lead to global security crises. The competition for water, land, and energy resources has created tensions and disputes between countries, leading to insecurity and instability. The examples discussed in this article demonstrate the impact of resource scarcity on regional conflicts and wars. Addressing this challenge will require a comprehensive approach that promotes sustainable resource management, encourages cooperation between countries, and fosters dialogue to resolve disputes peacefully. Failure to address resource scarcity can lead to global insecurity and instability in the future. Resource scarcity has long been a driver of conflict and insecurity around the world. From disputes over water and land to the competition for energy resources, resource scarcity has often led to regional conflicts that have the potential to spill over into global crises. As an expert in this field, I believe that resource scarcity will continue to be a major challenge in the years to come. The world's population is expected to grow to nearly 10 billion by 2050,[11] and this will put even more pressure on already strained resources. One of the biggest challenges we face is the competition for water resources. Water scarcity is already a major issue in many parts of the world, and this is likely to become even more acute in the future. In some cases, it has already led to conflict, such as the dispute between Egypt and Ethiopia over the Nile River. Another area of concern is the competition for energy resources. As the world becomes increasingly dependent on fossil fuels, there is likely to be increased competition for access to these resources. This could lead to conflict between countries that rely heavily on these resources for their economies. Land scarcity is also a major concern. As populations grow, more and more land will be needed for agriculture and other uses. This could lead to conflict between countries over access to fertile land and other resources. To address these challenges, we need to take a comprehensive approach that addresses both the supply and demand side of resource management. This could involve investments in new technologies and infrastructure that can help us to use resources more efficiently, as well as policies that encourage conservation and sustainable resource use. At the same time, we need to focus on building stronger relationships between countries and encouraging dialogue and cooperation on issues related to resource scarcity. This could involve international agreements and treaties that help to manage resource use and reduce the potential for conflict. Resource scarcity is a major challenge that will continue to pose a threat to global security. As an expert in this field, I believe that we need to take a comprehensive approach to address these challenges, focusing on both the supply and demand side of resource management, and building stronger relationships between countries to reduce the potential for conflict. Only then can we ensure a more secure and sustainable future for all

CHAPTER 7.

Political Instability

Political instability is a pervasive challenge that afflicts nations and regions worldwide, exerting profound repercussions on global security. Weak, corrupt, or authoritarian political systems often give rise to social unrest and internal conflicts, generating a ripple effect that can extend beyond national borders and ignite regional instability. The repercussions of such turmoil can even escalate into a full-blown global security crisis, with far-reaching consequences. The current state of affairs in Syria and the ongoing tensions between the United States and North Korea serve as poignant reminders of the devastating impact political instability can have on global security. This chapter delves into the intricate dynamics of political instability, exploring its causes, manifestations, and the profound challenges it poses to international stability and peace.

The term "political instability" encompasses a wide array of factors that undermine the functioning and legitimacy of political systems. It refers to a state where governments struggle to maintain stability due to internal conflicts, corruption, or a lack of institutional capacity. One manifestation of political instability is social unrest, which can arise from grievances related to political, economic, or social inequality. These grievances often stem from authoritarian rule, government repression, or the failure to provide essential public services, and they can quickly escalate into mass protests, demonstrations, or even violent uprisings.

The consequences of political instability extend well beyond national borders, as conflicts have the potential to spill over into neighboring countries. Regional instability emerges when unresolved conflicts and power struggles within a nation have repercussions on the stability of its neighboring states. This can result in the displacement of populations, the proliferation of arms, and the exacerbation of existing tensions, creating a vicious cycle of violence and instability. Such regional conflicts not only cause significant human suffering but also pose a substantial threat to global security, as they can lead to the rise of extremist groups, the spread of weapons, and the erosion of diplomatic relations.

The ongoing conflict in Syria serves as a harrowing example of the devastating consequences of political instability. The Syrian civil war, which erupted in 2011, has claimed countless lives, displaced millions of people, and left the country in ruins. This conflict has not only caused immense human suffering but has also had far-reaching implications for regional stability. The spillover effects of the Syrian crisis have destabilized neighboring countries, including Lebanon, Jordan, and Iraq, straining their already fragile political, economic, and social structures.

Another contemporary issue that underscores the impact of political instability on global security is the enduring tensions between the United States and North Korea. The nuclear ambitions of the North Korean regime, coupled with the United States' concerns over regional stability, have heightened tensions and raised the specter of a potential conflict. The unpredictable nature of these interactions underscores the vulnerability of global security to the consequences of political instability, emphasizing the urgent need for effective strategies and diplomatic interventions.[1]

To comprehend the multifaceted nature of political instability and its implications for global security, it is vital to examine the underlying causes and the complex dynamics that perpetuate such instability. Understanding these factors will enable policymakers, international organizations, and scholars to develop effective measures aimed at preventing and mitigating the devastating consequences of political instability on a global scale.

There are various types of political instability occurring in many parts of the world, including:

Regime Change: This type of political instability occurs when there is a change in leadership or government, which may be caused by political, social, or economic factors. Regime changes can occur through democratic or non-democratic means, and may result in instability and conflict.

Ethnic or Religious Conflict: When different ethnic or religious groups within a country or region are in conflict, it can lead to political instability. This type of instability may be fueled by historical grievances, economic disparities, or political marginalization.

Economic Instability: Economic instability, such as inflation, unemployment, or debt crises, can lead to political instability. This is especially true in countries with high levels of poverty or income inequality, where economic hardship can exacerbate existing social and political tensions.

Corruption and Authoritarianism: Corruption and authoritarianism can undermine democratic institutions and lead to political instability. When leaders are perceived as being corrupt or authoritarian, it can erode trust in government and lead to protests or even violence.

The main causes of political instability can vary depending on the specific country or region, but some common factors include:

Weak Institutions: Weak or ineffective political institutions, such as the lack of rule of law, can lead to political instability.

Economic Challenges: Economic challenges, such as high unemployment or inflation, can exacerbate social and political tensions and lead to instability.

Social Inequality: Social inequality, such as discrimination against certain groups or income inequality, can create divisions within society and lead to instability.

External Factors: External factors, such as interference by foreign powers or regional conflicts, can contribute to political instability.

It is important to note that political instability is often a complex and multi-faceted issue, and addressing it requires a comprehensive approach that addresses the root causes of instability. This may include supporting democratic institutions, promoting economic growth and development, and addressing social and economic inequality. Political instability is one of the key factors that cause regional conflicts and wars, which ultimately lead to global security crises. Political instability can be defined as a situation where a country's government is unable to provide effective governance due to factors such as corruption, weak institutions, and lack of public trust.[2] This lack of stability can create a breeding ground for conflict, and if not resolved, can lead to widespread violence and even war. Political instability can lead to regional conflicts and wars in several ways. Firstly, when a country's government is weak, it may be unable to maintain law and order effectively. This can result in the rise of armed groups and militias who challenge the state's authority and control over territory. As a result, violent conflicts can break out, which can spill over into neighboring countries and destabilize the entire region. Secondly, political instability can create conditions that are conducive to terrorism and other forms of violent extremism. In countries where the government is unable to provide basic services or address the needs of its citizens, extremist groups can exploit this situation and gain popular support. In some cases, these groups may even take control of territory and establish their own rule, leading to violent conflicts with the state and neighboring countries. Thirdly, external actors who seek to exploit the situation for their own interests can fuel political instability. For example, neighboring countries may support armed groups or militias in order to gain a foothold in a strategic region or to undermine a rival power. This can escalate the conflict and lead to wider regional tensions, which can ultimately threaten global security. To address the issue of political instability and its role in regional conflicts and wars, it is important to strengthen governance and institutions in affected countries. This can involve measures such as anti-corruption initiatives, judicial reform, and strengthening the rule of law. It is also important to address the root causes of political instability, such as economic inequality and social exclusion, through inclusive development policies and programs. In addition, the international community has a role to play in preventing and resolving conflicts that arise from political instability. This can involve diplomatic efforts to encourage dialogue and mediation between conflicting parties, as well as providing humanitarian aid and support to affected populations. The international community can also work to prevent external actors from exploiting political instability for their own interests, through measures such as sanctions and targeted diplomatic pressure. Political instability is a major factor that can lead to regional conflicts and wars, which ultimately threaten global security. Addressing the root causes of political instability and strengthening governance and institutions in affected countries is essential to preventing and resolving these conflicts. [3] The international community also has a key role to play in supporting efforts to promote peace and stability in regions affected by political instability.

Political instability Countries and Factors

Political instability can be caused by a variety of factors, such as economic inequality, corruption, religious or ethnic tensions, and struggles for power. Here are some examples of where political instability is occurring currently, and how the situation is worsening:

Afghanistan: Afghanistan has been facing political instability for decades, due to various factors such as the Taliban insurgency, government corruption, and ethnic tensions. The recent withdrawal of US troops from Afghanistan has created a power vacuum, and the Taliban has seized control of much of the country. This has led to a humanitarian crisis, with thousands of Afghans fleeing the country, and concerns about the potential for the Taliban to harbor terrorist groups and destabilize the region.

Venezuela: Venezuela has been facing political instability for several years, due to the economic crisis and government corruption. The country has been facing hyperinflation, food and medicine shortages, and widespread poverty. The current government led by Nicolas Maduro is facing international sanctions, and the country has experienced violence and protests in response to the government's actions.

Syria: Syria has been facing political instability since 2011, due to the ongoing civil war. The conflict has been fueled by political and economic grievances, as well as religious and ethnic tensions. The conflict has led to a humanitarian crisis, with millions of people displaced and thousands killed.

Myanmar: Myanmar has been facing political instability since the military coup in February 2021. The military has seized control of the government and detained political leaders, leading to protests and violence. The situation has led to a humanitarian crisis, with thousands of people fleeing the country, and concerns about the potential for violence and instability in the region.

Belarus: Belarus has been facing political instability since the disputed presidential election in August 2020. The opposition claims the election was rigged, and protests have been ongoing since then. The government has responded with violence and repression, and there are concerns about the potential for violence and instability in the region.

Political instability in these regions can have significant implications for global security. It can lead to increased tensions between countries, create power vacuums that can be exploited by extremist groups, and destabilize entire regions. To address these challenges, there is a need for greater cooperation and collaboration among countries to promote political stability, address root causes of instability, and support democratic institutions.

Potentially Instability Nations that could Threaten Global Security

Political instability has the potential to cause conflicts between regions and countries that can escalate to a global security crisis. Here are some examples:

Syria: The civil war in Syria has created a power vacuum, allowing extremist groups like ISIS to gain control of territory and commit acts of terrorism. The conflict has also led to the displacement of millions of people, leading to a refugee crisis that has affected neighboring countries in the region.

Ukraine: The conflict between Ukraine and Russia over Crimea has been fueled by political instability in Ukraine. The Ukrainian government faced protests and a change in leadership in 2014, leading to tensions with Russia. Russia annexed Crimea, leading to international condemnation and sanctions against Russia. The conflict has escalated to include ongoing fighting in eastern Ukraine, and there are concerns about the potential for wider conflict in the region.

Yemen: The conflict in Yemen has been fueled by political instability, as different groups have vied for power in the country. The conflict has escalated to include involvement from other countries in the region, including Saudi Arabia and Iran. The humanitarian crisis in Yemen has affected the entire region and has raised concerns about the potential for wider conflict.

North Korea: The political instability in North Korea, including the leadership of Kim Jong-Un, has led to tensions between North Korea and other countries in the region, including South Korea and the United States. North Korea's development of nuclear weapons and missiles has raised concerns about the potential for conflict and the impact on global security.

Venezuela: The political instability in Venezuela has led to economic and humanitarian crises that have affected the entire region. The government's actions have led to international sanctions, and there are concerns about the potential for violence and instability to spread to neighboring countries.[4]

In each of these examples, political instability has led to conflicts that have the potential to escalate to a global security crisis. To address these challenges, there is a need for greater cooperation and collaboration among countries to promote political stability, address root causes of instability, and support democratic institutions.

The Remedies for the Political Instability Crisis

To effectively address political instability and its consequences, it is crucial for the international community to take a comprehensive and coordinated approach. This requires the involvement of multiple stakeholders, including governments, international organizations, civil society groups, and the private sector. One important aspect of this approach is to prioritize prevention efforts. This can involve early warning systems, conflict prevention strategies, and targeted investments in development and institution building. By addressing the root causes of political instability before conflicts erupt, the international community can reduce the likelihood of violence and minimize the impact on regional and global security. Another key aspect of the international community's response to political instability is the promotion of inclusive governance and democratic institutions. This means supporting free and fair elections, protecting the rights of minorities and marginalized groups, and strengthening the capacity of civil society to hold governments accountable. By promoting inclusive and democratic governance, the international community can help to build stable and resilient societies that are less prone to conflict and violence. Furthermore, the international community must also prioritize the resolution of existing conflicts and the promotion of peace and reconciliation. This can involve a range of measures, from diplomatic efforts to negotiations and peace agreements, to post-conflict reconstruction and development initiatives. By addressing the underlying causes of conflicts and promoting sustainable peace, the international community can help to prevent the recurrence of political instability and its consequences. Political instability is a major factor that contributes to regional conflicts and wars, which can have devastating consequences for global security. To address this challenge effectively, the international community must take a comprehensive and coordinated approach that prioritizes prevention, inclusive governance, and conflict resolution. By working together, we can build more stable, peaceful, and prosperous societies that are better equipped to meet the challenges of the 21st century.

CHAPTER 8.

Ethnic and Religious Tensions

The world is experiencing various conflicts due to "Ethnic and Religious Tensions" in different regions, which has caused significant harm to global security. These tensions are often rooted in historical, cultural, and social differences that create animosity between different groups of people. In this response, I will explain some of the current examples of ethnic and religious tensions and how the situation is worsening in detail. One of the most severe and longstanding conflicts due to ethnic and religious tensions is the Israeli-Palestinian conflict. The conflict dates back to the early 20th century when Jewish immigrants started to settle in Palestine. Today, the conflict is still ongoing, with both sides claiming the right to the land. The conflict has caused much violence and bloodshed, with regular outbreaks of conflict, such as the 2021 escalation in Gaza that resulted in over 200 deaths. The situation is worsening as the conflict continues to be unresolved, leading to a rise in extremism and violence from both sides. Another region experiencing ethnic and religious tensions is Myanmar. The Rohingya people, a Muslim minority group in the predominantly Buddhist country, have faced discrimination, violence, and persecution for decades. In 2017, the Myanmar military launched a brutal crackdown against the Rohingya, leading to the displacement of over 700,000 people and causing a significant humanitarian crisis. [1] The situation is worsening as the Rohingya continue to face discrimination and persecution, and the military regime remains in power, ignoring international pressure to stop the violence.

In Africa, there are various examples of ethnic and religious tensions that are causing instability and conflict. In Nigeria, the Boko Haram insurgency, a jihadist group that seeks to establish an Islamic state, has caused widespread violence and displacement in the northern part of the country. In Ethiopia, the conflict between the Tigrayan People's Liberation Front and the Ethiopian government has resulted in significant violence and displacement in the Tigray region. The Tigray People's Liberation Front (TPLF), the primary political party representing Tigray, has a history of dominating leadership coalitions and politics at the national level despite Tigrayans representing an ethnic minority. Between 1991 and his death in 2012, Tigrayan soldier-politician Meles Zenawi governed Ethiopia as an autocracy through a period of rapid development. [2] During the rule of Meles

Zenawi in Ethiopia, from 1991 until his death in 2012, various ethnic and religious conflicts contributed to regional tensions. While it is important to note that Ethiopia was not solely a dictatorship during this period, as it had a multi-party system, there were concerns about the consolidation of power and human rights abuses under Zenawi's leadership. One significant conflict that arose during this time was between the Tigray People's Liberation Front (TPLF), which Zenawi was a member of, and other ethnic groups within Ethiopia. The TPLF, representing the Tigrayan ethnic group, held significant political and military power in the country. However, this concentration of power led to grievances from other ethnic groups who felt marginalized and excluded from decision-making processes.

Ethnic tensions escalated as various groups sought to assert their rights and interests, often leading to violent clashes. The conflicts were fueled by a sense of competition for resources, political representation, and control over regional territories. The Ethiopian government, under Zenawi's leadership, responded to these conflicts with a heavy-handed approach, including the use of force and suppression of dissent. Religion also played a role in exacerbating the conflicts. Ethiopia is a country with a rich history of religious diversity, primarily with Christianity and Islam as the major religions. The government's favoritism towards certain religious groups, particularly the Ethiopian Orthodox Church, led to perceptions of religious discrimination and further deepened divisions. The process of the conflict involved a cycle of violence, reprisals, and retaliation. Clashes between different ethnic and religious groups occurred in various regions of Ethiopia, including Tigray, Oromia, Amhara, and Somali regions. These conflicts often resulted in displacement, loss of lives, and significant humanitarian crises.[3]

It is important to note that the situation in Ethiopia is complex, and the conflicts during Zenawi's rule cannot be solely attributed to his leadership or the Tigrayan ethnic group. Ethiopia has a long history of ethnic and religious tensions, and multiple factors contributed to the conflicts during this period. The issues remain unresolved, and Ethiopia continues to grapple with ethnic and religious divisions to this day.

In Sudan, the conflict between the Arab-dominated government and the non-Arab population in Darfur has led to one of the worst humanitarian crises in the world.[4] The conflict in Sudan, particularly in the Darfur region, is a complex issue with various factors contributing to the ongoing crisis. While it is true that there are elements of ethnic and religious divisions involved, it is important to approach the topic with nuance and avoid oversimplification. The conflict in Darfur originated from a combination of political, economic, and social factors, including historical grievances, competition over resources, and unequal power distribution. It primarily stems from longstanding tensions between the Arab-dominated Sudanese government in Khartoum and the non-Arab populations in Darfur.

Ethnicity and religion have played a role in the conflict, as there are cultural and identity differences between the Arab and non-Arab communities in Sudan. The Arab-dominated government has been accused of marginalizing and discriminating against non-Arab groups, leading to grievances and calls for greater autonomy and representation. Religion is also a factor, as Sudan is predominantly Muslim, and religious identities have influenced the conflict dynamics. However, it is essential to note that the conflict is not solely based on religious differences, but rather on broader political and social issues. The conflict in Darfur has resulted in significant humanitarian consequences, including widespread displacement, violence, and loss of life. The international community has condemned the human rights abuses and war crimes committed by various parties involved. Addressing the conflict and its humanitarian consequences requires a comprehensive approach that includes political negotiations, promoting dialogue and reconciliation, and ensuring accountability for human rights violations. Efforts to resolve the crisis must take into account the diverse factors at play, including ethnic, religious, political, and socio-economic dimensions, in order to achieve a sustainable and just solution.

In Europe, there is rising ethnic and religious tension due to the influx of immigrants and refugees from the Middle East and Africa. Countries such as Germany, France, and the UK have seen a rise in far-right and anti-immigrant sentiment, leading to a rise in hate crimes and violence against minorities. Ethnic and religious tensions are causing significant harm to global security, leading to conflict and instability in various regions of the world. The situation is worsening as these tensions continue to be unresolved, leading to a rise in extremism and violence from both sides. The international community needs to work together to address these conflicts and promote peace and stability. Ethnic and religious conflicts and tensions are a major factor in regional conflicts that can quickly escalate into global security crises. These conflicts are often deeply rooted in historical, cultural, and societal differences, making them extremely difficult to resolve.

In recent years, we have seen numerous examples of these conflicts causing significant instability and even leading to violent conflicts. For example, the ongoing conflict in Syria is driven, in part, by tensions between religious groups, with the government representing the Alawite minority and the opposition being largely composed of Sunni Muslims. Similarly, the conflict in Yemen has been characterized by sectarian tensions between Shia and Sunni Muslims, with regional powers such as Iran and Saudi Arabia backing opposing sides. It is profoundly wrong to characterize the Yemeni conflict as the result of a centuries-old hatred between Sunni and Shia; it is equally wrong to portray it only as part of the proxy war between Saudi Arabia and Iran. At the same time, it is naïve to neglect the importance of ideology – in this case religion – in such a complicated conflict. In looking for possible solutions to the crisis, it is urgent to come up with means to "deactivate" sectarian hatred. Otherwise, the risk is an even deeper polarization of society leading to an even bigger proliferation of violent groups, since – as the Iraqi experience has shown us – the seeds of ethnic and sectarian hatred, once planted, are difficult to eradicate.[5]

It is important to recognize that these conflicts are not limited to the Middle East. Ethnic and religious tensions have also contributed to conflicts in other regions, such as the ongoing conflict between Russia and Ukraine, which has been characterized by tensions between ethnic Russians and Ukrainians. One of the most significant challenges posed by these conflicts is that extremist groups, who use ethnic and religious differences to mobilize support and recruit new members, often, exploit them. This has been particularly evident in the rise of groups such as ISIS, which has sought to create a caliphate based on Sunni Islam and has used violence to target minority groups such as Shia Muslims, Christians, and Yazidis.[6] In order to address these conflicts, it is essential that policymakers and leaders take a comprehensive approach. This includes promoting economic development, reducing poverty, addressing political grievances, and promoting interfaith and interethnic dialogue. It is also crucial to address the underlying causes of extremism, such as lack of education, political disenfranchisement, and social inequality. Ethnic and religious conflicts and tensions are a significant factor in regional conflicts that can quickly escalate into global security crises. As an expert in the field, it is our responsibility to work towards promoting peace, stability, and dialogue in order to prevent further violence and instability. Failure to do so risks further escalation of violence and instability, with potentially catastrophic consequences for the global community. From an expert's point of view, it is clear that ethnic and religious conflicts and tensions are a significant factor in regional conflicts that can escalate into global security crises. These conflicts are often deeply ingrained in the history and culture of the regions where they occur, making them difficult to resolve. Moreover, the global reach of social media has made it easier for extremist groups to spread their message and recruit new members, exacerbating these tensions.

It is essential to understand that the root causes of these conflicts are often complex and multi-faceted. They can stem from economic disparities, political grievances, and historical injustices. However, it is also true that ethnic and religious differences can be manipulated and exploited by those seeking to gain power or advance their own agendas.[7] In many cases, extremist groups will use these differences as a rallying cry, seeking to create divisions and foment violence. Therefore, it is imperative that governments and international organizations take a comprehensive and proactive approach to addressing these conflicts. This includes promoting economic development and reducing poverty, addressing political grievances, and promoting interfaith and interethnic dialogue. It is also crucial to address the underlying causes of extremism, such as lack of education, political disenfranchisement, and social inequality. Ethnic and religious conflicts and tensions are a significant factor in regional conflicts that can lead to global security crises. Therefore, I urge policymakers and leaders to take a proactive approach to addressing these conflicts and promoting peace and stability in the regions where they occur. Failure to do so risks further escalation of violence and instability, with potentially catastrophic consequences for the global community.

CHAPTER 9

The Role of Foreign Powers

The role of foreign powers in regional conflicts is a complex and ongoing issue in many parts of the world. The involvement of foreign powers often exacerbates existing tensions and can escalate conflicts to dangerous levels, leading to instability and insecurity on an international scale. One of the most pressing examples of foreign power involvement is the ongoing conflict in Syria. The Syrian civil war, which began in 2011, has been fueled by the involvement of numerous foreign powers. Russia, Iran, and Turkey have all backed different factions within the conflict, with Russia and Iran supporting the Syrian government and Turkey supporting opposition forces. The United States and other Western powers have also been involved, primarily through air strikes against ISIS targets.[1] This complex web of foreign involvement has only served to prolong the conflict and make it more deadly.

Another example is the conflict in Yemen, where a Saudi-led coalition has been fighting Houthi rebels since 2015. The involvement of foreign powers, including the United States and Iran, has contributed to the devastation of the country, with tens of thousands of civilians killed and millions displaced. Regarding the Yemeni civil war, it began when Houthi rebels occupied the northwestern Yemeni province of Sadah in early 2014 and captured the capital, Sana'a in September of the same year. In January of the following year, they took control of the presidential palace and ousted the Hadi government in Yemen. A month later, a provisional constitution was announced.

The existing parliament was dissolved and a new parliament was formed, and a presidential council was established to assume the role of government for two years[1]. The civil war in Yemen is not a simple 'fight within the family'. Behind the Houthi rebels is Iran, the suzerain of Shiites. Foreign media speculate that the Houthis are acquiring various missile technologies and drone technologies, including anti-ship missiles, anti-tank missiles, portable surface-to-air missiles, cruise missiles, and ballistic missiles, with technical assistance from Iran. On the other hand, the government forces are fully supported by Saudi Arabia, the suzerain of the Sunni sect. Saudi Arabia has formed an Arab coalition to restore the Sunni Hadi government, deter, and reduce Iran's growing influence in the region. In addition to Saudi Arabia, other countries such as UAE, Bahrain, Kuwait, Egypt, Jordan, Morocco, Sudan, Senegal and Qatar are joining the coalition.[2]

In Africa, foreign powers have also played a role in conflicts in countries such as Sudan, South Sudan, and the Democratic Republic of Congo. China has invested heavily in infrastructure projects across the continent, often with the aim of securing access to natural resources. This has led to accusations of neocolonialism, and China's involvement in African conflicts has been criticized for exacerbating existing tensions. China's investment in Africa has been driven by several factors, including a desire to secure access to natural resources, open new markets for Chinese goods and services, and establish political influence on the continent. Some analysts have also suggested that China's investment in Africa is part of a broader strategy to challenge Western dominance in global affairs. In recent years, China has been particularly active in investing in African countries such as Congo, Sudan, and South Sudan. These investments have been focused on a range of sectors, including infrastructure, mining, energy, and agriculture. China's infrastructure investments in Africa have been significant. One of the most prominent examples is the construction of a new railway line in Kenya, which was funded and built by Chinese companies.[3]

China has also invested heavily in port facilities, with Chinese firms owning or managing ports in several African countries, including Djibouti, Kenya, and Tanzania. In the mining sector, China has been involved in several high-profile projects in Africa, including the development of copper and cobalt mines in Congo. China has also invested in the energy sector, funding the construction of new power plants in several African countries. China's investments in African agriculture have also been growing. Chinese firms have been involved in large-scale agricultural projects in several African countries, including Zimbabwe and Zambia.[4] Despite the significant investments that China has made in Africa, there has been some criticism of China's approach. Some observers have argued that Chinese investments have not always been transparent or accountable, and that they have sometimes involved exploitative labor practices or environmental damage.

In terms of statistics, the exact figures for China's investment in Africa are difficult to determine, as Chinese investment data is often incomplete or unreliable. However, according to the China Africa Research Initiative at Johns Hopkins University, Chinese investment in Africa totaled $45 billion in 2019, up from $15 billion in 2010. This makes China the single largest investor in Africa, surpassing traditional partners such as the United States and the European Union.

As shown in the chart below, Chinese FDI flows to Africa have exceeded those from the U.S. since 2013, as U.S. FDI flows have generally been declining since 2010. The top five African destinations of Chinese FDI in 2021 were Democratic Republic of Congo, Zambia, Guinea, South Africa and Kenya. For American investment, it is South Africa, Egypt, Nigeria, Ethiopia and Republic of the Congo, although the US government has not disclosed FDI flows to nine African countries, including the DRC, to protect commercial data of individual companies.[5]

Comparative Analysis of Chinese and US Foreign Direct Investment (FDI) Flows to Africa (2011-2021)

Foreign direct investment (FDI) has played a crucial role in shaping economic relationships between countries, and Africa has emerged as an attractive destination for FDI from various global players. This comparative analysis focuses on Chinese FDI and US FDI flows to Africa from 2011 to 2021. The statistics presented here are derived from reputable sources, including the United Nations Conference on Trade and Development (UNCTAD) and the China Global Investment Tracker (CGIT).

Chinese FDI Flows to Africa (2011-2021):
Chinese FDI to Africa has witnessed significant growth over the past decade, reflecting China's economic engagement with the continent. According to data from the UNCTAD World Investment Report, Chinese FDI to Africa totaled approximately USD 46 billion in 2011, which increased to USD 51 billion in 2015 (UNCTAD, 2020, p. 85). Despite a slight decline in subsequent years, Chinese FDI rebounded strongly in 2018, reaching a peak of USD 55 billion (UNCTAD, 2020, p. 85). By 2021, Chinese FDI flows to Africa reached an estimated USD 50 billion.[6]

US FDI Flows to Africa (2011-2021):
In comparison to Chinese FDI, US FDI flows to Africa have been relatively stable, with fluctuations influenced by economic factors and policy changes. According to UNCTAD data, US FDI to Africa stood at USD 57 billion in 2011 and experienced minor variations in subsequent years, reaching USD 54 billion in 2015. By 2018, US FDI to Africa increased to USD 60 billion.[7] However, it should be noted that precise data for US FDI to Africa in 2021 is not yet available.

Comparative Analysis and Trends:

The comparative analysis of Chinese and US FDI flows to Africa reveals several noteworthy trends. Firstly, both countries have demonstrated a sustained interest in investing in Africa, as evidenced by the overall upward trajectory of FDI flows. However, Chinese FDI has displayed greater volatility compared to the relatively stable US FDI flows. The reasons behind this discrepancy can be attributed to different investment strategies and economic priorities pursued by China and the United States.

China's Belt and Road Initiative (BRI), launched in 2013, has been a key driver of Chinese FDI in Africa. The BRI focuses on enhancing infrastructure connectivity and promoting trade, providing opportunities for Chinese companies to invest in large-scale projects across the continent. On the other hand, US FDI to Africa is influenced by factors such as market considerations, political stability, and regulatory frameworks.[8]

Additionally, Chinese FDI in Africa has been primarily directed towards sectors such as energy, infrastructure, and manufacturing.[9] In contrast, US FDI in Africa has been more diversified, with investments spanning sectors such as finance, services, and technology.[10]

Chinese and US FDI flows to Africa have experienced notable growth over the past decade, albeit with differing patterns. Chinese FDI has displayed greater volatility, influenced by initiatives like the BRI, while US FDI flows have been relatively stable. The investment strategies of both countries have shaped the sectors and types of projects they prioritize within Africa. This analysis provides valuable insights into the evolving economic dynamics and foreign investment patterns between China, the United States, and Africa.

China has become a significant source of foreign direct investment in Africa. According to the Council on Foreign Relations, China invests in agriculture and develops special trade and economic cooperation zones in several African countries including Ethiopia, Nigeria, and Zambia. China has created 25 economic and trade cooperation zones in 16 African countries and has continued to invest heavily across the continent throughout the COVID-19 pandemic.[11] The top five African destinations of Chinese FDI in 2021 were Democratic Republic of Congo, Zambia, Guinea, South Africa and Kenya.[12]

China has been investing heavily in Africa for the past two decades, and it is now one of the continent's biggest investors. According to data from the China Africa Research Initiative at Johns Hopkins University, China's total investment in Africa between 2000 and 2020 was over $298 billion. This includes investment in various sectors such as infrastructure, energy, mining, agriculture, and manufacturing. The top five African countries that received the most investment from China during this period were:[13]

Angola: $43.4 billion, Ethiopia: $16.6 billion, Nigeria: $16.3 billion, Sudan: $14.4 billion, Zambia: $12.7 billion

It is worth noting that these figures are based on publicly available data and may not reflect the full extent of China's investment in Africa, as some investments may not be publicly disclosed. Additionally, the nature and impact of China's investments in Africa have been subject to debate, with some criticizing China's approach for its potential negative effects on African economies and societies. Based on the investment situation of China in Africa mentioned earlier, it appears that Angola has received the highest amount of investment among the suggested countries. What could be the reason behind this?

China's investment in Angola has been primarily driven by its interest in Angola's oil and gas sector. Angola is one of Africa's top oil producers, and China is one of its largest customers for oil exports. China has been investing heavily in Angola's oil industry since the early 2000s, with state-owned enterprises such as China National Petroleum Corporation (CNPC) and Sinopec establishing joint ventures with Angolan state-owned oil company Sonangol to explore and develop oil and gas fields in the country. Apart from oil and gas, China has also invested in other sectors in Angola, such as infrastructure, construction, and mining. China has financed and built several major infrastructure projects in Angola, including the Lobito-Luau Railway, the Catoca diamond mine, and the Kilamba New City housing project. In addition to economic interests, China's relationship with Angola has also been driven by geopolitical considerations. Angola is a key strategic partner for China in Africa, and the two countries have developed close political ties. China has provided significant financial and diplomatic support to Angola over the years, including during its civil war and post-war reconstruction.

China has been instrumental in the development of Angola's infrastructure through economic and commercial co-operation agreements resulting in huge investments in major projects in energy, transport, infrastructure, telecommunications and agro-business, as well as oil-backed loans.[14] As Angola became the leading supplier of crude oil to the Chinese economy in the early 2000s, it set up a barter model. The China-Africa Research Initiative reports that China delivered loans to Angola worth $42.8bn between 2000 and 2017.[15] The majority of Chinese investment in Africa has been in the form of loans, rather than direct investment or aid.

According to the same study, 70% of Chinese investment in Africa in 2019 was in the form of loans. While this has allowed African countries to fund large-scale infrastructure projects, it has also raised concerns about debt sustainability, particularly in countries with weaker economies. Overall, China's investment in Africa has been significant and has had a major impact on the continent's economic development. While there are some concerns about the transparency and accountability of Chinese investments, it is clear that China's presence in Africa is likely to continue to grow in the years ahead.

The situation in Ukraine is another example of how foreign power involvement can lead to dangerous levels of instability. Following the ousting of Ukraine's pro-Russian president in 2014, Russia annexed Crimea and backed separatist movements in eastern Ukraine. The conflict has resulted in thousands of deaths and has severely strained relations between Russia and the West. The conflict between Ukraine and Russia has a long history. Crimea is a part of Ukraine that has close historical ties to Russia mainly because it was originally a part of the Russian Federation from 1783 to 1954. Then in 1954, the Soviet leader, Nikita Khrushchev, gave the Crimean Peninsula to Ukraine. The historical ties between Crimea and Russia led many Ukrainians living in Crimea to have pro-Russian sentiments.

In 2014, protests in Kyiv's main square were a violent expression of Ukrainians' desire for closer ties with Europe and for an end to corruption. The protests led to the ousting of President Viktor Yanukovych and his pro-Russian government. This led to Russia annexing Crimea from Ukraine in March 2014. The conflict escalated in 2022 when Russia invaded Ukraine. The invasion constitutes the biggest threat to peace and security in Europe since the end of the Cold War. .

U.S. Involvement in the Russian-Ukrainian War

The United States has been involved in the war between Russia and Ukraine since the beginning of the conflict. The US has taken the lead in providing Ukraine with military equipment and training, economic aid, a near-blank check of diplomatic support, intelligence of use for stymying Russia's offensive, and threatening draconian consequences should Russia use nuclear weapons in its campaign. The US has also been coordinating Ukrainian missile strikes on Russian forces[1]. The US warned that Russia intended to invade Ukraine, citing Russia is growing military presence at the Russia-Ukraine border. President Putin then ordered troops to Luhansk and Donetsk, claiming the troops served a "peacekeeping" function. The US involvement in the war is driven by its interest in maintaining global security and stability. The US sees itself as a global leader and has a responsibility to protect its allies and promote democracy around the world. The US also has an interest in preventing Russia from expanding its sphere of influence and undermining international norms[3]. A crisis in global security could arise if the conflict between Russia and Ukraine escalates into a full-scale war. This could lead to a wider conflict involving other countries and could have serious implications for global security. Overall, the role of foreign powers in regional conflicts is a complex issue with no easy solutions. However, it is clear that foreign involvement often worsens conflicts and can have devastating consequences for civilians caught in the crossfire. It is important for the international community to work towards peaceful and diplomatic solutions to conflicts, rather than exacerbating them through military intervention and support for opposing sides.

As an expert in international relations, I can confidently say that the role of foreign powers is a significant factor that contributes to regional conflicts, which can lead to global security crises. It is essential to understand the dynamics of these conflicts and the involvement of foreign powers to develop effective strategies for preventing and resolving such crises. Foreign powers can be state or non-state actors that interfere in the internal affairs of a country, either directly or indirectly. These powers may be motivated for their involvement, including economic interests, geopolitical influence, ideological considerations, or a desire to protect their citizens or allies. One example of foreign powers' role in regional conflicts is the Syrian civil war, which began in 2011. The conflict started as a popular uprising against the authoritarian regime of Bashar al-Assad but soon escalated into a complex civil war, involving multiple domestic and foreign actors.[16] Foreign powers, such as Russia, Iran, Turkey, and the United States, provided military, financial, and diplomatic support to different sides of the conflict, further fueling the violence and prolonging the war.

Another example is the ongoing conflict between Israel and Palestine, which has been a source of tension and instability in the Middle East for decades. The conflict has multiple layers and involves various actors, including Israel, Palestine, Arab states, and other foreign powers. The involvement of external powers, such as the United States, has complicated the conflict and made it harder to find a lasting solution. The role of foreign powers in regional conflicts can also lead to unintended consequences and spillover effects, creating security risks beyond the conflict zone. For instance, the Syrian conflict has triggered a refugee crisis, destabilized neighboring countries, and provided fertile ground for terrorist groups like ISIS to flourish. Similarly, the Israeli-Palestinian conflict has fueled extremism and violence in the region and beyond.

To prevent and resolve regional conflicts caused by foreign powers, policymakers need to adopt a multifaceted approach that addresses the root causes of the conflict, reduces external interference, and promotes dialogue and cooperation among the conflicting parties. This approach requires a deep understanding of the local dynamics and the motivations and interests of external actors, as well as a commitment to international norms and principles of sovereignty and non-interference. The role of foreign powers is a critical factor that can exacerbate regional conflicts and create global security crises. To mitigate the risks of such conflicts, policymakers need to adopt a comprehensive and nuanced approach that balances the interests and concerns of all parties involved, including external actors. As an expert in international relations, I cannot stress enough the importance of addressing the role of foreign powers in regional conflicts that can potentially lead to global security crises.

The consequences of such conflicts are far-reaching and can have significant impacts on global peace and stability. To effectively address this issue, policymakers must recognize that external interference in internal conflicts is not a viable solution. Instead, they should focus on promoting dialogue and cooperation among conflicting parties, addressing the root causes of the conflict, and reducing external interference. This approach requires a concerted effort from all actors involved, including regional and international organizations, as well as individual states. It also requires a commitment to international norms and principles, such as the respect for sovereignty and non-interference.

In addition, policymakers must also take into account the unintended consequences of foreign involvement in regional conflicts. The spillover effects of such conflicts, such as refugee crises and the proliferation of extremist groups, can have significant security implications beyond the conflict zone. The role of foreign powers in regional conflicts cannot be underestimated. A critical factor can exacerbate tensions and lead to global security crises. Therefore, policymakers must adopt a comprehensive and nuanced approach that addresses the root causes of the conflict, reduces external interference, and promotes dialogue and cooperation among conflicting parties. Only then can we hope to prevent and resolve regional conflicts and ensure global peace and stability.

PART III

THE IMPACT OF REGIONAL CONFLICTS ON GLOBAL SECURITY

"Mankind must put an end to war or war will put an end to mankind."

- John F. Kennedy

CHAPTER 10.

The Displacement of Millions of People

Regional conflicts have become a recurring issue in various parts of the world. These conflicts have far-reaching consequences that extend beyond the boundaries of the affected regions, often leading to significant global security concerns. One of the most significant impacts of these conflicts is the displacement of millions of people who are forced to flee their homes to seek safety elsewhere. This mass displacement has grave consequences for the individuals involved, as well as for the broader global community.

For instance, the ongoing conflict in Syria has resulted in the displacement of millions of people, many of whom have fled to neighboring countries such as Lebanon, Turkey, and Jordan. This mass migration has put a significant strain on the resources and infrastructure of these host countries, exacerbating already existing economic and social challenges. Moreover, the influx of refugees from conflict-ridden regions has often resulted in social and political tensions in the host countries, further complicating the situation. Regional conflicts can lead to displacement of people and cause a humanitarian crisis.

One example is the Syrian refugee crisis. The Syrian civil war has caused millions of people to flee their homes and seek refuge in other countries. According to the United Nations High Commissioner for Refugees (UNHCR), there are currently over 6 million Syrian refugees and over 6 million internally displaced persons (IDPs) within Syria.

This has put a strain on the resources of the countries hosting the refugees and has led to a humanitarian crisis. The Syrian refugee crisis stems from the civil war in Syria that began in 2011. Pro-democracy protests against President Bashar al-Assad's regime triggered the conflict, which subsequently escalated into a full-scale war involving multiple factions. This ongoing war has caused immense devastation, widespread violence, and human rights violations, resulting in a humanitarian catastrophe.

The displacement of millions of Syrians can be attributed to several key factors. Firstly, the violence and conflict have made many areas uninhabitable due to intense fighting, aerial bombardments, and indiscriminate attacks. Both the Syrian government and armed opposition groups have been implicated in human rights abuses, including arbitrary detentions, torture, and killings. These factors have compelled many Syrians to flee their homes in search of safety. Moreover, the Syrian government has imposed sieges on opposition-held areas, cutting off essential supplies such as food, water, and medical aid. This has created severe humanitarian crises, prompting people to escape to neighboring countries. Additionally, the war has ravaged Syria's economy, resulting in high unemployment, inflation, and poverty. The deteriorating economic conditions have further pushed Syrians to seek better livelihoods elsewhere. The process of displacement has unfolded in three main phases. Initially, many Syrians sought refuge in safer areas within the country, away from the direct conflict. This included regions under government control, Kurdish-held territories, or areas controlled by other armed groups.

As the conflict persisted, a significant number of Syrians crossed the borders and sought refuge in neighboring countries, such as Turkey, Lebanon, Jordan, Iraq, and Egypt. These countries have faced substantial strain as they host the majority of Syrian refugees. Furthermore, due to prolonged instability and worsening conditions in the region, a significant number of Syrians have embarked on dangerous journeys to Europe and other regions. These perilous journeys often involve crossing the Mediterranean Sea in overcrowded boats, leading to numerous tragic incidents. The scale of this movement has drawn global attention and turned the crisis into a worldwide refugee issue. The Syrian refugee crisis has prompted significant international response. Humanitarian aid has been provided by various organizations, including the United Nations High Commissioner for Refugees (UNHCR) and non-governmental organizations. This assistance encompasses essential needs such as shelter, food, healthcare, and education for Syrian refugees.

Some countries have also implemented resettlement and relocation programs to offer permanent residence to a limited number of Syrian refugees. These programs involve processing asylum claims and providing support for integration into host societies. However, the crisis has presented challenges for host countries, leading to debates and political controversies. Concerns related to national security, economic burdens, and cultural integration have influenced the political response and policies regarding the acceptance and treatment of refugees. Accordingly, the Syrian refugee crisis has emerged from the ongoing civil war, characterized by violence, human rights abuses, and the collapse of infrastructure and the economy. This complex crisis has resulted in the displacement of millions of Syrians, who have sought refuge internally, in neighboring countries, and beyond. The international response has involved humanitarian aid, resettlement programs, and political deliberations, as nations grapple with the challenges posed by the crisis. The Syrian conflict, which began in 2011, has been one of the primary drivers of the global refugee crisis. Over 6.6 million Syrians have been internally displaced, while another 6.7 million have fled the country as refugees. Other major sources of refugees include Afghanistan, South Sudan, Myanmar, and Somalia.

Global Refugee Statistics and Status (1991-2021): A Comprehensive Analysis based on UNHCR Data[1]

According to the UNHCR statistical data, the issue of forced displacement has been a longstanding challenge in the realm of international politics, necessitating comprehensive analysis to understand the magnitude and trends of refugee populations worldwide. This article presents the latest statistics on refugees and forcibly displaced persons, derived from the United Nations High Commissioner for Refugees

Total Number of Forcibly Displaced Persons (End of 2021):
At the end of 2021, the total number of forcibly displaced persons worldwide reached a staggering 89.3 million individuals. These individuals were displaced because of persecution, conflict, violence, human rights violations, or events seriously disturbing public order.

Refugee Population:
a) Refugees under UNHCR's Mandate: Among the forcibly displaced, there were 27.1 million refugees globally. This includes 21.3 million individuals who fall under the mandate of the United Nations High Commissioner for Refugees (UNHCR). These refugees have been forced to flee their home countries due to conflict, persecution, or other compelling circumstances.

b) Palestine Refugees under UNRWA's Mandate: Within the overall refugee population, 5.8 million individuals are Palestine refugees who fall under the mandate of the United Nations Relief and Works Agency for Palestine Refugees in the Near East (UNRWA). These individuals have been displaced because of the Israeli-Palestinian conflict and its consequences.

Internally Displaced Persons (IDPs):
In addition to refugees, the phenomenon of internal displacement remains a significant concern. The global number of internally displaced persons stood at 53.2 million individuals. These individuals have been

uprooted from their homes but remain within the borders of their own countries.

Asylum Seekers Displaced Abroad:
Globally, there were 4.6 million individuals seeking asylum and displaced abroad. Asylum seekers are individuals who have fled their home countries and are seeking international protection but have not yet been recognized as refugees.

Venezuelans Displaced Abroad:
The ongoing political and economic crisis in Venezuela has led to a significant number of people being displaced abroad. As of the end of 2021, approximately 4.4 million Venezuelans were displaced outside their home country.

The statistics presented highlight the immense global challenge posed by forced displacement. The numbers underscore the urgent need for concerted international efforts to address the root causes of displacement, ensure the protection of refugees and internally displaced persons, and provide assistance and durable solutions to those affected by forced displacement.

As of 2021, the world is witnessing an unprecedented number of refugees and displaced persons due to various regional conflicts, wars, and ethnic conflicts. According to the United Nations High Commissioner for Refugees (UNHCR), there were over 82 million forcibly displaced people worldwide at the end of 2020, including 26.4 million refugees, 48 million internally displaced persons (IDPs), and 4.1 million asylum seekers. The UNHCR is the primary organization responsible for protecting and providing assistance to refugees worldwide. It works in partnership with governments, NGOs, and other international organizations to ensure that refugees have access to basic needs, such as food, shelter, healthcare, and education. One of the primary ways that the UNHCR provides assistance is through the provision of emergency relief, such as distributing food and shelter materials in refugee camps. The organization also works to ensure that refugees are protected from violence, exploitation, and discrimination. Another critical measure taken by the UNHCR is the resettlement of refugees in third countries. This involves identifying refugees who are unable to return to their home countries and finding suitable countries willing to accept them as permanent residents. In 2020, the UNHCR facilitated the resettlement of 22,770 refugees, primarily from Syria, the Democratic

Republic of Congo, and Afghanistan.[2] The UNHCR also works to advocate for the rights of refugees and to raise awareness of the challenges they face.

In last year's Global Trends report, UNHCR predicted, "The question is no longer if forced displacement will exceed 100 million people – but rather when". The when is now. With millions of Ukrainians displaced and further displacement elsewhere in 2022, total forced displacement now exceeds 100 million people. This means one in every 78 people on earth has been forced to flee – a dramatic milestone that few would have expected a decade ago. As new refugee situations emerge and intensify, and as existing ones reignite or remain unresolved, there is an acute need for durable solutions at increasing scale. The Global Compact on Refugees notes that one strategic priority for UNHCR and the humanitarian community is to identify and support durable solutions that enable refugees to rebuild their lives and live in safety and dignity.[3]

It seeks to promote durable solutions, including voluntary repatriation, resettlement, and local integration, as well as to address the root causes of displacement. The global refugee crisis is a significant challenge that requires a coordinated international response. The UNHCR and other organizations are working tirelessly to provide assistance and protection to refugees and to advocate for their rights. However, more needs to be done to address the root causes of displacement and to find durable solutions for refugees worldwide. The displacement of millions of people due to regional conflicts is a crucial factor that can have significant implications for global security. Regional conflicts can arise from a range of factors, including historical grievances, territorial disputes, ethnic and religious tensions, and economic disparities. [4] These conflicts can escalate rapidly, leading to violence, displacement, and humanitarian crises. One of the most significant consequences of regional conflicts is the displacement of millions of people. Displaced populations are forced to flee their homes and seek refuge in other countries or within their own borders. This displacement can have several impacts on global security, including:

Spread of Violence: The displacement of millions of people can contribute to the spread of violence beyond national borders. Displaced populations may be forced to cross international borders to seek safety, which can create tensions with neighboring countries. This can result in further conflict, leading to an escalation of violence and instability in the region.

Humanitarian Crises: The displacement of millions of people can result in humanitarian crises, including food shortages, lack of shelter, and inadequate medical care. These crises can lead to the spread of disease and other health problems, further exacerbating the situation.

Social and Economic Dislocation: Displaced populations face significant challenges in integrating into new communities. This can result in social tensions and economic dislocation, as refugees may compete with local populations for jobs and resources.[5]

Radicalization: Displaced populations may be vulnerable to radicalization by extremist groups.[6] This can lead to the emergence of new security threats, as these groups may seek to exploit the vulnerability of displaced populations to further their own objectives.

To address these challenges, international political scientists emphasize the importance of finding sustainable solutions for displaced populations. This can include providing humanitarian assistance, supporting refugee integration into host communities, and addressing the root causes of regional conflicts. Effective collaboration among regional and international actors is crucial to addressing these challenges and promoting stability and security in the region.

The Numerous and Complicated Issues by the Displacement of Millions of People

The displacement of millions of people due to regional conflicts can have a significant impact on global security crises. The movement of large numbers of refugees can lead to a range of complex and interconnected problems, including social, economic, and political challenges. One of the immediate concerns is the strain on the host country's resources, particularly in areas with limited capacity to accommodate and provide for refugees. This can create tensions between refugees and host communities and exacerbate existing economic and social inequalities.

In some cases, the influx of refugees can also lead to environmental degradation and resource depletion, further contributing to instability and conflict. The displacement of millions of people can also have broader security implications. For example, refugees may be more susceptible to recruitment by extremist groups and criminal organizations, particularly in situations where they lack access to necessities such as food, shelter, and healthcare.[7] This can further exacerbate regional conflicts and contribute to the spread of violence beyond national borders.

Moreover, the displacement of millions of people can have long-term economic and social impacts. Refugees may struggle to reintegrate into their home communities after the conflict has ended, particularly if the conflict has resulted in the destruction of infrastructure, the loss of livelihoods, and the breakdown of social networks. This can lead to a cycle of poverty and insecurity, which can in turn fuel further conflict and instability. The displacement of millions of people due to regional conflicts has far-reaching consequences for global security. Addressing the root causes of these conflicts and finding sustainable solutions for refugees is essential to preventing the spread of violence and promoting peace and stability on a global scale.

The migration of millions of refugees and others resulting from regional conflicts presents complex challenges that extend beyond the borders of the affected regions. The security implications of such mass movements cannot be underestimated, as they have the potential to pose a threat to global stability and global security. The displacement of large numbers of people due to regional conflicts creates multifaceted problems that require comprehensive and coordinated solutions. It is imperative for the international community to recognize the urgency of addressing these issues and to work together to mitigate the risks, they pose.

Firstly, there is a need for enhanced cooperation and burden sharing among nations to ensure the safety and well-being of the displaced populations. This involves providing adequate humanitarian assistance, including shelter, food, healthcare, and education, to alleviate their immediate suffering and facilitate their integration into host communities. Furthermore, efforts should be focused on addressing the root causes of these regional conflicts to prevent future waves of displacement. This entails diplomatic negotiations, conflict resolution, and peacebuilding initiatives, aimed at fostering stability and reconciliation in the affected regions. By addressing the underlying grievances and promoting inclusive governance, the international community can contribute to sustainable solutions and reduce the risk of further migration and conflict. In addition, it is crucial to strengthen international mechanisms for managing and responding to refugee and migration flows.

This involves improving coordination between states, international organizations, and non-governmental actors to ensure a coherent and effective response. Shared responsibility and burden-sharing frameworks can help distribute the challenges associated with refugee influxes more equitably among nations. Ultimately, addressing the complex problems arising from the migration of millions of refugees and others caused by regional conflicts is not only a humanitarian imperative but also a matter of global security. By investing in conflict prevention, resolution, and humanitarian assistance, we can create a more secure and stable world that upholds the principles of human rights, dignity, and peace for all. Only through collective action and a commitment to global solidarity can we navigate the challenges posed by regional conflicts and their far-reaching consequences.

CHAPTER 11.

The Spread of Violence and Extremism

The world is currently facing a significant threat to global security - the spread of violence and extremism that is causing regional conflicts in various parts of the world. These conflicts, fueled by religious, political, and ideological differences, have far-reaching consequences that extend beyond the borders of the affected regions, threatening the stability and security of the entire world. From the rise of extremist groups such as ISIS in the Middle East to the ongoing conflict in Afghanistan and the growing tensions between North Korea and its neighbors, the global community is facing a complex and multifaceted challenge. These conflicts have resulted in the displacement of millions of people, the loss of countless lives, and the destruction of vital infrastructure, further exacerbating the challenges faced by the affected regions. There have been numerous regional conflicts that have been fueled by the spread of violence and extremism, ultimately posing a threat to global security. Here are some examples and statistics:

Middle East and North Africa (MENA) Region: The rise of extremist groups such as ISIS and al-Qaida in the MENA region has led to widespread violence and regional conflicts. According to the United Nations, the Syrian conflict has resulted in the displacement of over 6.7 million people as refugees, while over 6.6 million people have been internally displaced. The conflict has also caused the death of an estimated 500,000 people. The ongoing conflict in Yemen, which began in 2014, has also resulted in the displacement of over 3.6 million people and the death of over 233,000 people.[1]

Afghanistan: The ongoing conflict in Afghanistan has been one of the longest-lasting conflicts, with roots in the Cold War. According to the UN, there were over 10,000 civilian casualties in 2020 alone. IOM (the International Organization for Migration) explained that last year, Afghans increasingly crossed the border into Iran and Pakistan, describing it as a trend that is likely to continue in the coming months. The UN agency warned that as needs continue to grow, failure to sustain and improve access to essential services, restore livelihoods, and effectively address the vulnerabilities of populations affected by the crisis, would cause a surge in displacement and migration. To respond to the urgent humanitarian and protection needs of more than 3.6 million people in the conflict-stricken country, IOM is appealing for $589 million.[2]

South Asia: The ongoing conflict between India and Pakistan over Kashmir has been a major source of tension and violence in the region. According to the UN, there were over 2,300 civilian casualties in Kashmir in 2020.

Sub-Saharan Africa: The Boko Haram insurgency in Nigeria has resulted in the displacement of over 2.7 million people and the death of over 30,000 people since 2009. The conflict has also spilled over into neighboring countries, such as Cameroon and Niger.[3]

Southeast Asia: The ongoing conflict between the Myanmar military and ethnic minority groups, particularly the Rohingya in Rakhine state, has resulted in the displacement of over 1.1 million people as refugees and the death of thousands of people. The UN has described the situation as a "textbook example of ethnic cleansing."

These regional conflicts pose a threat to global security in various ways. The displacement of millions of people as refugees can lead to a strain on resources and infrastructure in neighboring countries, as well as social and political tensions. Moreover, the spread of violence and extremism can fuel further conflicts and instability, leading to the potential for the formation of new extremist groups that may pose a threat to global security. To address these issues, international organizations such as the UN and regional organizations such as the African Union and the Organization of American States have taken measures to prevent and resolve conflicts, such as promoting peace and dialogue, providing humanitarian assistance, and supporting post-conflict reconstruction efforts. However, the challenges remain significant, and sustained international efforts are necessary to ensure global security and stability.

The Causes of the Spread of Violence and Extremism

The causes of the spread of violence and extremism leading to regional conflicts around the world are complex and multifaceted. Some of the root causes include poverty, inequality, political instability, and social exclusion. The consequences of these conflicts can be devastating and long lasting, including displacement of people, loss of life, and destruction of infrastructure.

According to the United Nations, violent extremism is a growing threat to international peace and security. The impact of violent extremism on communities can be long lasting and can inflict harm beyond physical violence. The spread of violence and extremism leading to regional conflicts around the world has been a persistent problem for several decades. There are several causes of this phenomenon, including political, social, economic, and ideological factors. These factors can create an environment that fosters extremism and violence, leading to regional conflicts. Additionally, the consequences of these conflicts can be severe and far-reaching, affecting both the immediate region and the world at large.

Causes and Consequences of Violence and Extremism Leading to Regional Conflicts

Regional conflicts arise due to violence and extremism, which ultimately pose a threat to global security. What are the underlying causes of this violence and extremism? It is necessary to identify several causes.

Political factors: Political instability, weak governance, and political corruption can create an environment of uncertainty and instability. This instability can lead to extremist groups taking advantage of the situation, exploiting people's grievances and turning them towards violence.[4]

Social factors: Social inequality, discrimination, and marginalization can also fuel extremist ideologies. Groups that feel left behind or excluded from society may turn towards extremist groups that promise to address their grievances through violence.

Economic factors: Economic disparities and poverty can create an environment that fosters extremism. Unemployment and poverty can lead to frustration and despair, which can be channeled towards extremist ideologies.[5]

Ideological factors: Religious, political, or cultural ideologies that promote intolerance and extremism can fuel regional conflicts. These ideologies often use violent tactics to achieve their goals.

Violence and extremism have many consequences. To name a few representative ones, they include loss of life and displacement, economic damage, political instability, and global negative impacts

Loss of life and displacement: The most obvious consequence of regional conflicts is the loss of life and displacement of people. Civilians are often the most affected by these conflicts, leading to the loss of homes, livelihoods, and communities.

Economic damage: Regional conflicts can also lead to severe economic damage, including loss of infrastructure, businesses, and tourism. The economic impact of regional conflicts can be long lasting, with some countries struggling to recover for years or even decades.

Political instability: Regional conflicts can also create political instability, leading to weak governance, corruption, and a breakdown in the rule of law. This instability can further fuel extremist ideologies, creating a cycle of violence and instability.

Global impact: The impact of regional conflicts can also be felt globally. These conflicts can destabilize entire regions, leading to the spread of violence, extremism, and terrorism beyond national borders. This global impact can lead to the destabilization of entire regions and affect global security.

The spread of violence and extremism leading to regional conflicts around the world is a complex issue with several underlying causes. The conflicts can have severe consequences that affect both the immediate region and the world at large. It is essential to address the root causes of these conflicts and work towards building stable, peaceful, and inclusive societies.

Roles of International Organizations and Governments

International organizations and governments can take several steps to prevent and resolve regional conflicts in the future. These steps include:

Addressing root causes: Addressing the underlying causes of conflict, such as political, economic, and social factors, is essential for preventing future conflicts. This requires investments in development, poverty reduction, and promoting good governance and human rights.

Promoting inclusive and participatory governance: Promoting inclusive and participatory governance is essential for preventing conflicts. This includes ensuring that all groups are represented in decision-making processes, promoting transparency and accountability, and respecting human rights and the rule of law.

Building trust and reconciliation: Building trust and promoting reconciliation between conflicting parties is essential for resolving conflicts. This requires promoting dialogue and understanding, addressing grievances, and promoting justice and accountability.

Strengthening conflict resolution mechanisms: Strengthening conflict resolution mechanisms, including mediation and arbitration, is essential for preventing and resolving conflicts. This includes investing in training and capacity building for mediators and arbitrators, promoting the use of international law, and strengthening regional and international conflict resolution mechanisms.

Preventing and resolving regional conflicts and the spread of violence and extremism requires a comprehensive and multi-faceted approach that involves diplomacy, conflict prevention, peacekeeping, humanitarian assistance, and counterterrorism. It also requires addressing the underlying causes of conflict, promoting inclusive and participatory governance, building trust and reconciliation, and strengthening conflict resolution mechanisms. The spread of violence and extremism is one of the key factors that contribute to regional conflicts eventually becoming global security crises. The rise of violent extremist groups in a region can exacerbate existing tensions and conflicts, as well as create new ones. Extremist groups often use violence as a means to achieve their objectives, whether they are political, ideological, or religious. This violence can take many forms, from terrorist attacks to armed insurgencies, and it can quickly escalate and spread beyond the confines of a single region. In some cases, extremist groups have even declared their intention to establish a global caliphate or engage in violent jihad against perceived enemies around the world.

The spread of violence and extremism can also have a destabilizing effect on neighboring regions and countries. As violence spreads, it can create refugee flows and trigger mass migrations, leading to a further strain on resources and exacerbating existing tensions. Neighboring countries may also feel compelled to intervene, either to protect their own interests or to prevent the violence from spreading further. Moreover, the global nature of modern communication and media means that violent incidents in one region can quickly become known worldwide. This can lead to increased scrutiny and pressure on the international community to respond, through either diplomatic efforts or military intervention. Accordingly, it is clear that the spread of violence and extremism is a serious threat to global security.

Addressing this threat requires a multifaceted approach that includes efforts to address the root causes of extremism, such as poverty, political repression, and social inequality, as well as targeted measures to disrupt and dismantle extremist networks and prevent the spread of extremist ideology. It also requires a coordinated international response that includes diplomatic efforts, economic sanctions, and, in some cases, military intervention.

In the face of mounting challenges posed by violence and extremism, the international community united in a concerted effort to safeguard global peace and security. Recognizing the urgency of the situation, nations put aside their differences and joined hands to develop comprehensive strategies to counter this pervasive threat. It began with a series of high-level meetings and summits, where world leaders gathered to discuss the gravity of the situation and the need for collaborative action. Through these dialogues, they identified common objectives, shared intelligence, and pledged unwavering support for each other in the pursuit of peace. One of the main strategies adopted by the international community was enhanced intelligence sharing and cooperation. Countries recognized that the fight against violence and extremism required a collective approach, transcending national borders. Intelligence agencies established dedicated channels to exchange vital information, enabling a more comprehensive understanding of the evolving threats.

This collaborative effort allowed them to identify and disrupt potential terrorist plots, apprehend high-profile extremists, and dismantle their networks. Another critical aspect of the international community's strategy was focused on addressing the root causes of violence and extremism.

Governments realized that sustainable peace could only be achieved by tackling the underlying conditions that fuel these ideologies. To that end, they invested in social and economic development programs, aiming to alleviate poverty, marginalization, and inequality—factors that extremists often exploit to recruit vulnerable individuals. Education played a crucial role in this endeavor, with renewed efforts to promote tolerance, critical thinking, and respect for diversity. Additionally, diplomatic efforts were intensified to foster dialogue and resolve conflicts peacefully. Diplomats and mediators engaged in shuttle diplomacy, facilitating negotiations and peace agreements in regions riddled with violence and extremism.

International organizations, such as the United Nations, played a central role in coordinating these efforts, providing a neutral platform for dialogue and conflict resolution. Moreover, the international community recognized the significance of engaging with civil society organizations, religious leaders, and local communities. These stakeholders were crucial in countering violent narratives, promoting interfaith dialogue, and empowering communities to resist extremist ideologies. Governments supported grassroots initiatives that focused on rehabilitation and reintegration of former extremists, aiming to provide them with alternatives and prevent further radicalization. The internet and social media platforms posed unique challenges in combating the spread of violence and extremism.

Recognizing this, the international community worked closely with technology companies to develop effective strategies to counter online radicalization. Governments encouraged cooperation between law enforcement agencies and tech firms to remove extremist content promptly, monitor online activities, and identify potential threats. Simultaneously, initiatives were launched to promote positive narratives, utilizing social media platforms to amplify messages of peace, tolerance, and inclusion. By combining these multifaceted strategies, the international community sought to create a global network of cooperation, underpinned by shared values and a resolute commitment to counter violence and extremism. Recognizing that this was an ongoing battle, nations understood the need for sustained collaboration and adaptability in the face of evolving threats. Through their collective efforts, they aimed to build a safer and more secure world for present and future generations.

CHAPTER 12.

The Disruption of Global Trade and Commerce

Commerce and trade are vital to the global economy, as they serve as the driving force behind growth and prosperity, as well as the connection between people and businesses worldwide. Nevertheless, what occurs when these engines cease operating? What are the repercussions of a collapse in trade, a cessation in commerce, and a chaotic spiral of the global economy? The disruption of trade and commerce around the world can have wide-ranging economic, political, and social consequences.

This Chapter aims to offer a comprehensive overview of the prevailing situation, identify the key factors contributing to the disruption, and propose potential strategies to mitigate the adverse impact on global trade and commerce. Regional disputes have long been recognized as significant challenges to the stability and growth of global trade and commerce. These disputes encompass a wide range of conflicts, including territorial disputes, trade barriers, political tensions, and economic sanctions among countries or regions. The disruptions caused by such disputes impede the smooth flow of goods, services, and investments across borders, exerting detrimental effects on businesses and economies worldwide. As of 2023, numerous regional disputes have profoundly disrupted global trade and commerce. Some notable examples include:

Regional disputes have prompted the imposition of trade barriers and tariffs, impeding international trade flows. For instance, ongoing trade tensions between major economies such as the United States and China have resulted in the imposition of tariffs on a wide array of goods, leading to disruptions in global supply chains and adversely affecting businesses across diverse industries. Political tensions between countries or regions often precipitate the imposition of economic sanctions, further exacerbating the disruption of global trade and commerce. Recent examples include the sanctions imposed on Russia by the United States and the European Union, influencing various industries and businesses operating in those regions. Territorial disputes can significantly influence global trade and commerce, particularly in regions where crucial trade routes are involved. Disputes in the South China Sea, for instance, have raised concerns regarding the freedom of navigation and access to vital maritime trade routes. These disputes have the potential to disrupt global supply chains and trade flows.

Several factors contribute to the disruption of global trade and commerce resulting from regional disputes:

Regional disputes create an atmosphere of policy uncertainty, making it challenging businesses to plan and make informed decisions. The unpredictability of government policies and regulations hampers cross-border investments and impedes the establishment of long-term trade relationships. Disputes between countries or regions disrupt supply chains by impeding the movement of goods, components, or raw materials. This disruption leads to delays, increased costs, and reduced efficiency in production processes, adversely affecting businesses' ability to meet customer demand and fulfill contractual obligations. Heightened regional tensions can diminish investor confidence, resulting in reduced foreign direct investment (FDI) and capital flows. The lack of investment restricts economic growth, hinders technological advancements, and impedes the development of new markets, thereby negatively affecting global trade and commerce.

To mitigate the disruptions caused by regional disputes, the following strategies can be considered: Firstly, promoting diplomatic efforts and dialogue between conflicting parties is crucial to finding peaceful resolutions and preventing further escalation. Engaging in constructive negotiations and encouraging diplomatic solutions can help alleviate tensions and create a conducive environment for trade and commerce. Secondly, businesses should consider diversifying their supply chains by identifying alternative suppliers and markets to reduce dependence on regions prone to disputes. Developing robust contingency plans and establishing resilient supply networks can help mitigate the adverse effects of trade disruptions caused

The factors that can be influenced by the disruption of trade and commerce encompass economic, political, and social dimensions, each contributing to a comprehensive understanding of the implications arising from such disruptions. Within the realm of economic factors, the loss of jobs stands out as a significant consequence resulting from the disruption of trade and commerce. This disruption precipitates a decline in economic activity, leading to job losses across a multitude of industries and sectors. Consequently, individuals find themselves grappling with the repercussions of unemployment, which permeates various aspects of their lives. Moreover, the disruption of trade and commerce exerts an adverse impact on economic growth. These fundamental drivers of economic progress, when disrupted, impede growth rates, subsequently engendering long-term negative effects on the economy. The decline in growth rates poses challenges for businesses, hampers investment opportunities, and diminishes the overall economic vitality of a nation. A disruption in trade and commerce can further manifest through the mechanism of price increases. When the normal flow of trade is impeded, the accessibility of goods and services becomes more arduous. As a result, consumers and businesses encounter difficulties in obtaining the necessary commodities, leading to price hikes. This inflationary effect, borne out of disrupted trade, compounds the economic strain faced by individuals and exacerbates the challenges faced by businesses.

Additionally, supply chains become susceptible to disruptions when trade and commerce are impeded. The intricate network that supports the flow of goods and services is disrupted, resulting in delays and shortages. The repercussions of disrupted supply chains reverberate through various sectors, adversely affecting the availability of essential commodities and stymying economic activities. In the realm of political factors, a disruption of trade and commerce can catalyze the rise of nationalism and protectionism.

Faced with the challenges posed by disrupted trade, nations endeavor to protect their own industries and markets, leading to an upsurge in nationalist sentiments and protectionist policies. This shift in the political landscape further complicates international trade dynamics and shapes the trajectory of global economies. Furthermore, regional conflicts may be exacerbated by disruptions in trade and commerce.

As countries vie for resources and markets, the disruption of these vital economic channels intensifies competition, which, in turn, can spark or escalate regional conflicts. The interplay between economic interests and political dynamics becomes increasingly pronounced, underscoring the far-reaching consequences of trade disruptions.

Moreover, the disruption of trade and commerce can erode international cooperation and trust among nations. When the mechanisms that facilitate economic exchange are disrupted, the foundation for cooperation becomes fragile. The ensuing decline in trust and cooperation renders the resolution of disputes and conflicts more intricate, potentially impeding diplomatic efforts and exacerbating tensions. On the social front, increased poverty emerges as a distressing outcome of trade and commerce disruptions. Job losses and price increases combine to create a precarious environment, wherein individuals and families face heightened difficulty in meeting their basic needs. The rising tide of poverty exacerbates social inequalities, compounding the challenges faced by vulnerable populations. Economic hardships and job losses, because of trade and commerce disruptions, can ignite social unrest. The grievances borne out of economic strain find expression through protests and demonstrations, as individuals seek redress for their concerns. This social unrest becomes an important indicator of the social ramifications arising from the disruptions to trade and commerce. Lastly, the disruption of trade and commerce diminishes individuals and communities' access to essential goods and services. Disrupted trade channels create obstacles in procuring vital commodities such as food, medicine, and energy. The limited availability of these essential resources poses significant challenges, particularly for disadvantaged communities, potentially exacerbating existing social inequalities. Accordingly, the disruption of trade and commerce reverberates through multiple dimensions, including economic, political, and social factors. These disruptions manifest as job losses

The disruption of trade and commerce can have far-reaching consequences for the global economy, international relations, and social well-being.[1] Policymakers and stakeholders must work together to find solutions that can mitigate the negative impacts of such disruptions and promote economic stability and sustainable growth. As we have seen so far, trade and commerce are essential components of the global economy, connecting people and businesses across borders and driving economic growth and development. However, the stability and predictability of the global trading system is under threat from a range of challenges, including rising protectionism, economic nationalism, and geopolitical tensions. Disruptions in trade and commerce are important as they can affect regional conflicts and global security.[2] The weakening of the world trade system can have a cascading effect on the collapse of international relations, the rise of protectionism, and ultimately the increase in regional conflicts and threats to global security.

The COVID-19 pandemic, which has disrupted global supply chains and trade flows, has highlighted the fragility of the global trading system.[3] This crisis has brought to the forefront the potential consequences of a breakdown in trade and commerce, including shortages of essential goods and services, increased reliance on domestic production, and a rise in protectionism. At the same time, geopolitical tensions, particularly between major powers such as the United States and China, have intensified in recent years, leading to trade disputes and tit-for-tat tariffs. These tensions have the potential to escalate into regional conflicts, particularly in regions such as Asia and the Middle East, where the interests of major powers intersect and overlap. Against this backdrop, this dissertation aims to provide a comprehensive analysis of the causes and consequences of the collapse of trade and commerce, and to explore potential strategies for mitigating its impact on regional conflicts and global security.

One concrete and detailed example of how trade and commerce were disrupted is the ongoing trade dispute between the United States and China. The conflict began in 2018, when the US imposed tariffs on Chinese goods in an effort to address the trade deficit between the two countries. In response, China imposed retaliatory tariffs on US goods, leading to a cycle of escalating tariffs and counter-tariffs.

The Disruption of Global Trade and Commerce

It is clear that trade disputes have far-reaching economic, political, and social consequences. Here are some examples of how trade and commerce have been disrupted.

Economic Consequences: The tariffs imposed by both countries have led to a decline in bilateral trade and investment. US exports to China fell by 16.2% in 2019, while Chinese exports to the US fell by 20.9%. This decline in trade has had a negative impact on both economies, with some estimates suggesting that the dispute has cost the global economy up to $700 billion. However, China still maintains significant share of the U.S. – World Trade. In 2019, 6.5 % of total U.S. exports of $1.6 trillion to the World were exported to China and 18.1% of total U.S. Imports of $2.5 trillion were imported from China. In 2019, U.S. exports of Agriculture products to China have increased significantly from $8.7 billion in 2018 to $13.4 billion, a 54.8% ($4.7 billion) increase. In 2019, U.S. exports to China, the imports from China and the trade deficit all below the prior five-year average level by value not adjusted for inflation.

In 2019, BIS has processed a total of 2,677 license applications valued at $7.8 billion for tangible items, software and technology for China. BIS has approved 2,677, 78.3% of the total applications valued at $5.4 billion. RWA totaled 56 valued at $85.1 million. There were 130 denials valued at $85.1 million. In 2019, BIS received 657 applications from Chinese nationals for deemed exports and approved 583. There were 74 RWA and no denials.[4]

The top approved ECCNs, including ECCN for deemed exports are 3A233 for Mass spectrometers with 538 approvals; 5E001 for Technology with 514 approvals, and 2B350 for Chemical manufacturing facilities and equipment with 400 approvals.

Political Consequences: The trade dispute has led to a rise in nationalism and protectionism in both countries, with each side accusing the other of unfair trade practices. The conflict has strained diplomatic relations between the US and China, and has led to an increase in regional tensions.

Social Consequences: The tariffs imposed by both countries have led to price increases for consumers, particularly in the US. For example, the US tariffs on Chinese goods have led to price increases on a range of consumer products, including electronics, clothing, and home appliances.[5]

In addition to these consequences, the trade dispute has also led to a disruption of supply chains, particularly in industries such as electronics and manufacturing. This disruption has led to delays in the production and delivery of goods, which has had a negative impact on businesses and consumers.[6]

The US-China trade dispute is a concrete and detailed example of how trade and commerce disruptions can have wide-ranging consequences for the global economy, international relations, and social well-being. The ongoing conflict highlights the need for international cooperation and dialogue to address trade disputes and promote sustainable economic growth.

Expert Insights and a Few Measurements

There are several measures and expert insights from international organizations and governments to prevent trade and commerce disruption. Some of them are:

Strengthening International Trade Rules: International organizations such as the World Trade Organization (WTO) and the United Nations Conference on Trade and Development (UNCTAD) have called for a strengthening of international trade rules and regulations to prevent trade and commerce disruptions. This can involve reducing trade barriers, streamlining customs procedures, and increasing transparency in trade agreements.[7]

Diversifying Supply Chains: Governments and businesses can take steps to diversify their supply chains, reducing reliance on a single country or region. This can help to mitigate the impact of trade disruptions, as production can be shifted to alternative suppliers in the event of a disruption.

Promoting Free Trade Agreements: International organizations and governments can promote the use of free trade agreements to increase trade between countries. These agreements can help to reduce trade barriers, increase market access, and promote economic growth and development.

Investing in Infrastructure: Governments can invest in infrastructure projects such as ports, roads, and railways to improve connectivity and reduce trade barriers. This can help to facilitate trade and commerce and reduce the likelihood of disruptions.

Maintaining Economic Stability: Governments can take measures to maintain economic stability, such as maintaining low inflation rates and stable exchange rates. This can help to reduce the likelihood of economic shocks and disruptions.

Fostering International Cooperation: International organizations and governments can work together to foster international cooperation, dialogue, and trust. This can help to reduce the likelihood of trade disputes and conflicts, and promote peaceful resolution of disputes.

According to the WTO, countries should work towards reducing trade barriers and increasing market access to prevent trade disruptions. The organization has also called for the strengthening of international trade rules and regulations. The UNCTAD has called for greater cooperation between countries to address trade disruptions, particularly in developing countries. According to the International Chamber of Commerce (ICC), businesses can take steps to mitigate the impact of trade disruptions by diversifying their supply chains and investing in alternative suppliers.

The World Bank has emphasized the importance of maintaining economic stability and investing in infrastructure to reduce the likelihood of trade disruptions.[8] Preventing trade and commerce disruptions requires a multi-faceted approach that involves cooperation between international organizations, governments, and businesses. By implementing measures such as strengthening trade rules, diversifying supply chains, and investing in infrastructure, countries can reduce the likelihood of disruptions and promote economic stability and sustainable growth.

As mentioned earlier, the disruption of global trade and commerce is a significant effect of regional conflicts that can lead to a global security crisis. Regional conflicts can cause disruptions in supply chains, trade routes, and commerce, which can have a profound impact on the global economy. The resulting economic instability can exacerbate already fragile geopolitical situations, creating a vicious cycle of conflict and insecurity.[9]

One example of the impact of regional conflicts on global trade and commerce is the ongoing conflict in Syria. The conflict has caused the displacement of millions of people and has led to the destruction of critical infrastructure, including roads, bridges, and ports. This has severely disrupted trade and commerce, affecting both regional and global supply chains. The disruption of global trade and commerce due to the conflict in Syria has led to a significant economic impact.

The United Nations estimates that the conflict has caused over $1 trillion in economic losses, with damage to infrastructure, business closures, and lost trade opportunities. This has affected the livelihoods of millions of people and has contributed to the worsening of the humanitarian crisis in the region. The impact of the Syrian conflict has extended beyond the region, with the disruption of supply chains affecting global markets. The conflict has led to disruptions in oil and gas supplies, affecting energy prices worldwide. The crisis has also disrupted the flow of goods and services, affecting industries such as manufacturing, transportation, and tourism.

As above, the example of the conflict in Syria highlights how regional conflicts can have a profound impact on global trade and commerce, leading to economic instability and potential global security crises. The disruption of trade and commerce due to regional conflicts can exacerbate already fragile geopolitical situations, leading to increased tensions and the potential for further conflict. Addressing the root causes of regional conflicts and promoting effective conflict resolution mechanisms is essential to preventing the disruption of global trade and commerce and ensuring global peace and stability.

The Disruption of Global Trade and Commerce between the US and China: Unfair Practices and Retaliatory Tariffs

This section examines the phenomenon of mutual competition, characterized by unfair trade practices and retaliatory tariffs, between the United States and China over the past five years (2018-2022). Through an analysis of academic research and credible sources, this study explores the disruptive impact of trade disputes on global commerce. It highlights the emergence of unfair practices, such as intellectual property theft and forced technology transfers, and the subsequent imposition of retaliatory tariffs by both countries. By shedding light on these issues, this paper seeks to enhance our understanding of the complex dynamics and consequences of US-China trade tensions on the global economic landscape.

The economic relationship between the United States and China has experienced significant turbulence in recent years, marked by trade disputes and escalating tensions. This paper aims to provide an academic analysis of the disruptions caused by mutual competition, focusing on unfair trade practices and retaliatory tariffs. By examining scholarly research and credible sources, this study aims to deepen our understanding of the consequences of US-China trade tensions on global trade and commerce.

Unfair Trade Practices:

Unfair trade practices have been a significant source of contention between the United States and China. One prominent issue is intellectual property theft, wherein Chinese entities have been accused of infringing upon American companies' patents, copyrights, and trade secrets. Research by the United States Trade Representative (USTR, 2018) reveals that China's intellectual property theft has resulted in substantial economic losses for US businesses.

Another contentious practice is forced technology transfers, whereby foreign companies operating in China are coerced into sharing their technological expertise with Chinese partners. This practice has raised concerns about the protection of intellectual property rights and fair competition. The USTR (2019) highlights the detrimental impact of forced technology transfers on American businesses and innovation.

Retaliatory Tariffs:

In response to perceived unfair practices, both the United States and China resorted to the imposition of retaliatory tariffs, escalating trade tensions further. The US initiated a series of tariff measures, targeting a wide range of Chinese goods. The Office of the United States Trade Representative (USTR, 2020) reports that these tariffs aimed to address issues such as intellectual property theft, forced technology transfers, and trade imbalances.

China, in turn, retaliated by imposing tariffs on American goods, focusing on sectors that could potentially inflict economic and political pressure. Research by the Peterson Institute for International Economics (PIIE, 2021) highlights the negative consequences of retaliatory tariffs, including higher costs for businesses and disruptions to global value chains.[10]

Consequences for Global Trade and Commerce:

The disruptions in trade and commerce between the United States and China have reverberated globally. These tensions have disrupted global value chains, leading to increased costs and uncertainties for businesses operating in both countries. Research by the World Trade Organization (WTO, 2021) emphasizes the adverse impact of US-China trade tensions on global economic growth and stability.

Furthermore, the disruptions have prompted countries to reassess their trade policies and diversify their supply chains, with potential long-term implications for global trade patterns. The International Monetary Fund (IMF, 2022) underscores the need for countries to find collaborative solutions and address the underlying issues to mitigate the adverse effects on the global economy.

The disruption of global trade and commerce between the United States and China, characterized by unfair trade practices and retaliatory tariffs, has had significant consequences for the global economic landscape. The emergence of unfair practices and the subsequent imposition of tariffs have disrupted supply chains, increased costs for businesses, and raised concerns about intellectual property rights and fair competition. Resolving these trade tensions requires constructive dialogue and collaborative efforts to create a more stable and predictable trade environment.

This provides a comprehensive analysis of the total trade in goods between the United States and China from 2018 to 2022. The statistical data presented in this study is derived from reliable public institutions such as the U.S. Department of Commerce. By examining the trade trends and exploring, the key factors that influence bilateral trade, this analysis aims to shed light on the status of the US-China economic relationship.

The economic relationship between the United States and China is one of the most crucial and complex in the world. Trade in goods between these two countries has experienced significant growth and turbulence in recent years. Understanding the dynamics of this relationship is essential for policymakers, businesses, and researchers alike. This paper aims to provide a detailed examination of the total trade in goods between the United States and China, covering the years 2018 to 2022.

The statistical data utilized in this analysis is obtained from the U.S. Department of Commerce, specifically from their official reports on international trade. These reports provide comprehensive information on the value of goods traded between the United States and China, categorized by specific sectors and product groups. The data is reported on an annual basis, allowing for a comprehensive overview of the trends and fluctuations in bilateral trade over the specified period.

The total trade in goods between the United States and China exhibited both growth and volatility during the period under consideration. In 2018, the total trade volume amounted to $660 billion, with China being the United States' largest trading partner. However, due to escalating trade tensions, the total trade volume experienced a decline in 2019, reaching $559 billion. This downward trend continued into 2020, as the trade volume further decreased to $538 billion. However, in 2021 and 2022, there was a modest recovery in trade, with the volume increasing to $561 billion and $586 billion, respectively.

Several factors played a significant role in shaping the trade dynamics between the United States and China during this period. Notably, trade policy changes and tariff impositions had a profound impact on the bilateral trade relationship. The trade tensions between the two nations, characterized by retaliatory tariffs, influenced the overall trade volume and market access. Additionally, macroeconomic conditions, such as changes in exchange rates and economic growth rates, also influenced the trade patterns.

Analyzing the sectoral composition of US-China trade provides valuable insights into the dynamics of the economic relationship. Throughout the studied period, the top sectors of trade included machinery, electrical machinery, and vehicles. These sectors accounted for a significant proportion of the total trade in goods. However, there were variations in sectoral trade performance, influenced by factors such as technological advancements, consumer demand, and regulatory changes.

As of the latest available data, the US-China total trade in goods has shown signs of recovery and stabilization in recent years. While trade tensions persist, efforts to negotiate trade agreements and manage conflicts have contributed to a modest rebound in trade volume. Furthermore, changes in trade policies and evolving global economic conditions are likely to affect the future trajectory of US-China trade.

This analysis of the US-China total trade in goods from 2018 to 2022 highlights the complexities and fluctuations in the bilateral economic relationship. The statistical data presented in this study, obtained from the U.S. Department of Commerce, provides a comprehensive overview of trade trends and key factors influencing bilateral trade. Understanding the dynamics of this economic relationship is crucial for policymakers and businesses seeking to navigate the challenges and opportunities presented by US-China trade. Future research and policy analysis should continue to monitor and assess the evolving trends and developments in this important economic relationship.

CHAPTER 13.

The Outbreak of War

The outbreak of war remains a persistent and concerning phenomenon in the realm of international politics, with far-reaching consequences that extend beyond the regions directly affected. In recent years, a troubling trend has emerged, characterized by regional conflicts escalating into full-scale wars, posing a significant threat to global security. These conflicts, such as the ongoing crisis in Syria and the territorial disputes in the South China Sea, have resulted in widespread displacement, the proliferation of weapons, and the exacerbation of terrorism, thereby creating a complex web of challenges for the international community to address. This essay seeks to examine the causes and consequences of these conflicts, highlighting the interconnectedness between regional hostilities and their potential to disrupt global security.

According to the UNHCR, the conflict in Syria stands as a stark example of how a regional dispute can spiral into a devastating war with wide-ranging implications. The war, which began in 2011 as a series of protests against the Assad regime, quickly escalated into a full-scale armed conflict involving various factions and external actors. According to the United Nations High Commissioner for Refugees, the conflict has resulted in the displacement of over 13 million people, both internally and externally, creating a massive humanitarian crisis. The prolonged nature of the conflict has also allowed extremist groups, such as the Islamic State of Iraq and Syria (ISIS), to exploit the power vacuum and establish a foothold, perpetuating the threat of terrorism in the region.

Similarly, the territorial disputes in the South China Sea have escalated tensions among states in the region and pose a significant challenge to global security. The South China Sea, a vital maritime trade route, is subject to overlapping territorial claims by several countries, most notably China, Vietnam, the Philippines, and Taiwan. These disputes have led to increased militarization, with nations asserting their claims through the construction of military facilities and the deployment of naval forces. The potential for miscalculation, accidental clashes, or intentional provocations raises concerns about the stability of the region and the possibility of a large-scale conflict with global ramifications.

To fully grasp the implications of these regional conflicts on global security, it is essential to recognize the interconnected nature of today's world. In an era characterized by globalization and advanced communication technologies, the ripple effects of regional conflicts are no longer confined within geographical boundaries. The proliferation of weapons, particularly small arms and light weapons, from conflict zones to neighboring countries and beyond, has contributed to the rise of transnational criminal networks, fostering instability and threatening international security.[1] Furthermore, the displacement of millions of people fleeing conflict zones has created a strain on neighboring countries, exacerbating existing socioeconomic challenges and potentially causing tensions that can spill over into new conflicts.

As such, the outbreak of war in regional hotspots poses a significant challenge to global security, necessitating a comprehensive understanding of the root causes, dynamics, and consequences of these conflicts. By analyzing the complex interplay between regional hostilities, terrorism, displacement, and the proliferation of weapons, policymakers and international actors can better address the multifaceted threats and strive towards promoting peace and stability on a global scale.

In recent years, we have witnessed an alarming trend of regional conflicts escalating to full-scale wars and threatening global security. From the ongoing conflict in Syria to the territorial disputes in the South China Sea, these conflicts have led to the displacement of millions of people, the proliferation of weapons, and the spread of terrorism. The consequences of these conflicts are not limited to the regions in which they occur, but can have a ripple effect that threatens global security.

In this chapter, I have been following these conflicts closely, and I have been struck by the complexity and interconnectedness of the issues at play. Economic, political, and social factors all contribute to these conflicts and the stakes are high for the people involved and the world at large.

War Damage

Human casualties, economic and political impacts of regional conflicts and wars, and their impact on global security are complex and multifaceted issues.[2] Here is an example of how to provide a detailed explanation of these impacts and the role of local and international organizations in preventing wars:

Firstly, the impact of regional conflicts and wars on human casualties cannot be overstated. These conflicts often result in the displacement of millions of people, who are forced to flee their homes and seek refuge in other countries. These refugees face numerous challenges, including a lack of access to necessities such as food, water, and shelter, as well as the risk of violence and exploitation.[3] In addition, civilians caught in the crossfire of these conflicts often withstand the worst of the violence, with many losing their lives or suffering serious injuries.

Secondly, regional conflicts and wars also have significant economic impacts. These conflicts disrupt trade and commerce, leading to a loss of income and employment opportunities. They also damage infrastructure and property, making it difficult for affected areas to rebuild and recover. In addition, the cost of supporting refugees and displaced persons can place a significant burden on the economies of neighboring countries, leading to further economic instability and social unrest.

Thirdly, the political impact of regional conflicts and wars is also significant. These conflicts often exacerbate existing political tensions and can lead to the collapse of political systems. They also provide opportunities for extremist groups to gain power and influence, leading to increased violence and instability. Additionally, the international community often becomes divided along political lines, making it difficult to find effective solutions to these conflicts.

Fourthly, the impact of regional conflicts and wars on global security cannot be ignored. These conflicts can have a ripple effect that destabilizes entire regions, leading to increased terrorism, arms proliferation, and the spread of radical ideologies. Additionally, the political and economic impact of these conflicts can spill over into other parts of the world, exacerbating existing tensions and potentially leading to new conflicts.

Role of Local and International Organizations:

Local and international organizations play a critical role in preventing regional conflicts and wars. Governments must work together to find peaceful solutions to these conflicts, while non-governmental organizations can provide assistance and support to affected communities.[4] The media can also play a role in raising awareness about these conflicts and holding governments accountable for their actions. Additionally, international organizations such as the United Nations and the International Criminal Court can provide a framework for resolving these conflicts through diplomacy and legal means. The impact of regional conflicts and wars on human casualties, economic and political stability, and global security is profound. It is essential that local and international organizations work together to prevent and resolve these conflicts, and to support affected communities in rebuilding their lives.

There are many concrete and detailed examples of threats to global security due to the outbreak of war in the region. Here are a few:

Spread of Terrorism: Regional conflicts can provide a breeding ground for terrorist groups to gain strength and spread their influence. For example, the civil war in Syria has created a power vacuum that has allowed groups like ISIS to thrive.[5] These groups can pose a threat to global security by carrying out attacks and destabilizing regions.

Displacement of People: War and conflict can lead to the displacement of large numbers of people, who may become refugees and seek asylum in other countries. This can create humanitarian crises and strain the resources of neighboring countries. For example, the Syrian civil war has led to the displacement of millions of people, many of whom have sought refuge in neighboring countries like Turkey and Lebanon.

Proliferation of Weapons: Regional conflicts can lead to the proliferation of weapons, which can pose a threat to global security. For example, the conflict in Yemen has led to the spread of weapons, including missiles and drones that have been used in attacks on neighboring countries like Saudi Arabia.[6]

Economic Disruption: Regional conflicts can disrupt trade and commerce, which can have a negative impact on the global economy. For example, the conflict in Ukraine has led to sanctions being imposed on Russia, which has had a negative impact on the Russian economy and has affected trade relations with other countries.[7]

Regional Instability: Regional conflicts can destabilize entire regions, leading to increased tensions and the potential for further conflict. For example, the ongoing conflict between Israel and Palestine has led to tensions in the Middle East and has the potential to draw in regional and international actors.

These are just a few examples of how the outbreak of war in a region can pose a threat to global security. It is important for the international community to work together to prevent and resolve regional conflicts to ensure stability and security for all.

Regional conflicts have long been recognized as a potential source of instability and insecurity in international relations. These conflicts can arise from a variety of factors, such as ethnic, religious, or territorial disputes, and can quickly escalate into violent confrontations that threaten regional and global security. One of the most severe impacts of these conflicts is the outbreak of war, which can have devastating consequences for human lives, economic stability, and political order. For instance, the ongoing conflict in Yemen is a prime example of how a regional conflict can escalate into a global security crisis. What began as a local uprising against the Yemeni government in 2011 soon evolved into a full-blown civil war,[8] pitting Houthi rebels against government forces and their allies? The conflict quickly drew in regional powers, with Saudi Arabia leading a coalition of Arab states to support the government's efforts to crush the rebellion.

As the conflict has dragged on, it has become increasingly complex and destructive, with both sides accused of war crimes and violations of human rights. The humanitarian toll has been catastrophic, with millions of people displaced, and thousands killed or injured. The conflict has also created a security vacuum that has allowed extremist groups such as Al-Qaeda in the Arabian Peninsula (AQAP) and ISIS to flourish in the country, further exacerbating the crisis. The impact of the conflict has also spilled over into neighboring countries, with Houthi rebels launching attacks on Saudi Arabia and threatening the stability of the entire region.

Furthermore, the conflict has drawn in external actors, with Iran supporting the Houthis and the United States providing military and logistical support to the Saudi-led coalition. This has further heightened tensions between these powers and complicated efforts to resolve the conflict. The conflict in Yemen illustrates how a regional conflict can have far-reaching and severe consequences that can lead to an global security crisis. The outbreak of war is one of the most severe impacts of these conflicts, and it underscores the urgent need for effective conflict resolution mechanisms and international cooperation to prevent these conflicts from spiraling out of control and threatening global peace and security.

The international community has various dispute resolution mechanisms in place to address conflicts and promote peaceful resolutions. One of the primary mechanisms is the United Nations (UN), which serves as a platform for member states to discuss and resolve disputes through diplomatic channels. The UN Charter, the organization's founding document, outlines principles and procedures for peaceful settlement of disputes among member states.

The UN Security Council plays a crucial role in addressing international conflicts. It has the authority to impose sanctions, authorize peacekeeping missions, and even authorize the use of force in cases of threats to international peace and security. However, the Security Council's effectiveness can be limited due to the veto power held by its permanent members—China, France, Russia, the United Kingdom, and the United States. This can sometimes hinder swift and decisive action in resolving conflicts. In addition to the UN, regional organizations and initiatives play a significant role in dispute resolution. For example, the African Union (AU), the Organization of American States (OAS), and the European Union (EU) have established mechanisms to address regional conflicts within their respective spheres of influence.[9]

These organizations often work in collaboration with the UN and play a crucial role in mediating disputes and promoting peaceful settlements. International cooperation for dispute resolution has seen mixed progress. While there have been successful examples of conflict resolution and prevention, such as peace agreements and diplomatic negotiations, there are ongoing conflicts that have proven challenging to resolve. The effectiveness of international cooperation depends on several factors, including the willingness of conflicting parties to engage in dialogue, the commitment of member states to uphold international law and norms, and the availability of resources and political will to support peacekeeping and mediation efforts.

It is important to note that dispute resolution and conflict prevention require a multifaceted approach, including political, economic, and social measures. Efforts to address the root causes of conflicts, promote inclusive governance, and support sustainable development play an essential role in preventing and resolving disputes. While there are mechanisms and frameworks in place for international cooperation and dispute resolution, the effectiveness of these mechanisms can vary depending on the specific conflict and the commitment of involved parties to pursue peaceful solutions. Continued efforts to strengthen international cooperation, enhance diplomatic dialogue, and promote peaceful settlements remain crucial to preventing and resolving conflicts at both regional and international levels.

Local War Outbreak and Global Security Crisis

The outbreak of war is one of the most severe impacts of regional conflicts that can lead to a global security crisis. One of the most prominent examples of this phenomenon is the Syrian Civil War, which began in 2011 as a local conflict between the government and opposition forces but quickly escalated into a complex regional and international crisis. The war has not only caused a humanitarian catastrophe in Syria, with millions of people displaced and hundreds of thousands killed, but it has also destabilized the entire Middle East region. The conflict has drawn in regional powers, such as Iran and Saudi

Arabia, who have backed opposing sides in the conflict, and has led to the emergence of extremist groups, such as ISIS, which have threatened regional and global security. Moreover, the Syrian Civil War has had a ripple effect that has affected other parts of the world. The refugee crisis that emerged because of the conflict has led to a mass migration of people to neighboring countries and Europe, which has strained the resources and capabilities of those countries and sparked political and social tensions.

Furthermore, the conflict has had international implications, as major powers such as the United States, Russia, and China have become involved in the conflict, either directly or indirectly, to pursue their strategic interests. This has led to increased tensions and rivalries among these powers, and has complicated efforts to resolve the conflict. More than any case, the Syrian Civil War is a stark example of how regional conflicts can escalate into global security crises, with severe consequences for human lives, regional stability, and global security. It underscores the need for effective international cooperation to prevent and resolve regional conflicts before they spiral out of control and threaten international peace and security.

The alarming trend of regional conflicts escalating into full-scale wars and posing a threat to global security demands urgent attention from the international community. The cases of Syria's ongoing conflict and the territorial disputes in the South China Sea vividly illustrate the grave consequences that arise from such conflicts. These crises have resulted in the displacement of millions of individuals, the proliferation of weapons, and the propagation of terrorism, ultimately reverberating far beyond the confines of the regions in which they occur.

The conflict in Syria has created a humanitarian catastrophe, with over 13 million people displaced, both internally and externally. This displacement crisis has strained neighboring countries and, in turn, has the potential to spark new conflicts if left unaddressed. Moreover, extremist groups like ISIS have exploited the chaos, exacerbating the threat of terrorism and fostering instability not only in the region but also beyond.

The territorial disputes in the South China Sea have introduced heightened tensions among states and have the capacity to disrupt global security. The competing claims over this vital maritime trade route have prompted militarization efforts, including the construction of military facilities and the deployment of naval forces. [10] The potential for miscalculations and accidental clashes looms large, highlighting the fragility of the situation and the risk of an escalation into a large-scale conflict.

It is imperative to recognize the interconnected nature of the world we live in today. The consequences of regional conflicts extend well beyond their immediate geographical boundaries. The proliferation of weapons from conflict zones to neighboring regions and the rise of transnational criminal networks perpetuate instability and jeopardize international security. [11] Furthermore, the displacement of millions of individuals has far-reaching implications, straining resources and potentially fueling new tensions.

Addressing the outbreak of war and its implications for global security requires a comprehensive and collaborative approach. The international community must work together to mitigate the underlying causes of conflicts, address the humanitarian crises they create, and foster sustainable peacebuilding efforts. Multilateral organizations such as the United Nations, regional bodies, and individual states must actively engage in preventive diplomacy, mediation, and conflict resolution to prevent further escalation and mitigate the repercussions of these conflicts.

By addressing the root causes of regional conflicts, promoting dialogue, and providing humanitarian aid and support to affected populations, the international community can contribute to a more secure and stable world. Sustained efforts in diplomacy, peacebuilding, and conflict resolution are essential to break the cycle of violence and foster conditions for lasting peace. Only through collective action and a shared commitment to global security can we hope to prevent the outbreak of war and ensure a more peaceful future for all.

PART IV

THE CHALLENGES OF RESOLVING REGIONAL CONFLICTS

"If you want peace, you don't talk to your friends. You talk to your enemies."

- Desmond Tutu

CHAPTER 14

The Lack of International Cooperation

International cooperation can be traced back to ancient times when people formed alliances for trade, defense, and other purposes. However, the modern system of international cooperation dates back to the Treaty of Westphalia in 1648,[1] which ended the Thirty Years' War in Europe and established the principle of state sovereignty. In the 20th century, international cooperation became more formalized with the establishment of organizations such as the League of Nations (1919) and the United Nations (1945). These organizations aimed to promote cooperation and prevent war through diplomacy and international law. Today, international cooperation takes place on a wide range of issues, from trade and economic development to climate change and global health. It involves the participation of governments, international organizations, civil society groups, and the private sector.

International cooperation can be an effective means of resolving regional disputes and wars, but it also faces several challenges. Firstly, international cooperation requires the agreement and participation of all parties involved in the conflict. If one party is unwilling to cooperate, the process can be derailed. For example, efforts to resolve the conflict in Syria have been hampered by the refusal of some parties to engage in diplomatic efforts. Secondly, international cooperation can be slow and difficult to achieve, especially when the parties have deep-rooted differences. Negotiations may take years or even decades, and progress may be slow. For example, the Israeli-Palestinian conflict has been ongoing for decades despite numerous attempts at international mediation. Thirdly, international cooperation may be undermined by geopolitical rivalries and power imbalances.

Stronger nations may use their influence to sway negotiations in their favor, and weaker nations may feel marginalized or ignored. For example, the ongoing conflict in Yemen has been fueled by regional power struggles between Saudi Arabia and Iran.[2] Despite these challenges, international cooperation remains an important tool for resolving regional disputes and promoting peace. By engaging in diplomacy, building trust, and working together, nations can achieve solutions that benefit all parties involved.

Albert Einstein once said, "The world is a dangerous place to live; not because of the people who are evil, but because of the people who don't do anything about it."[3] The connotation of this quote emphasizes the necessity of international cooperation to prevent regional conflicts from occurring worldwide. After all, Albert Einstein's quote highlights the importance of taking action in the face of danger, rather than simply ignoring it. He suggests that the danger of the world does not come from inherently evil people, but rather from those who fail to take action to prevent harm.

If we interpret this quote as emphasizing the need for international cooperation to prevent regional conflicts from occurring all over the world, then its connotation becomes even more significant. In this context, the quote suggests that the world is a dangerous place not only because of natural disasters or unpredictable events but also because of the potential for conflicts between nations or regions. By emphasizing that, the danger comes not from inherently evil people but rather from those who do nothing about it, Einstein may be suggesting that all nations have a responsibility to take action to prevent conflicts and promote peace. This may involve working together through international organizations, such as the United Nations, to address conflicts before they escalate into full-blown wars.

In light of various quotes stressing the significance of cross-border collaboration, former UN Secretary-General Kofi Annan proclaimed, "The greatest challenge of the twenty-first century is to ensure that everyone has access to the benefits of globalization and international cooperation." This statement implies the utmost importance of international cooperation, as it may not be feasible to resolve global issues independently. This is due to the fact that, in the current complex international environment, no country can succeed unilaterally in resolving inter-state challenges.[4] From an international political perspective, the complexity of the current international environment necessitates international cooperation to address various problems and disputes between countries. There are several reasons why it is nearly impossible to solve these issues unilaterally:

Interconnectedness: In today's globalized world, countries are intricately interconnected through trade, economics, security, and communication networks. Issues like climate change, terrorism, nuclear proliferation, and pandemics transcend national borders. Therefore, addressing such challenges requires collective action and cooperation among multiple countries.

Power diffusion: Power in the international system is distributed among multiple actors, including states, international organizations, non-state actors, and multinational corporations. No single country possesses the capability to unilaterally address all global problems. International cooperation helps pool resources, expertise, and capabilities from various actors, making it more effective in resolving complex issues.

Sovereignty and self-interest: States are driven by their national interests and sovereignty concerns. Unilateral actions by a single country can often be viewed as infringing on the sovereignty of other nations, leading to tensions and conflicts. International cooperation provides a platform for countries to negotiate and find mutually acceptable solutions that respect the sovereignty and interests of all parties involved.

Multifaceted nature of problems: Many contemporary global challenges are multifaceted and require a comprehensive approach. For example, addressing climate change requires coordination on emissions reduction, technology transfer, financing, and adaptation measures. Such complex problems cannot be adequately tackled by a single country acting alone, as they demand diverse perspectives, expertise, and contributions from multiple actors.

Norms and international law: The international system is guided by norms, principles, and international law. International cooperation helps ensure adherence to these norms, resolve disputes through diplomatic channels, and promote peaceful resolutions. Unilateral actions often undermine the legitimacy of international norms and can lead to a breakdown of trust and cooperation among nations.

In practice, there are numerous examples that can highlight the need for international cooperation to address global challenges. Upon examining some of these examples, one can recognize the importance and necessity of international cooperation in solving problems.

Climate change: The Paris Agreement, a multinational accord adopted in 2015, aims to mitigate greenhouse gas emissions and limit global warming. Its success hinges on the collaboration and commitments of numerous countries working together to achieve common goals.

Nuclear non-proliferation: The Treaty on the Non-Proliferation of Nuclear Weapons (NPT) seeks to prevent the spread of nuclear weapons. It relies on cooperation between nuclear and non-nuclear states to promote disarmament, nuclear energy cooperation, and non-proliferation efforts.

Global health crises: The COVID-19 pandemic demonstrated the need for international collaboration in combating infectious diseases. Countries have worked together through the World Health Organization (WHO) and other platforms to share information, coordinate response efforts, and develop vaccines.

Trade and economic cooperation: International trade agreements, such as the World Trade Organization (WTO), facilitate negotiations, dispute settlements, and the removal of trade barriers. These agreements promote economic growth and stability through cooperation among multiple countries.

Conflict resolution: Many conflicts around the world require multilateral efforts to achieve lasting peace. Examples include peacekeeping missions by the United Nations (UN), mediation efforts by regional organizations, and international peace conferences aimed at resolving protracted conflicts. As can be seen from these practical examples, the complex international environment requires international cooperation to resolve various problems and disputes between countries. The interconnectedness of the world, power diffusion, the multifaceted nature of issues, sovereignty concerns, and adherence to international norms and law all contribute to the need for collaborative approaches in addressing global challenges.

A book that comes to mind when it comes to international cooperation is "The Future of Power" by Joseph S. Nye. . The book explores the shifting nature of power in the 21st century and the importance of international cooperation in addressing global problems. Nye argues that power is no longer solely held by nation-states, but also by non-state actors such as multinational corporations, non-governmental organizations, and individuals. This diffusion of power has led to a more complex global landscape, in which traditional power politics are less effective.

One of the key themes of the book is the concept of "soft power," which Nye defines as the ability to attract and persuade others to align with one's interests. Soft power is distinct from traditional "hard power," which relies on military or economic coercion. Nye argues that soft power is becoming increasingly important in international relations, as the power of attraction and persuasion becomes more important than the threat of force. Nye also discusses the concept of "smart power," which is the combination of both soft and hard power. Smart power is the ability to use a combination of strategies to achieve desired outcomes.[5]

Nye argues that smart power is necessary for addressing complex global problems, such as climate change, nuclear proliferation, and terrorism. Throughout the book, Nye emphasizes the importance of international cooperation in solving these global problems. He argues that no single nation or actor can address these issues alone, and that effective cooperation requires a deep understanding of the interests and motivations of other actors.

He also emphasizes the importance of building relationships of trust and understanding, as these are necessary for effective cooperation. In conclusion, the book suggests that the nature of power is changing in the 21st century, and that traditional power politics are becoming less effective. The concept of soft power, and the importance of international cooperation and smart power, are key to addressing global problems in this new global landscape.[6]

Accordingly, "The Future of Power" hints at the need for international cooperation. In this book, Nye argues that international cooperation is becoming increasingly important as power shifts from states to non-state actors. In other words, the book emphasizes the importance of international cooperation in solving global problems.

Another book that comes to mind is "The Clash of Civilizations and the Remaking of World Order" by Samuel P. Huntington. It emphasizes the importance of international cooperation in resolving conflicts between different cultures and civilizations. Particularly, the book underscores the critical role of international cooperation in resolving regional disputes and conflicts. Huntington argues that the world has shifted from ideological battles to cultural clashes, with conflicts primarily driven by cultural and religious differences between major civilizations.

The book examines various historical and contemporary conflicts, such as those between the Islamic world and the West, to demonstrate the repercussions of civilization clashes. However, rather than dwelling on pessimism, Huntington emphasizes the need for international cooperation as a means to mitigate conflicts and establish a more stable world order.

He stresses that true international cooperation should not be based on imposing Western ideals on others, but rather on understanding and respecting the diversity of civilizations. The West, according to Huntington, should foster dialogue that promotes mutual understanding and compromise, rather than enforcing its values on others. Huntington also explores the role of international organizations, particularly the United Nations, in facilitating global cooperation. While acknowledging the UN's limitations, he believes it can serve as a platform for dialogue and negotiation. He advocates for reforms within the UN to ensure the representation of different civilizations, promoting a more inclusive and balanced approach to international relations.

The book concludes by recognizing the challenges that lie ahead but remains steadfast in its call to action. It highlights that international cooperation is not a panacea but underscores the importance of understanding cultural differences and engaging in dialogue to manage conflicts effectively. By doing so, the book envisions a future where nations transcend their differences and work together towards a more harmonious and peaceful world.

In essence, "The Clash of Civilizations and the Remaking of World Order" emphasizes the imperative of international cooperation as a means to resolve regional conflicts, fostering understanding, dialogue, and compromise across diverse civilizations.

Entering the 21st century, regional conflicts and wars have become a great threat to global security. In order to find sustainable solutions to these disputes, international efforts are being made to resolve issues through bilateral and multilateral cooperation. What is the reason for such a lack of international cooperation and failure? There are several reasons why international cooperation to resolve regional conflicts may fail, even when it is urgently needed. One of the main reasons is that countries often prioritize their own national interests over the common good, which can lead to a lack of willingness to cooperate. Another reason is that there may be deep-rooted historical, cultural, or political differences between conflicting parties that make it difficult to find common ground.

Additionally, the involvement of external factors, such as great powers or regional powers, can further complicate the situation and make cooperation more difficult. Examples of failures of international cooperation to resolve regional conflicts include the ongoing conflict in Syria. Despite multiple attempts by the international community to broker a peace deal, including several rounds of talks in Geneva and the Astana process led by Russia, Iran, and Turkey, the conflict has persisted for over a decade.

This is largely due to the involvement of multiple regional and global powers, each with their own interests in the conflict, as well as the deep divisions within the Syrian society. Another example is the Israeli-Palestinian conflict, which has been ongoing for decades despite numerous attempts at international mediation and cooperation. The conflict is complicated by deep-seated historical and religious differences, as well as the involvement of external factors, such as the United States and Iran.

However, there have also been successes in international cooperation to resolve regional conflicts. One example is the peace process in Northern Ireland, which was facilitated by the international community, including the United States and the European Union. The process involved extensive negotiations and compromise between the conflicting parties, which eventually led to the Good Friday Agreement in 1998. This agreement established a power-sharing government in Northern Ireland and largely put an end to the decades-long sectarian violence in the region. Another example is the peace agreement between the Colombian government and the Revolutionary Armed Forces of Colombia (FARC) in 2016, which was facilitated by the United Nations and several other countries.[7] The agreement ended over five decades of armed conflict, which had resulted in the deaths of over 200,000 people. The peace process involved extensive negotiations and compromise between the parties, as well as the establishment of transitional justice mechanisms to address past human rights abuses.

While international cooperation is essential to resolving regional conflicts and ensuring global security, many factors can hinder its success. Historical, cultural, and political differences, the involvement of external actors, and competing national interests can all make cooperation more difficult. However, as demonstrated by the successes in Northern Ireland and Colombia, with persistence and the right conditions, international cooperation can lead to lasting peace and stability. The lack of international cooperation is a major obstacle in resolving wars and regional conflicts that can lead to global security crises. Without the support of the international community, mediators may lack the resources and legitimacy needed to effectively facilitate a resolution to the conflict. Here are some concrete steps that can be taken to address this issue:

Establish a Strong International Coalition: In order to effectively resolve a regional conflict, it is important to establish a strong international coalition that can provide political and financial support to the mediation efforts. This coalition can include neighboring countries, regional organizations, and global powers like the United States and Russia. By working together, these actors can provide the necessary resources and legitimacy to facilitate a resolution to the conflict.

Develop a Comprehensive Strategy: In order to garner international support, mediators must develop a comprehensive strategy for resolving the conflict that addresses the underlying issues driving the conflict. This strategy should be based on a thorough analysis of the political, economic, and social dynamics of the conflict and should identify concrete steps that can be taken to build trust and promote reconciliation between the warring parties.

Engage in Diplomatic Outreach: Mediators should engage in active diplomatic outreach to key actors in the international community in order to build support for their mediation efforts. This can include meeting with diplomats, policymakers, and civil society organizations in order to explain the issues at stake in the conflict and make the case for why international support is essential for a successful resolution.

Mobilize Public Opinion: In addition to engaging with policymakers and diplomats, mediators should also work to mobilize public opinion in support of their mediation efforts. This can include using social media and other communication channels to raise awareness of the conflict and its impact on the region and the world. By building a groundswell of public support for their efforts, mediators can help to pressure governments and other actors to provide the necessary support for a successful resolution to the conflict.

Utilize International Institutions: Finally, mediators can also utilize international institutions like the United Nations and other regional organizations to build support for their mediation efforts. These institutions can provide a framework for dialogue and negotiation between the warring parties and can help to build the necessary trust and cooperation needed to resolve the conflict.

The lack of international cooperation is a major challenge that often undermines efforts to resolve wars and regional conflicts. In order to effectively address this issue, a number of concrete steps can be taken:

Increase Diplomatic Engagement: One of the key ways to address the lack of international cooperation is by increasing diplomatic engagement between the warring parties and the international community. This can involve regular dialogue and communication between diplomats, policymakers, and civil society groups in order to identify areas of common ground and develop a shared understanding of the conflict.

Utilize International Mediators: Another effective way to address the lack of international cooperation is by utilizing international mediators to facilitate dialogue and negotiation between the warring parties. These mediators can bring a neutral perspective to the conflict, and can help to build trust and understanding between the parties.

Leverage Economic Pressure: Economic pressure can also be used to encourage greater international cooperation in resolving conflicts. Sanctions and other economic measures can be used to incentivize warring parties to come to the negotiating table and to encourage international actors to support mediation efforts.

Promote Regional Cooperation: Regional cooperation can also play an important role in addressing the lack of international cooperation. By encouraging neighboring countries to work together to promote peace and stability in the region, it may be possible to build a more supportive and collaborative environment for resolving conflicts.

Foster a Shared Vision of the Future: Finally, in order to address the lack of international cooperation, it is important to foster a shared vision of the future among the warring parties and the international community. By working together to articulate a clear and compelling vision for a peaceful and prosperous future, it may be possible to build greater cooperation and collaboration in the pursuit of peace.

Despite many efforts made so far by international organizations such as the United Nations to resolve global security threats, conflict situations that threaten global security are still taking place all over the world International organizations, including the United Nations (UN), have been working for decades to resolve global security threats. Here are some of the efforts made by the UN in recent years:

Peacekeeping Operations: The UN has established peacekeeping operations in various conflict zones around the world, deploying thousands of military and civilian personnel to maintain peace and security in these regions. These operations are aimed at preventing conflicts from escalating, protecting civilians, and promoting stability.

Nuclear Non-Proliferation: The UN has been working to prevent the spread of nuclear weapons and promote disarmament through various initiatives such as the Non-Proliferation Treaty (NPT) and the International Atomic Energy Agency (IAEA). The NPT aims to prevent the spread of nuclear weapons, while the IAEA helps to ensure the peaceful use of nuclear energy.[8]

Counterterrorism: The UN has established various bodies and initiatives to combat terrorism, including the Counter-Terrorism Committee (CTC) and the Office of Counter-Terrorism (OCT). The CTC helps member states to implement measures to prevent and combat terrorism, while the OCT coordinates and strengthens the UN's overall efforts to counter terrorism.

Sanctions: The UN Security Council has the authority to impose sanctions on states or entities that pose a threat to international peace and security. These sanctions may include travel bans, asset freezes, and arms embargoes.

Peaceful Dispute Resolution: The UN provides a forum for peaceful resolution of disputes between states, including mediation, arbitration, and judicial settlement. The International Court of Justice (ICJ) is the UN's main judicial body, which hears cases between states and gives advisory opinions on legal questions.

Humanitarian Assistance: The UN provides humanitarian assistance to those affected by conflict and natural disasters, including food, water, shelter, and medical care. The UN Office for the Coordination of Humanitarian Affairs (OCHA) coordinates the UN's response to humanitarian crises around the world.[9]

In general, the endeavors undertaken by the United Nations and other international organizations to address global security threats are diverse and encompass a broad spectrum of strategies and initiatives. The overarching objective of these endeavors is to foster peace, stability, and security on a global scale. In this context, the lack of international cooperation poses significant challenges to the resolution of regional disputes and wars. As mentioned earlier, for international cooperation to be effective, it requires the agreement and participation of all parties involved in the conflict. However, when one party is unwilling to cooperate, the entire process can be derailed, impeding progress towards peace and stability.

Numerous endeavors undertaken by the United Nations (UN) and other international organizations reflect the multifaceted nature of addressing global security threats. These initiatives encompass a broad spectrum of strategies aimed at fostering peace, stability, and security on a global scale. The UN, as the principal international body responsible for maintaining international peace and security, employs various mechanisms such as diplomacy, mediation, peacekeeping operations, and sanctions to promote cooperation among nations and resolve conflicts.

Despite the efforts put forth by international organizations, the lack of cooperation continues to hinder the resolution of regional disputes and wars. This is evident in conflicts such as the ongoing Syrian civil war, where the involvement of multiple international actors with competing interests has complicated efforts to achieve a peaceful settlement.[10] In cases where certain parties prioritize their national interests over collective action, the potential for finding sustainable solutions becomes increasingly elusive.

Moreover, divergent geopolitical interests among major powers can further exacerbate the challenges of international cooperation. Competition for influence, resources, and strategic positioning can lead to rivalries and conflicts that impede cooperative efforts.[11] This can be seen in situations where geopolitical considerations overshadow the imperative of resolving regional disputes, such as in the South China Sea territorial disputes.[12]

Addressing the lack of international cooperation requires a comprehensive approach that involves diplomatic negotiations, mediation, and sustained dialogue among all parties involved. Incentives for cooperation, such as economic and political benefits, need to be effectively employed to encourage reluctant actors to engage in cooperative efforts.[13] Additionally, enhancing the capacity of international organizations and strengthening their legitimacy can contribute to fostering an environment conducive to cooperation and conflict resolution.[14]

To overcome the challenges of the lack of international cooperation, it is crucial for states and international organizations to remain committed to the principles and objectives outlined in the UN Charter. Furthermore, sustained political will, effective leadership, and inclusive diplomacy are essential to overcoming differences and fostering an environment conducive to international cooperation in the pursuit of peace, stability, and global security.

CHAPTER 15.

The Difficulty of Building Trust between Warring Parties

Building trust between parties involved in regional conflicts is often a challenging and complex task, presenting a significant obstacle to resolving such conflicts. The parties involved in these conflicts often carry a burden of historical grievances, resulting in deep-seated mistrust and suspicion towards one another. This mistrust is often fueled by a myriad of factors, including cultural, religious, or ideological differences, as well as political and economic interests. Overcoming these barriers to establish confidence and trust becomes a crucial factor in the resolution of regional conflicts, especially considering their potential to escalate into global security crises. Nevertheless, this endeavor demands patience, persistence, and a genuine willingness to engage in dialogue and compromise.

Regional conflicts have plagued our world throughout history, leaving lasting scars on the collective consciousness of nations and peoples involved. These conflicts can be rooted in territorial disputes, ethnic tensions, or struggles for power and resources. The complexities of such conflicts are further compounded by their impact on national and regional security, often involving multiple actors, both state and non-state, with varying agendas and interests.

One of the primary obstacles in building trust amidst regional conflicts is the long-standing history of grievances between the parties involved. These grievances are often rooted in perceived injustices, historical injustices, or past conflicts that have left deep wounds in the social fabric. As a result, the parties hold on to their grievances, which perpetuate a cycle of mistrust and animosity, making it challenging to establish a foundation for dialogue and cooperation.

Cultural, religious, and ideological differences also contribute significantly to the difficulties in building confidence. These differences can lead to misunderstandings, stereotypes, and biases, further fueling animosity and preventing effective communication. These conflicts often become entangled with identity politics, as parties cling to their cultural or religious heritage, intensifying divisions and inhibiting the development of a shared understanding.

Moreover, political and economic interests play a crucial role in sustaining regional conflicts. Competing for power, control over resources, or geopolitical influence often drives parties to adopt zero-sum approaches, where one's gain is perceived as another's loss. Such a win-lose mindset perpetuates hostility, making it difficult to build the necessary trust for conflict resolution. Economic factors, such as control over trade routes or access to valuable resources, can exacerbate tensions and incentivize parties to maintain a confrontational stance.

Building trust requires a comprehensive and multifaceted approach that goes beyond mere rhetoric. It demands persistent efforts to bridge divides, promote mutual understanding, and foster empathy among the conflicting parties. Engaging in dialogue, both formal and informal, is crucial to dispelling misconceptions, challenging stereotypes, and finding common ground.

Successful strategies for building confidence often include the involvement of impartial mediators or international organizations capable of facilitating dialogue and negotiations. These mediators can provide a neutral platform where grievances can be addressed, concerns can be heard, and compromises can be explored. They play a vital role in helping conflicting parties overcome barriers, promoting reconciliation, and nurturing an environment conducive to trust-building.

Furthermore, confidence-building measures such as ceasefire agreements, arms control initiatives, and the implementation of joint projects can contribute to fostering trust. These measures not only demonstrate a commitment to peaceful resolution but also provide tangible evidence of cooperation and shared interests. Incremental steps towards building confidence can create a positive momentum, gradually transforming the dynamics of the conflict and paving the way for more substantial agreements.

In fact, building trust between parties involved in regional conflicts is a complex and demanding task. The historical grievances, cultural, religious, and ideological differences, as well as political and economic interests, act as formidable barriers to confidence-building. However, recognizing the importance of trust in resolving conflicts and the potential consequences of failure motivates stakeholders to persist in their efforts. By embracing patience, engaging in meaningful dialogue, and exploring compromises, it becomes possible to overcome these challenges and foster an environment where peace and reconciliation can prevail.

The ongoing conflict between Israel and the Palestinians serves as an illustrative instance of a regional dispute in which the establishment of trust between the involved parties has presented a significant obstacle. Spanning decades, this conflict has engendered deep dissatisfaction and mutual distrust. For Israel, the roots of the conflict lie in the historical trauma of the

Holocaust and the conviction that Israel represents the homeland for Jews. On the other hand, Palestinians view the conflict as stemming from the movement and occupation of their land by Israel, driven by a desire for self-determination and statehood. Efforts aimed at resolving the conflict have been impeded by a lack of trust between the parties. Both sides have accused each other of violating agreements and acting in bad faith. Numerous attempts at achieving a lasting peace agreement, including the Oslo Accords in 1993 and the Camp David Summit in 2000, have proven unsuccessful.

A primary impediment to confidence-building in this conflict lies in the lack of communication and interaction between Israel and the Palestinians. Opportunities for personal interaction between the two sides are scarce, resulting in a deficiency of understanding and empathy on both ends. Furthermore, external actors with vested interests and agendas, including the United States and other regional countries, exacerbate the conflict by intervening in the dispute.

In protracted conflicts such as the Israeli-Palestinian struggle, where long-standing discontent and deep-rooted distrust prevail, constructing trust becomes an especially formidable task but is essential for achieving lasting peace. Building trust is fundamental to a successful negotiation or arbitration process. Without trust, effective communication, information sharing, and concession-making become exceedingly challenging for the parties involved. Several factors contribute to the difficulty of establishing trust in conflicts or wars. Firstly, the parties may harbor disparate goals and objectives, impeding the identification of common ground and agreement. Secondly, a history of hostility and distrust can hinder the parties from transcending the past and moving forward. Thirdly, external actors seeking to disrupt the peace process may influence the conflict, perpetuating it for their own gain.

The task of building trust is by no means facile, as evidenced by the Israeli-Palestinian conflict. Evidently, the two sides have remained at odds for decades, and a profound mistrust stands as a significant stumbling block. Only by addressing and rectifying these deep-seated misgivings can negotiations for a peace agreement proceed smoothly. I firmly believe that such confidence-building measures are indispensable for successfully concluding the terms of the agreement between the parties and advancing the prospects of peace. As exemplified by the Israeli-Palestinian conflict, the challenge of building trust represents one of the most arduous aspects involved in resolving regional conflicts. The two sides have been fighting for decades with no sign of resolution. It is imperative to examine the historical context of these disputes and the underlying reasons and instances of trust erosion. Israelis and Palestinians have clashed over claims to the Holy Land for decades, a conflict that has long been one of the world's most intractable. Although the United States is a strong supporter of Israel, it has traditionally tried to advance a diplomatic solution that would reconcile the competing claims of the two parties. Numerous United States' governments have suggested plans for a peaceful resolution that would create two separate states - one for Israel and one for Palestine.

Nevertheless, some commentators argue that the possibility of a two-state solution became less likely during the presidency of Donald Trump. This is because Trump's policies concerning fundamental elements of the conflict were highly contentious. Although the current Joe Biden administration has restated the United States' backing for a two-state solution, it has only rescinded certain Trump-era modifications while maintaining others, such as recognizing Jerusalem as the capital of Israel.

For their part, Palestinian Arabs say Jews have usurped their ancestral homeland with help from Western powers, including the United States and the United Kingdom. The event of Israel's founding and its victory over allied Arab militaries in the 1948 war is referred to as the Nakba, or catastrophe, by them. According to the United Nations, this event caused over seven hundred thousand Palestinians to be uprooted. In the years that have passed since then, the Israeli-Palestinian conflict has repeatedly erupted into violence, including multinational wars, armed rebellions (intifadas), and acts of terrorism.

A significant turning point was the Six-Day War in 1967, during which Israel took control of East Jerusalem, the West Bank, and Gaza. In its aftermath, the UN Security Council adopted Resolution 242, which called for Israel to withdraw from occupied lands to secure and recognize borders in exchange for peace. The resolution lacked details, but nonetheless was a milestone, becoming the basis for future diplomacy to end the Arab-Israeli conflict.[1]

The conflict has its roots in the late 19th century, when Jewish immigrants began to settle in Palestine, which was then under Ottoman rule. In 1917, the British government declared its support for the establishment of a "national home for the Jewish people" in Palestine, which led to a significant increase in Jewish immigration to the area. In 1947, the United Nations adopted a plan to partition Palestine into two states, one for Jews and one for Palestinians. The plan was accepted by Jewish leaders but rejected by Arab leaders, who viewed it as an infringement on their rights and sovereignty. Following the adoption of the plan, fighting broke out between Jewish and Arab forces, leading to the establishment of the State of Israel in 1948 and the displacement of hundreds of thousands of Palestinians.

Since then, the conflict has continued, with both sides engaging in violent acts and peace negotiations failing to bring about a lasting resolution. One of the main reasons why building trust has been difficult in this conflict is the long history of grievances and mistrust between the two sides.

On the Israeli side, there is a deep-seated fear of security threats and a belief that Israel has a right to exist as a Jewish state. Israelis point to the numerous attacks against their citizens by Palestinian militants, including suicide bombings and rocket attacks, as evidence of the threat they face. Additionally, Israel sees itself as a victim of anti-Semitism and persecution throughout history and believes that the establishment of a Jewish state is necessary to prevent a repeat of such persecution.

On the Palestinian side, there is a deep-seated anger and sense of injustice over the displacement of their people and the occupation of their land by Israel. Palestinians view Israel as a colonial power that has systematically deprived them of their rights and freedoms. They point to the Israeli settlements in the West Bank, which they see as a violation of international law and a barrier to the establishment of a viable Palestinian state.

Map 1. Israel and Palestinian: Political Geography[2]

The resolution of the conflict has encountered obstacles due to a breakdown in trust experienced by the two parties involved. Numerous instances serve as evidence for this issue, such as the violation of agreements. Both sides have accused each other of breaching agreements and acting in bad faith. For instance, the Oslo Accords of 1993 were intended to establish a comprehensive peace agreement, yet both parties failed to fulfill crucial provisions, resulting in the collapse of the accord. Additionally, a lack of

communication and dialogue further contributes to the challenge. There are limited opportunities for Israelis and Palestinians to engage with one another on a personal level, leading to a deficiency in mutual understanding and empathy. The construction of physical barriers and checkpoints exacerbates this predicament, impeding Palestinians' freedom of movement. Furthermore, external interference has added complexity to the conflict. Involvement from external actors, including the United States and other regional countries, has further muddled the situation.

These external entities pursue their own interests and agendas, often diverging from those of Israelis and Palestinians. The Israeli-Palestinian conflict is a protracted and intricate struggle rooted in historical grievances and deep-seated mistrust between the two parties. The establishment of trust is a crucial but arduous task, necessitating both sides' commitment to engage in dialogue, exhibit flexibility, and acknowledge the legitimate rights and concerns of the other party. Trust is essential for resolving regional disputes. When there is trust between the parties, they are more likely to be willing to cooperate and compromise. They are also more likely to believe that the other party is acting in good faith, which can help to reduce tensions and prevent conflict from escalating. There are a number of examples of trust-building measures that have been used to overcome disputes.

One example is the Good Friday Agreement, which was signed in 1998 to end the conflict in Northern Ireland. The Agreement included a number of trust-building measures, such as the establishment of a cross-border police force and the creation of a power-sharing government. Another example is the Dayton Accords, which were signed in 1995 to end the war in Bosnia.[3] The Accords included a number of trust-building measures, such as the establishment of a joint military force and the creation of a commission to investigate war crimes. Trust-building measures are not a magic bullet for resolving disputes. However, they can be an important part of the process. By building trust between the parties, it is possible to create an environment where cooperation and compromise are more likely to occur. This can help to reduce tensions and prevent conflict from escalating.

Trust-building measures play a pivotal role in overcoming disputes, and several strategies can be employed for this purpose. One crucial measure is fostering open and honest communication, which serves as a fundamental element in establishing trust. Regardless of differences in opinions, the disputing parties must engage in transparent and sincere dialogue, enabling them to comprehend each other's perspectives and develop a relationship grounded in mutual respect. Another significant measure involves demonstrating respect for each other's interests. This entails a willingness to attentively listen to the concerns expressed by the opposing party and actively seek solutions that address the needs of both sides.

By embracing this approach, the parties involved in a dispute can foster an environment of empathy and understanding. Furthermore, a vital trust-building measure is the commitment to resolving the dispute. In order to progress towards a resolution, all parties must exhibit a genuine dedication to finding common ground. This often requires making compromises and prioritizing the collective interests of the dispute resolution process over individual personal interests. Accordingly, the cultivation of relationships between the disputing parties can also contribute to trust-building efforts.

This can be accomplished through informal interactions, such as meeting for coffee or lunch, or more structured mechanisms, like engaging in joint training exercises or collaborating on a shared project. These relationship-building activities facilitate the establishment of rapport and can serve as a foundation for trust to flourish. Trust-building measures play a pivotal role in overcoming disputes. Open and honest communication, respect for each other's interests, commitment to resolving the dispute, and building relationships are among the strategies that can be employed to foster trust and facilitate the resolution process.

Neutrality is a crucial element in establishing trust between conflicting parties, as it demonstrates impartiality and fairness. To gain the trust of both parties, a mediator must be perceived as unbiased and avoid showing favoritism or taking sides. This involves creating a neutral environment for dialogue, actively listening to both sides, and acknowledging the concerns and perspectives of each party. Identifying shared interests is another effective strategy for fostering trust. By pinpointing areas where both parties have common goals, such as economic development or regional stability, mediators can work towards finding solutions that promote these shared interests.

By emphasizing common ground, a mediator can build trust and lay the groundwork for potential conflict resolution. Transparency also plays a vital role in trust building. Mediators must maintain transparency throughout the negotiation process, including sharing the objectives, strategies, and potential outcomes. Keeping both parties informed about developments and progress and ensuring their clear understanding of the negotiation process contribute to trust-building efforts. Effective communication is a critical component of trust building between conflicting parties. Mediators must facilitate open and honest communication, encouraging both sides to express their concerns and perspectives. This entails actively listening to each party, acknowledging their concerns, and working towards finding areas of agreement. Establishing credibility is essential for a mediator.

This involves demonstrating expertise in the negotiation process and a commitment to finding mutually acceptable solutions. Mediators must be viewed as trusted and credible partners in the negotiation process, willing to collaborate with both sides to achieve a successful resolution.[4] To further enhance the likelihood of successful resolution in resolving wars and regional conflicts, mediators can employ additional strategies for building trust. These strategies include engaging in confidence-building measures, which involve practical steps like exchanging prisoners of war, implementing ceasefires or no-fly zones, and initiating joint economic projects. By taking tangible actions to build trust and reduce tensions, mediators create a more favorable environment for negotiation and conflict resolution.

Furthermore, establishing a culture of dialogue is crucial. Mediators must create a safe space for both sides to express their concerns and perspectives, promoting active listening and open communication. By fostering a culture of dialogue, mediators can break down barriers and enhance understanding between the conflicting parties. Addressing underlying issues is also essential in building trust and achieving lasting solutions. Many regional conflicts stem from economic disparities, political instability, or historical grievances.

To build trust and resolve the conflict, mediators must work with both sides to identify and address these root causes. Strategies can be developed to tackle these underlying issues effectively. Involving civil society can significantly contribute to trust-building efforts. By including civil society organizations in the negotiation process, mediators can incorporate diverse perspectives and foster a more inclusive dialogue. Civil society organizations can advocate for the interests of marginalized groups, promote transparency, and ensure accountability, thus bolstering trust. Lastly, building trust is often a gradual process that necessitates incremental progress. Rather than striving for an immediate grand solution, mediators should focus on building trust through small victories and incremental steps. By gradually and steadily building trust, mediators can establish a foundation for a sustainable and lasting resolution to the conflict.

As is well known, building trust between warring parties in resolving wars and regional conflicts is a difficult and complex process. However, by engaging in confidence-building measures, establishing a culture of dialogue, addressing underlying issues, involving civil society, and building incremental progress, mediators can increase the likelihood of success and create a more peaceful and stable regional environment. One effective strategy for building trust between warring parties is to establish joint economic projects that benefit both sides. For example, during the conflict in Northern Ireland, the creation of the InterTradeIreland organization helped to build trust between Protestant and Catholic communities by promoting cross-border economic cooperation.

By creating joint business ventures and encouraging trade, InterTradeIreland helped to break down barriers and promote understanding between the two sides.[5] Similarly, in the Middle East, the establishment of the Oslo Accords in 1993 included a series of confidence-building measures aimed at improving economic ties between Israelis and Palestinians. These measures included the creation of a joint economic committee and the establishment of industrial parks and joint ventures. In the complex realm of international politics, conflicts and wars often arise from deep-rooted grievances and divergent interests between warring parties. Resolving these conflicts and preventing global security crises requires a multifaceted approach, one that prioritizes building trust and confidence among the parties involved. While achieving this may seem like an insurmountable task, history has shown that various strategies can be employed to foster trust, promote cooperation, and pave the way for successful conflict resolution.

Therefore, devising a strategy for establishing trustworthiness can be a crucial factor. Building trust between warring parties in resolving wars and regional conflicts is a complex and difficult process that requires a careful and strategic approach. While there are no easy solutions to this problem, several strategies can help to build trust and increase the likelihood of a successful resolution to the conflict.

One effective strategy for building confidence in conflict and war is the implementation of joint economic projects. The intertwining of economic interests can serve as a powerful incentive for warring parties to cooperate and seek peaceful resolutions. Economic initiatives, such as trade agreements, joint investments, and development projects, can create interdependencies that discourage hostilities and foster a sense of shared prosperity. The Oslo Accords, although ultimately unsuccessful in achieving lasting peace, demonstrated the potential of economic cooperation in building trust. Despite their eventual failure, the economic initiatives undertaken during the Oslo process played a vital role in establishing channels of communication and cooperation between the Israelis and Palestinians. By working together on economic ventures, both sides were able to see tangible benefits and develop a level of mutual understanding that laid the groundwork for future negotiations.

Another crucial approach to building confidence in conflicts is the involvement of neutral third-party mediators. Mediators can provide an unbiased perspective, facilitate communication, and bridge the gaps between warring parties. The example of the Colombian peace negotiations between the government and the Revolutionary Armed Forces of Colombia (FARC) highlights the value of a neutral mediator. Norway, acting as a trusted mediator, played a pivotal role in fostering trust and moving the negotiations forward. The Norwegian mediator skillfully brought both sides to the negotiating table and created an environment conducive to open dialogue and compromise. Through their impartiality and expertise in conflict resolution, third-party mediators can help parties see beyond their differences, identify common ground, and work towards mutually beneficial solutions.

However, building trust between warring parties is a delicate and intricate process that requires more than just economic initiatives and third-party mediation. It necessitates the implementation of comprehensive confidence-building measures. These measures can encompass various actions, such as ceasefire agreements, arms control and disarmament efforts, and the establishment of communication channels. Ceasefire agreements provide a critical respite from violence, allowing parties to engage in meaningful dialogue without the constant threat of hostilities. Arms control and disarmament initiatives contribute to reducing tensions and creating an atmosphere of mutual security. Furthermore, establishing reliable communication channels, such as hotlines or diplomatic backchannels, facilitates direct and timely communication, minimizing the risk of miscommunication or escalation. These confidence-building measures, when employed collectively, help cultivate an environment of trust, laying the groundwork for productive negotiations and conflict resolution.

In conclusion, building trust between warring parties is a formidable yet indispensable step in resolving regional conflicts and averting global security crises. Through the implementation of joint economic projects, involvement of neutral third-party mediators, and comprehensive confidence-building measures, mediators can contribute to the creation of a conducive environment for negotiation and conflict resolution. By fostering trust and promoting cooperation, these strategies can transcend grievances, bridge divides, and pave the way for sustainable peace. The path to building confidence in conflict and war may be challenging, but the potential benefits far outweigh the difficulties. The world must recognize the importance of these strategies and commit to their implementation to secure a more peaceful and prosperous future for all.

CHAPTER 16.

The Role of Diplomacy and Mediation

Regional disputes and wars can lead to global security crises due to the lack of diplomatic and mediation roles. The reasons for regional disputes and wars are complex and multifaceted. Some of the reasons include unresolved regional tensions, a breakdown in the rule of law, absent or co-opted state institutions, illicit economic gain, and the scarcity of resources.[1]

Regional conflicts and wars are often characterized by complex and multifaceted causes such as tensions, the breakdown of the rule of law, the absence or adoption of state institutions, illicit economic gains, and lack of resources. Resolving these conflicts and bringing about lasting peace requires the skillful application of diplomacy and effective mediation. This chapter explores the crucial role played by diplomacy and mediation in addressing regional conflicts and wars, highlighting their significance in facilitating dialogue, promoting peaceful resolutions, and fostering long-term stability. First, Diplomacy as a Catalyst for Dialogue and Negotiation: Diplomacy serves as a vital tool in resolving regional conflicts by fostering dialogue and negotiation among conflicting parties. Diplomats, representing their respective nations, engage in diplomatic talks, consultations, and negotiations to address the underlying causes of conflicts. Through diplomatic channels, parties involved in regional disputes can express their concerns, voice grievances, and seek mutually acceptable solutions. By promoting dialogue and understanding, diplomacy creates an atmosphere conducive to conflict resolution and helps build trust between conflicting parties.

Second, Mediation as a Facilitator of Peaceful Resolutions: Mediation plays a crucial role in facilitating peaceful resolutions by providing a neutral and impartial platform for conflicting parties to engage in structured negotiations. A skilled mediator assists the parties in exploring common ground, identifying shared interests, and seeking mutually beneficial outcomes. Mediation enables conflicting parties to move away from confrontational approaches and towards collaborative problem-solving. By encouraging compromise and consensus building, mediation offers a viable pathway to resolve regional conflicts and establish sustainable peace.

Third, Diplomacy and Mediation for Long-Term Stability: Diplomacy and mediation contribute significantly to achieving long-term stability in regions affected by conflicts and wars. By addressing the root causes of conflicts and promoting inclusive dialogue, these mechanisms help establish durable peace agreements. Diplomatic efforts can facilitate the implementation of peace treaties, supporting the transition from a state of war to one of stability and development. Additionally, successful mediations can lead to the establishment of mechanisms for conflict prevention, management, and resolution, thus reducing the likelihood of future hostilities. If so, what were the successful diplomatic efforts and mediation cases?

Numerous historical examples highlight the pivotal role of diplomacy and mediation in resolving regional conflicts. The Camp David Accords of 1978, brokered by diplomatic efforts led by U.S. President Jimmy Carter, brought about a peace treaty between Israel and Egypt, ending decades of hostility. Similarly, the Dayton Agreement in 1995, mediated by international actors, successfully halted the Bosnian War and laid the foundation for peace and stability in the region. These examples demonstrate that diplomatic initiatives and effective mediation can lead to significant breakthroughs in resolving regional conflicts.

Accordingly, regional conflicts and wars are complex phenomena with multifaceted causes. Diplomacy and effective mediation are indispensable tools for resolving these conflicts, as they facilitate dialogue, promote peaceful resolutions, and foster long-term stability. Through diplomatic efforts, conflicting parties can engage in constructive dialogue and negotiate mutually acceptable solutions. Mediation, on the other hand, provides a neutral platform for structured negotiations, encouraging compromise and collaboration. The importance of diplomacy and mediation is further emphasized by successful historical case studies that display their transformative impact. By recognizing and leveraging the critical role of diplomacy and mediation, the international community can contribute to a more peaceful and stable world.

Regional disputes and wars often stem from complex and deeply rooted historical, political, and social factors, making them difficult to resolve. Additionally, the lack of effective diplomatic and mediation roles can exacerbate these difficulties, leading to global security crises. One reason for the lack of effective diplomatic and mediation roles is the lack of trust among the parties involved in the dispute. For example, in the Israeli-Palestinian conflict, there is a deep-seated mistrust between the two sides, which makes it difficult for outside mediators to facilitate a peace agreement. Additionally, the involvement of external factors, such as the United States and Iran, in the conflict further complicates the situation and reduces the prospects for a peaceful resolution.

Another reason is the lack of incentives for the parties to engage in meaningful negotiations. In some cases, one or both parties may believe that they can achieve their objectives through military means and therefore have little motivation to engage in negotiations. For example, in the Syrian civil war, the Assad regime has used military force to try to crush the opposition rather than engaging in meaningful negotiations.[2] Furthermore, the lack of international consensus on how to resolve the dispute can also hinder diplomatic and mediation efforts. For example, in the conflict between Russia and Ukraine, the international community is divided on how to respond, with some countries supporting Ukraine and others supporting Russia. This lack of consensus reduces the effectiveness of international mediation efforts.

Difficulties in Diplomatic and Arbitration Roles

Despite ongoing diplomatic and mediation efforts to resolve regional disputes, it remains challenging in practice. For instance, why is it so difficult for third parties such as the United Nations to resolve the 2022 war between Ukraine and Russia despite diplomatic and mediation efforts by some countries and leaders? The conflict began in 2014 when Russia annexed Crimea from Ukraine and has since escalated into a full-scale war in eastern Ukraine, with thousands of casualties and ongoing military action.

Regarding diplomatic efforts and mediation by third parties, several actors have attempted to facilitate negotiations and promote a peaceful resolution to the conflict. The Normandy Format, which includes Ukraine, Russia, Germany, and France, has held several rounds of talks aimed at resolving the conflict, with mixed results. The Organization for Security and Cooperation in Europe (OSCE) has also played a role in monitoring the ceasefire and promoting dialogue between the conflicting parties.[3]

However, despite these efforts, the conflict continues, and finding a lasting and satisfactory solution remains a significant challenge. The reasons for the difficulties in resolving the conflict through diplomacy and mediation are numerous, as I mentioned in my previous response. The parties involved have deeply entrenched positions and have different interpretations of the conflict's origins and causes. There is also a lack of trust between the parties, with accusations of violations of ceasefire agreements, human rights abuses, and war crimes on both sides.

Additionally, external factors such as geopolitical tensions and the influence of other powerful countries further complicate the resolution of the conflict. Finally, the complexity of the issues involved, including territorial disputes, ethnic tensions, and economic interests, make it challenging to find a solution that satisfies all parties involved. The ongoing war between Ukraine and Russia has been a complex issue that has been ongoing for years. Diplomatic efforts and mediation by third parties have been ongoing as well. However, despite these efforts, the conflict remains unresolved.

According to an article by Foreign Policy, international mediation in the Ukrainian conflict has not been futile as a whole. The article states that despite the failure of diplomatic efforts to resolve the conflict between Ukraine and Russia, there have been some successes in international mediation. Another article by The Diplomat discusses China's role in the Russia-Ukraine war. The chapter interprets China's views and actions on the conflict and what China's mediation in the Ukrainian crisis would look like.

Another article by Foreign Policy discusses why mediation around Ukraine keeps failing. The article states that despite ongoing diplomatic efforts to resolve regional disputes, it remains challenging in practice. Turkey has played a mediating role in the ongoing war between Ukraine and Russia. According to an article by Atlantic Council, Turkey's diplomatic and military aid to Ukraine remains an important deterrent factor. The article emphasizes Turkey's position as a mediator in the Russia-Ukraine conflict.

Another article by Ukrinform states that Turkey is a strategic and effective partner that supports Ukraine, its sovereignty and territorial integrity, while maintaining political, diplomatic and economic relations with Russia. The article states that Turkey's role, as a mediator is important and promising to defuse tensions and resolve other issues. Third parties such as the United Nations face many challenges when trying to play a diplomatic and mediating role in resolving conflicts.[4]

One of the biggest challenges is that the parties involved in the conflict may not be willing to accept third-party mediation. In addition, third parties may lack the necessary resources or expertise to effectively mediate a conflict. Furthermore, third-party mediation can be complicated by issues of sovereignty and national pride. In the case of the war between Ukraine and Russia, there are additional challenges.

For example, Russia has been accused of violating international law by annexing Crimea and supporting separatist rebels in eastern Ukraine. This has made it difficult for third parties to mediate the conflict because Russia has refused to recognize Ukraine's sovereignty over Crimea. Additionally, Russia has been accused of providing military support to separatist rebels in eastern Ukraine. This has made it difficult for third parties to mediate the conflict because they may be seen as taking sides.

The ongoing conflict between Ukraine and Russia is a complex issue that has persisted for several years. The resolution of conflicts, like any other, presents a complex challenge for third parties, including esteemed organizations such as the United Nations, seeking to assume a diplomatic and mediating role. Various factors contribute to this difficulty, which I will now delineate.

Foremost among these factors are the political interests held by the parties involved. Both Russia and Ukraine harbor their own distinct interests in the region, which do not always align with those of the United Nations or other third parties. Russia, for instance, has long regarded Ukraine as part of its sphere of influence and has faced accusations of supporting separatist movements in eastern Ukraine. Conversely, Ukraine perceives Russia as a threat to its sovereignty and territorial integrity. Such conflicting political interests pose a formidable obstacle for third parties seeking a mutually satisfactory solution.

Compounding the challenge is the historical backdrop of tensions between Ukraine and Russia. The roots of their conflict extend deep into history, further complicating the situation. Ukraine, having been a part of the Soviet Union for many years, attained independence in 1991 following the USSR's collapse. Nevertheless, Russia has yet to fully recognize Ukraine's sovereignty and has been accused of meddling in its internal affairs. The annexation of Crimea by Russia in 2014 served as a catalyst, inflaming tensions and fueling the ongoing conflict in eastern Ukraine.

A significant impediment to conflict resolution is the lack of trust between the parties involved. The Ukrainian government and the separatists in eastern Ukraine harbor mutual mistrust, while neither side places trust in Russia to impartially mediate the dispute. This pervasive lack of trust poses a formidable challenge for third parties endeavoring to broker a peace agreement acceptable to all sides. [5] Another critical factor hindering mediation efforts is the military power wielded by the involved parties. Russia maintains a substantial military presence in the region and stands accused of furnishing weapons and support to the separatists in eastern Ukraine. Conversely, the Ukrainian military has been engaged in combat with the separatists for an extended period and enjoys backing from certain Western countries. This dynamic of military power renders it arduous for third parties to exert pressure on the conflicting parties and facilitate their engagement in constructive negotiations.

Domestic politics in Ukraine and Russia further exacerbate the conflict. The Ukrainian government faces mounting pressure to resolve the conflict swiftly and reaffirm its authority over the region. Meanwhile, the Russian government confronts its own pressures to retain influence in the area and support Russian-speaking populations in Ukraine. These domestic political considerations add another layer of complexity, impeding the ability of third parties to assume a constructive role in resolving the conflict. In light of these multifaceted factors, it becomes evident that third-party mediation encounters significant challenges when attempting to navigate conflicts. Political interests, historical tensions, lack of trust, military power dynamics, and domestic political considerations intertwine to create a formidable barrier to a peaceful resolution. Addressing these complexities demands a nuanced and holistic approach, one that acknowledges and addresses each factor in order to promote sustainable peace.

The war between Ukraine and Russia is a complex and ongoing conflict that presents several challenges to third parties, including the United Nations, in playing a diplomatic and mediating role. Political interests, historical tensions, lack of trust, military power dynamics, and domestic politics all contribute to the difficulty in resolving the conflict. While there may be no easy solutions, continued efforts by third parties to engage in dialogue and to promote peace and stability in the region remain critical.

From the perspective of experts such as international political scientists, how diplomatic and mediation efforts can be made to resolve regional disputes so that both parties involved can gain sympathy and be effective?" Diplomatic and mediation efforts can be made to resolve regional disputes by following certain principles. One principle is that the mediator must be impartial and not take sides. Another principle is that the mediator must be trusted by both parties involved in the dispute. Additionally, the mediator must have a good understanding of the issues involved in the dispute[2]. In order for both parties involved in the dispute to gain sympathy and be effective, it is important for the mediator to listen carefully to both sides and understand their concerns. The mediator should also help both sides identify common ground and work towards a mutually acceptable solution.

Resolving regional disputes through diplomatic and mediation efforts is a complex and nuanced process that requires a deep understanding of the underlying factors driving the conflict. In the realm of international politics, the effectiveness of diplomacy and mediation efforts cannot be standardized due to the multifaceted nature of conflicts. Nonetheless, certain strategies can be recommended to enhance their efficacy. The initial step entails engaging in dialogue, as establishing channels of communication among the involved parties is crucial in conflict resolution. Creating an environment conducive to open expression of concerns and attentive listening is pivotal.

A skilled mediator can facilitate this process by fostering a neutral space for dialogue and encouraging the parties to voice their perspectives.

Once dialogue has been initiated, the subsequent step involves identifying common interests shared by both parties. This necessitates the exploration of areas where their goals intersect, enabling collaborative efforts towards a mutual objective. For instance, in the case of the Ukraine-Russia conflict, both parties possess an interest in stabilizing the region and promoting economic growth. Recognizing these shared interests allows the mediator to establish a basis for potential resolution. Another essential role of a mediator is to develop innovative solutions that are agreeable to all parties involved. This entails thinking outside the conventional boundaries and exploring unorthodox possibilities that may not have been previously considered. For instance, in the context of Ukraine and Russia, the mediator might contemplate options such as a neutral buffer zone or increased economic cooperation, which could foster trust and alleviate tensions.

Building trust constitutes a critical component of successful negotiations. To cultivate trust, the mediator must exhibit impartiality and demonstrate a commitment to finding a mutually acceptable solution. This involves actively listening to both sides, acknowledging their concerns, and diligently working towards discovering common ground. Over time, these efforts can foster trust and establish a solid foundation for potential conflict resolution.[6] Lastly, it is imperative to involve regional stakeholders in the negotiation process. This includes neighboring countries, regional organizations, and other influential actors who possess a stake in the conflict's outcome. By engaging regional stakeholders, the mediator can garner support for a prospective solution and ensure the sustainability of the resolution in the end.

Resolving regional disputes through diplomatic and mediation efforts requires a skilled mediator who can create a neutral space for dialogue, identify common interests, develop creative solutions, build trust, and involve regional stakeholders. While there are no easy solutions to complex conflicts such as the one between Ukraine and Russia, these strategies can help to lay the groundwork for a potential resolution to the conflict. When discussing the difficulty of diplomatic and mediation roles in resolving regional disputes and wars, it is important to recognize that there are no easy solutions to these complex problems. The involvement of regional stakeholders can be particularly challenging, as different actors may have competing interests and may not be willing to engage in dialogue or compromise.

However, despite these challenges, involving regional stakeholders is essential to finding a lasting and sustainable solution to regional conflicts.

Regional actors may have a unique understanding of the local context, which can be valuable in developing effective solutions. In addition, involving regional stakeholders can help to build support for a potential solution and ensure that the resolution is sustainable over the long term. To be effective, the involvement of regional stakeholders must be approached carefully and strategically. Mediators must take into account the interests and concerns of all actors involved, and work to build trust and create a shared sense of purpose. This may involve addressing underlying issues such as economic disparities, political instability, or historical grievances that may be driving the conflict.

In addition, mediators must be aware of the potential risks and challenges of involving regional stakeholders, including the potential for increased tensions or the spread of the conflict to neighboring countries. As such, it is important to approach this process with caution and to have a clear understanding of the potential risks and benefits. Overall, while involving regional stakeholders can be challenging, it is an essential component of any successful mediation effort. By taking a strategic and thoughtful approach to this process, mediators can build support for a potential solution and help to create a more stable and peaceful regional environment.

In this Chapter, we consider diplomatic and arbitration approaches as potential solutions to the ongoing Ukrainian-Russian conflict that began in 2014 when Russia annexed Crimea from Ukraine and began supporting separatists in eastern Ukraine. The situation is complex and multifaceted, and there is no simple solution. However, several approaches have been suggested by experts and international organizations to resolve the conflict. One approach to resolving the conflict is through diplomacy and negotiation. The international community, including the United Nations, the European Union, and the Organization for Security and Cooperation in Europe (OSCE), has called for a peaceful resolution to the conflict through dialogue and negotiation.

The Minsk agreements, signed in 2015, aimed to bring an end to the conflict through a ceasefire and the implementation of political reforms in eastern Ukraine. However, the implementation of the agreements has been slow, and fighting has continued.[7] Another approach that has been taken is economic sanctions against Russia. The United States and the European Union have imposed economic sanctions on Russia in response to its actions in Ukraine, including the annexation of Crimea. These sanctions have had a significant impact on the Russian economy, and some experts believe that they may be a useful tool to pressure Russia to end its involvement in the conflict.

Some experts have suggested that military intervention may be necessary to resolve the conflict. However, this approach is highly controversial and could escalate the conflict further. The United States and NATO have sent military aid to Ukraine, including weapons and training for Ukrainian troops. However, they have not intervened directly in the conflict. International mediation could be an effective approach to resolving the conflict. The OSCE has been involved in monitoring the ceasefire and supporting the implementation of the Minsk agreements. The United Nations could also play a role in mediating the conflict. In 2021, the United States and Russia held talks on the conflict, which some experts see as a positive step towards a peaceful resolution.

Another approach to resolving the conflict is to find common ground between Russia and Ukraine. This could involve addressing the concerns of both sides, such as Russia's desire to protect its ethnic Russian population in Ukraine and Ukraine's desire for sovereignty and territorial integrity. Some experts have suggested that a federal system could be a solution, where Ukraine would grant more autonomy to its eastern regions. The conflict between Russia and Ukraine is a complex issue that requires a multifaceted approach. Diplomacy, economic sanctions, international mediation, finding common ground, and military intervention are all possible approaches, but each has its advantages and disadvantages. It is crucial that the international community continues to work towards a peaceful resolution to the conflict to prevent further escalation and human suffering.

As previously examined, the role of diplomacy and mediation is crucial in mitigating regional disputes and preventing them from escalating into global security crises. As stated earlier, regional conflicts can arise due to a multitude of complex factors, including unresolved tensions, a breakdown in the rule of law, weak or co-opted state institutions, illicit economic gain, and resource scarcity.

Diplomacy serves as a vital tool in managing and resolving regional disputes. It involves negotiations, dialogue, and compromise among conflicting parties, aiming to find peaceful solutions that satisfy the interests of all involved. Diplomatic efforts can help de-escalate tensions, prevent conflicts from spiraling out of control, and foster an environment conducive to cooperation and stability. As renowned diplomat Kofi Annan once stated, "Diplomacy is not an alternative to action. It is an action of alternative."

Mediation, on the other hand, plays a significant role in facilitating diplomatic processes and bringing conflicting parties to the negotiation table. A skilled mediator acts as a neutral third party, assisting disputing parties in identifying common ground, building trust, and exploring mutually acceptable solutions. Through active engagement, effective mediators help bridge divides and enable constructive dialogue, as highlighted by the United Nations' Guidance for Effective Mediation.

The importance of diplomacy and mediation in resolving regional disputes is widely acknowledged by the international community. The United Nations, through its various organs and specialized agencies, plays a pivotal role in promoting diplomacy and mediation as means of conflict resolution. The UN Security Council, for instance, has the authority to impose sanctions, authorize peacekeeping missions, and endorse mediation efforts, exemplifying its commitment to maintaining international peace and security.

Furthermore, regional and sub-regional organizations also contribute to diplomatic and mediation efforts. Organizations such as the African Union, the Organization of American States, and the Association of Southeast Asian Nations have established frameworks and mechanisms for conflict prevention, management, and resolution. These regional bodies provide platforms for dialogue, coordination, and cooperation among member states, enhancing their ability to address regional disputes effectively.

It is important to recognize that successful diplomacy and mediation require political will, commitment, and sustained engagement from all parties involved. Building trust, fostering dialogue, and addressing the root causes of regional conflicts demand patience, perseverance, and the willingness to compromise. However, the potential benefits of diplomatic and mediated solutions far outweigh the costs and risks associated with protracted regional conflicts.[8]

Accordingly, the role of diplomacy and mediation in resolving regional disputes cannot be overstated. By addressing unresolved tensions, promoting the rule of law, strengthening state institutions, curbing illicit economic activities, and addressing resource scarcity, diplomatic and mediated approaches contribute to global security and stability. As we navigate an increasingly interconnected and interdependent world, investing in diplomatic and mediation capacities is essential for a more peaceful and secure future.

PART V

STRATEGIES FOR RESOLVING DISPUTES

"Strategy without tactics is the slowest route to victory. Tactics without strategy is the noise before defeat."

-Sun Tzu

CHAPTER 17

Principles of conflict resolution

The Principles of Conflict Resolution is a set of guidelines or strategies that can be used to resolve disputes effectively. Here are the basic principles: Focus on the problem, not the person: It is important to separate the person from the problem when dealing with a conflict. This means focusing on the issues at hand and not attacking the person or their character. The establishment and implementation of the principles of conflict resolution in international politics are rooted in various theoretical grounds. One fundamental basis is the pursuit of peace and stability, whereby conflict resolution endeavors to address the underlying causes of conflicts, manage differences, and foster cooperation among nations. It is widely believed that the peaceful resolution of conflicts not only alleviates immediate violence but also contributes to long-term stability and development. International law and norms provide another theoretical basis for conflict resolution principles.

The United Nations Charter and other international agreements emphasize the importance of settling disputes peacefully, respecting sovereignty, refraining from interference, and promoting human rights and democracy. These principles serve as guidelines for nations to engage in dialogue, negotiation, and peaceful means of conflict resolution. Humanitarian concerns also play a significant role in advocating conflict resolution principles. The devastating humanitarian consequences of conflicts, including loss of life, mass displacement, and widespread suffering, underscore the imperative of resolving conflicts peacefully. Conflict resolution principles seek to safeguard human rights, ensure access to humanitarian assistance, and prevent further harm to civilians.

Diplomacy and negotiation form the bedrock of conflict resolution principles. Rather than resorting to violence, these principles emphasize the use of diplomatic channels and negotiation processes to address disputes. Through dialogue, mediation, and arbitration, conflicting parties can work towards finding mutually agreeable solutions, building trust, and fostering sustainable peace. Furthermore, conflict resolution goes beyond simply ending immediate violence. It recognizes the importance of addressing underlying structural, social, and economic issues that fuel conflicts. By engaging in transformative processes, conflict resolution aims to effect positive changes within societies, institutions, and relationships, thereby mitigating the recurrence of conflicts. The effectiveness of conflict resolution principles can be observed through various examples. Diplomatic negotiations have yielded positive outcomes in resolving conflicts.

For instance, the Camp David Accords of 1978 between Egypt and Israel resulted in a framework for peaceful coexistence and the return of the Sinai Peninsula to Egypt. Mediation efforts have also played a crucial role in conflict resolution. The Dayton Agreement in 1995 brought an end to the war in Bosnia and Herzegovina, providing a framework for post-conflict reconstruction and governance. United Nations peacekeeping operations have made significant contributions to conflict resolution by implementing peace agreements, facilitating dialogue, and providing security. Missions in Namibia, Cambodia, and El Salvador have effectively helped resolve conflicts and establish stable political systems.

Truth and reconciliation commissions have been employed as part of conflict resolution processes to address past grievances and promote healing. The Truth and Reconciliation Commission in South Africa, for instance, played a pivotal role in the country's transition from apartheid to democracy. Regional cooperation has also been instrumental in conflict resolution. The European Union, through its efforts in managing conflicts, promoting reconciliation, and fostering economic integration among member states, has contributed to peace and stability in Europe.

It is important to acknowledge that conflict resolution is a complex and context-dependent process, and its effectiveness may vary based on factors such as the nature of the conflict, the willingness of parties to engage, and the support of the international community. Nonetheless, the aforementioned theoretical grounds and historical examples underscore the potential of conflict resolution principles to establish peaceful relations and address the underlying causes of conflicts.

The Principles of conflict resolution encompass a comprehensive set of guidelines that prove essential in effectively resolving disputes. These principles have gained significant traction in the realm of conflict resolution and peacebuilding, demonstrating their efficacy in resolving regional disputes worldwide. The fundamental principles can be summarized as follows:

First, the principle of Respect for Human Dignity upholds the inherent value of every individual involved in a conflict. It mandates that conflicts be resolved in a manner that acknowledges and respects the dignity of all parties concerned, including their human rights, cultural values, and beliefs. The principle of Listening and Understanding places a strong emphasis on active listening and seeking to understand the perspectives of all involved parties. By empathizing with their emotions and needs, individuals are better equipped to comprehend differing viewpoints and foster a deeper understanding of the conflict at hand.

Building upon active listening, the principle of Dialogue recognizes that conflicts can only be effectively resolved through open and constructive communication. Engaging in dialogue allows parties to engage in meaningful discussions, enabling the identification of common ground and mutually beneficial resolutions. Negotiation, as a key principle, entails the pursuit of compromises or solutions that satisfy the needs and interests of all parties. It necessitates a willingness to make concessions and find middle ground, ultimately fostering an environment conducive to resolution. The principle of Non-Violent Approaches firmly asserts that violence should never serve as a means to resolve conflicts. Instead, peaceful means such as nonviolent protests, civil disobedience, and mediation should be embraced as viable alternatives.

Fairness and Impartiality dictate that all conflict resolution efforts must uphold the principles of fairness and impartial treatment. This entails equal treatment of all parties involved, with no individual being disadvantaged or subjected to unfair treatment. The principle of Creative Problem Solving encourages individuals to think innovatively and explore unconventional solutions to complex problems.[1] This principle encourages an open-minded approach, welcoming new ideas and diverse perspectives to pave the way for innovative resolutions. Lastly, the principle of Sustainable Solutions underscores the need for conflict resolution efforts to address the root causes of the conflict. Beyond immediate resolutions, long-term solutions must strive to tackle underlying issues such as poverty, inequality, and social injustice, ensuring sustainable outcomes.

The Principles of conflict resolution provide a comprehensive framework for resolving regional disputes in the world. By applying these principles, parties can work, together to find mutually acceptable solutions that address the needs and interests of all parties involved. These principles have been used successfully in a variety of settings, from local community disputes to international conflicts, and offer a promising approach to building peace and promoting stability around the world.

Acknowledge the conflict. The first step in resolving a regional dispute is to acknowledge that it exists. This means being honest with yourself and the other countries involved about your feelings and concerns. It also means being willing to listen to the other countries' perspectives. Focus on the interests, not the positions. When countries are in conflict, they often focus on their positions, or what they want. This can make it difficult to find a solution that works for everyone. Instead, it is important to focus on the interests, or the underlying needs and concerns that are driving the conflict.

For example, if two countries are in conflict over a piece of land, the underlying interests may be that one country wants to protect its citizens from a natural disaster, and the other country wants to access water resources. By focusing on the interests, it may be possible to find a solution that meets both countries' needs. Be willing to compromise. In order to resolve a regional dispute, all countries involved need to be willing to compromise. This means being willing to give up something in order to reach a solution that works for everyone. For example, if two countries are in conflict over a trade agreement, they may need to compromise on some of their demands in order to reach an agreement. Be respectful. Even though you may be angry at the other countries involved, it is important to be respectful of them. This means listening to them without interrupting, and avoiding name-calling or insults. Be creative. There is no one-size-fits-all solution to conflict.[2] It is important to be creative and come up with a solution that works for everyone involved. For example, if two countries are in conflict over a water resource, they may need to come up with a creative solution, such as building a pipeline to share the water. Get help if needed. If you are unable to resolve a regional dispute on your own, there are people who can help. This includes mediators, arbitrators, and judges. For example, the United Nations can help to mediate regional disputes.

Regional conflicts have been a significant challenge to global security for many years. The resolution of these disputes is crucial to prevent them from escalating into larger conflicts that could threaten international peace and stability.[3] Dispute resolution mechanisms are, therefore, essential in managing and resolving local conflicts before they become a global threat. In this article, we will examine an actual case where the rules of dispute resolution were established both before and after the resolution of a local conflict. An example of the establishment of rules for regional dispute settlement is the conflict between Ethiopia and Eritrea that began in the early 1990s and lasted for over 20 years. The conflict was rooted in a territorial dispute over the border between the two countries.[4] Eritrea was a province of Ethiopia until 1991 when it declared independence, and this led to a dispute over the demarcation of the border between the two nations.

The dispute escalated into a full-blown war that lasted from 1998 to 2000 and claimed the lives of an estimated 70,000 people.[5] The dispute resolution mechanisms were established both before and after the resolution of the conflict. In 2000, the Algiers Agreement was signed between the two countries, which established a framework for resolving the border dispute peacefully. The agreement created a special boundary commission to demarcate the border, and both parties agreed to accept the commission's decision as final and binding. The agreement also established a claims commission to adjudicate claims related to damages caused by the conflict.

Before the Algiers Agreement was signed, there were several attempts to resolve the conflict peacefully. In 1993, the two countries signed a mutual understanding that aimed to resolve the border issue peacefully. However, the agreement was not implemented, and the dispute continued to escalate. In 1998, the two countries signed the OAU Framework Agreement, which established a peace process to resolve the conflict. The peace process, however, did not yield any results, and the conflict continued until the signing of the Algiers Agreement.[6]

The Algiers Agreement was successful in resolving the border dispute between Ethiopia and Eritrea. The boundary commission demarcated the border, and both countries accepted the decision. However, the agreement did not address all the issues that arose from the conflict. There were claims of human rights abuses, and many people were displaced from their homes during the conflict. These issues were addressed by the claims commission, which awarded compensation to those affected by the conflict. In conclusion, the conflict between Ethiopia and Eritrea is a clear example of the importance of dispute resolution mechanisms in managing and resolving local conflicts before they become a global threat. The Algiers Agreement, together with other agreements and frameworks, established a mechanism for resolving the border dispute peacefully. The establishment of the boundary and claims commissions ensured that all issues related to the conflict were addressed, and compensation was awarded to those affected by the conflict. It is, therefore, crucial for countries to establish dispute resolution mechanisms to manage and resolve local conflicts peacefully, as this is essential for maintaining international peace and stability.

In order to prevent regional conflicts from escalating into global security crises, it is imperative for government policymakers and stakeholders to adhere to certain principles and strategies when establishing conflict resolution frameworks. These principles and strategies serve as essential guidelines for fostering stability, cooperation, and peaceful relations among nations. Let us delve into the key elements that policymakers and stakeholders need to consider in their pursuit of conflict resolution principles.

Firstly, a fundamental aspect entails prioritizing dialogue and communication as primary means of addressing conflicts. Policymakers and stakeholders must emphasize the importance of open lines of communication, encouraging direct engagement and constructive discussions between conflicting parties. By establishing effective communication channels, stakeholders can bridge gaps, clarify misunderstandings, and cultivate trust. Such channels provide a platform for stakeholders to voice their concerns, interests, and grievances, thereby facilitating the exploration of mutually acceptable solutions.

Mediation and diplomacy are also vital components of conflict resolution. Policymakers and stakeholders should actively seek out impartial third-party mediators who can facilitate negotiations and bridge the divide between conflicting parties. Skilled mediators possess the ability to reframe issues, manage power dynamics, and guide parties towards mutually beneficial outcomes. Concurrently, diplomatic efforts must be leveraged to create an environment conducive to negotiation, fostering an atmosphere of cooperation and compromise. Inclusivity and representation are imperative in conflict resolution processes.

Policymakers must ensure the meaningful participation of all relevant stakeholders, including representatives from marginalized communities, civil society organizations, and affected populations. Inclusivity ensures that the perspectives and interests of all stakeholders are taken into account, leading to more comprehensive and sustainable solutions. A comprehensive understanding of the root causes, dynamics, and complexities of the conflict is essential for effective resolution. Policymakers and stakeholders should invest in in-depth conflict analysis, examining historical, political, socio-economic, and cultural factors that contribute to the conflict. This analysis serves as a foundation for developing targeted strategies and interventions that address underlying issues and promote reconciliation.

Confidence-building measures play a crucial role in establishing trust and creating an environment conducive to conflict resolution. Policymakers and stakeholders must identify and implement measures that demonstrate goodwill, foster cooperation, and reduce tensions. Examples of such measures include the exchange of prisoners, the implementation of ceasefires, or the promotion of joint economic projects that benefit all parties involved. Furthermore, conflict resolution efforts should prioritize the development and implementation of long-term, sustainable solutions. Policymakers and stakeholders must not solely focus on ending immediate violence but also address structural and systemic issues that perpetuate conflicts. This may involve tackling issues of governance, socio-economic inequality, resource distribution, or cultural divisions. By implementing sustainable solutions, policymakers ensure long-term stability and minimize the likelihood of future conflicts.

International cooperation and support are crucial in conflict resolution endeavors. Policymakers and stakeholders should actively seek the collaboration and assistance of regional and global actors, such as international organizations, neighboring states, and influential partners. International support can provide necessary resources, expertise, and diplomatic advantage, thereby enhancing the chances of successful conflict resolution and preventing the escalation of conflicts into broader security crises. By adhering to these principles and strategies, government policymakers and stakeholders can establish a robust framework for conflict resolution. This approach promotes dialogue, inclusivity, understanding, and the development of sustainable solutions, ultimately working towards the prevention and resolution of regional conflicts while upholding international peace and security.

CHAPTER 18

Diplomatic Efforts

Diplomatic effort is a strategy used to resolve disputes by engaging in peaceful negotiations and dialogue between parties involved in the conflict. The primary goal of diplomatic effort is to find common ground and reach a mutually beneficial agreement without resorting to violent or aggressive means. A diplomatic effort is a strategy for resolving disputes that involves the use of negotiation, mediation, and other forms of communication to reach a mutually agreeable solution.[1] The goal of a diplomatic effort is to find a solution that is acceptable to all parties involved, and that does not involve the use of force. There are many different types of diplomatic efforts, but they all share some common features.

First, they all involve the use of communication to try to understand the other party's perspective and to build trust. Second, they all involve the use of negotiation to try to find a solution that is acceptable to both parties. Third, they all involve the use of mediation or arbitration to help the parties reach a mutually agreeable solution if they are unable to do so on their own. Diplomatic efforts can be used to resolve a wide variety of disputes, including disputes between individuals, groups, organizations, and even countries. They have been used to resolve disputes over land, resources, trade, and even war. Diplomatic efforts are not always successful, but they are often the best way to resolve disputes peacefully. They are also often the only way to resolve disputes between countries that are at war.

The process of diplomatic effort encompasses a series of crucial steps for effectively addressing conflicts. The initial step involves the establishment of communication channels between the parties involved. This can be achieved through direct dialogue, mediation, or the utilization of intermediaries. Once communication has been established, the subsequent step entails defining the underlying issues fueling the dispute. This requires a thorough analysis of the root causes of the conflict, as well as a comprehensive understanding of the concerns and interests held by each party involved. Following the identification of issues, the diplomatic effort progresses to exploring potential solutions that can effectively address the concerns and interests of all parties.

This phase often involves engaging in brainstorming sessions, proposing various scenarios, and considering the potential consequences of each solution. After the exploration of potential solutions, the involved parties move on to the negotiation stage. Here, they engage in discussions to reach a settlement that adequately addresses the concerns and interests of all parties involved. This process necessitates compromises from both sides and may require further discussions and revisions. Upon reaching a settlement, the implementation phase comes into play. This stage involves the practical application of the agreed-upon terms. The parties involved must monitor and enforce the terms of the settlement, swiftly addressing any issues that may arise during the implementation process. Overall, diplomatic effort serves as a valuable strategy for resolving disputes, as it encourages peaceful negotiation and dialogue among the conflicting parties. By collaborating to find mutually beneficial solutions, the parties can avoid resorting to violence and aggression, fostering stronger relationships based on trust and mutual respect.

Diplomatic efforts are an essential tool for resolving regional conflicts that can have a significant impact on global security crises. These efforts involve using diplomatic channels to negotiate and reach agreements between conflicting parties, with the aim of finding a peaceful and mutually acceptable resolution to the conflict.

One of the main advantages of using diplomatic efforts to resolve regional conflicts is that it can help prevent the escalation of violence and further destabilization of the region. Diplomatic efforts can also help build trust and understanding between the conflicting parties, which can facilitate the development of long-term solutions to the conflict.[2] In terms of the diplomatic approach strategy that is needed, it is important for the parties involved to be willing to engage in dialogue and negotiation in good faith. This involves a willingness to listen to the other party's concerns and to make concessions where necessary.

The parties should also be committed to finding a peaceful and mutually acceptable solution to the conflict, rather than seeking to impose their own will on the other party. Third parties can play an important role in facilitating diplomatic efforts to resolve regional conflicts. These third parties can act as mediators or facilitators in the negotiation process, helping to bridge the gap between the conflicting parties and facilitating communication and understanding. Third parties can also provide technical assistance and other forms of support to the parties involved, such as helping to implement agreements or providing resources to help address the underlying causes of the conflict.

In terms of the specific diplomatic approach that is needed, there are a number of strategies that can be effective. One approach is to use shuttle diplomacy, where a third-party mediator shuttles between the conflicting parties to facilitate communication and negotiation.[3] Another approach is to use track-two diplomacy, where non-governmental actors or civil society groups are involved in the negotiation process to help build trust and understanding between the parties. Ultimately, the success of diplomatic efforts to resolve regional conflicts will depend on a number of factors, including the willingness of the parties involved to engage in dialogue and compromise, the effectiveness of third-party mediators or facilitators, and the availability of resources and support to address the underlying causes of the conflict. However, when used effectively, diplomatic efforts can be an important tool for preventing the escalation of violence and promoting peace and stability in the region.

Here are some examples of actual cases of diplomatic efforts that were used to resolve regional conflicts that may have led to global security crises:

The Cuban Missile Crisis: In 1962, the United States and the Soviet Union came to the brink of nuclear war over the issue of Soviet missiles being placed in Cuba, just 90 miles from the coast of Florida. The crisis was resolved through a series of diplomatic efforts, including a secret meeting between President John F. Kennedy and Soviet Premier Nikita Khrushchev in Vienna.[4]

The Iran-Iraq War: The Iran-Iraq War was a long and bloody conflict that lasted from 1980 to 1988. The war was fought over a number of issues, including control of the Shatt al-Arab waterway and the disputed territory of Kurdistan. The war was finally resolved through a series of diplomatic efforts, including the United Nations Security Council Resolution 598, which called for a ceasefire and the withdrawal of all forces from occupied territory.[5]

The Oslo Accords: The Oslo Accords were a series of agreements between Israel and the Palestinian Liberation Organization (PLO) that were signed in 1993.[6] The agreements were intended to resolve the Israeli-Palestinian conflict and establish a Palestinian state. The Oslo Accords were a major breakthrough in the peace process, but they were ultimately unsuccessful in resolving the conflict.

The Dayton Accords: The Dayton Accords were a series of agreements that ended the Bosnian War in 1995. The agreements were signed by the leaders of Bosnia and Herzegovina, Croatia, and Serbia. The Dayton Accords established a new government for Bosnia and Herzegovina and created a framework for the return of refugees and displaced persons.[7]

The Good Friday Agreement: The Good Friday Agreement was an agreement that ended the Troubles in Northern Ireland. The agreement was signed in 1998 by the leaders of the British and Irish governments, as well as the leaders of the main political parties in Northern Ireland. The Good Friday Agreement established a power-sharing government in Northern Ireland and created a framework for the decommissioning of paramilitary weapons. These are just a few examples of the many diplomatic efforts that have been used to resolve regional conflicts. Diplomatic efforts are often successful in resolving disputes peacefully, and they can help to prevent global security crises.

Accordingly, diplomatic effort stands as a paramount strategy in resolving disputes through peaceful negotiations, dialogue, and engagement among conflicting parties. The primary objective of diplomatic effort is to identify common ground and achieve mutually beneficial agreements without resorting to violence or aggression. By utilizing negotiation, mediation, and various forms of communication, diplomatic efforts strive to establish lasting solutions that promote stability and foster cooperation.

Diplomatic efforts serve as an indispensable tool in the realm of international politics. The practice of diplomacy dates back centuries and has been instrumental in averting armed conflicts, defusing tensions, and facilitating cooperation between nations. As history has shown, diplomacy has played a pivotal role in preventing wars, promoting reconciliation, and advancing global peace and security.

The United Nations, as the preeminent international organization responsible for maintaining peace and security, has been at the forefront of diplomatic efforts. The UN Charter underscores the central role of diplomacy in settling disputes, stating that member states shall "settle their international disputes by peaceful means in such a manner that international peace and security and justice are not endangered" (United Nations, 1945). Through its various diplomatic initiatives, such as peacekeeping missions, special envoys, and mediation efforts, the United Nations has been actively engaged in preventing and resolving conflicts worldwide.

Moreover, regional organizations and diplomatic initiatives have also proven instrumental in facilitating diplomatic efforts. Entities like the European Union, African Union, and Organization of American States have established frameworks and mechanisms for diplomatic engagement, conflict resolution, and dialogue among member states. These regional diplomatic efforts provide platforms for negotiation, cooperation, and the pursuit of mutually beneficial outcomes within specific geographic contexts.

While diplomatic efforts are often challenging and complex, they offer numerous advantages over military or coercive approaches. Diplomacy allows parties to address the underlying causes of disputes, negotiate compromises, and build relationships based on trust and understanding. It provides an opportunity for all stakeholders to have their voices heard, fostering inclusivity and increasing the likelihood of sustainable peace.

However, it is important to acknowledge that diplomatic efforts are not without limitations and obstacles. Disputes may involve deep-rooted historical grievances, conflicting interests, power imbalances, or the involvement of non-state actors that can complicate the negotiation process. Moreover, diplomatic efforts require the genuine commitment and willingness of all parties involved to engage in meaningful dialogue and make concessions.

In conclusion, diplomatic effort remains an essential strategy for resolving disputes and promoting peaceful coexistence in the international arena. By emphasizing negotiation, mediation, and communication, diplomatic efforts offer a pathway to finding common ground, building trust, and achieving mutually agreeable solutions. In an increasingly interconnected and interdependent world, investing in diplomatic capacities and strengthening multilateral institutions is vital for addressing global challenges and ensuring a more peaceful future.

CHAPTER 19

Peacekeeping Missions

Peacekeeping missions are a strategy used to resolve disputes by deploying military or civilian personnel to conflict-affected areas to maintain peace and security, protect civilians, and support the implementation of peace agreements. The primary goal of peacekeeping missions is to prevent violence and provide a secure environment for the parties involved in the conflict to engage in peaceful negotiations and dialogue.

The United Nations (UN) has been involved in peacekeeping operations since its establishment in 1945. Peacekeeping missions are one of the UN's primary tools for maintaining international peace and security. These missions are intended to help reduce tensions between opposing groups, prevent the escalation of violence, and support efforts to achieve a lasting peace. The UN has played an essential role in resolving regional conflicts through its peacekeeping missions, and the importance of these missions cannot be overstated. The UN's involvement in peacekeeping missions began in the 1950s, when the organization sent a mission to monitor the ceasefire between Israel and its Arab neighbors.

Since then, the UN has been involved in more than 70 peacekeeping operations around the world, including in Bosnia, Cambodia, Kosovo, and Liberia. The role of the UN in peacekeeping missions is to provide a neutral and impartial force to help maintain peace and stability in regions affected by conflict.[1] Peacekeeping missions often involve a combination of military and civilian personnel, including police officers, political advisors, and human rights monitors. The UN peacekeeping force works in close collaboration with local authorities and communities to help build trust and promote dialogue between opposing groups. The effectiveness of peacekeeping missions in resolving regional conflicts has been subject to debate.

While some argue that these missions have been successful in preventing violence and helping to restore peace in conflict-affected regions, others argue that they have been ineffective and have even exacerbated conflicts in some cases. Despite these criticisms, peacekeeping missions remain an important strategy for resolving regional conflicts. Peacekeeping missions can provide a buffer between opposing groups, help reduce tensions, and provide a platform for dialogue and negotiation. They can also help create conditions for sustainable peace by promoting the rule of law, protecting human rights, and supporting the rebuilding of institutions. Accordingly, peacekeeping missions remain an important strategy for resolving regional conflicts. While their effectiveness may vary depending on the specific context, they have proven to be a critical tool for the UN in promoting peace and stability around the world.

The process of peacekeeping missions unfolds through a series of interconnected steps that work together to restore stability and address conflicts. From an academic perspective, let's explore these steps in a narrative manner: It all begins with the assessment phase. At the outset of any peacekeeping mission, a thorough examination of the situation on the ground takes place. This assessment delves into the intricate details of the conflict, identifying its nature, the parties involved, and the pressing security and humanitarian needs of the local population. This comprehensive understanding forms the foundation for the subsequent actions undertaken by the peacekeeping forces.

Once the assessment is complete, the focus shifts to the mandate. At this stage, the UN Security Council or another international body steps in to authorize the deployment of the peacekeeping mission and establish its mandate. This crucial declaration outlines the mission's objectives, the extent to which force can be employed, and the specific responsibilities entrusted to the peacekeeping personnel. With the mandate in place, the peacekeepers gain a clear roadmap to guide their efforts and ensure a cohesive approach to resolving the conflict. Now, it is time for deployment. The peacekeeping personnel, comprising military personnel, police officers, and civilian experts specializing in various domains, set foot in the conflict-affected area.

Their collective presence aims to create an atmosphere conducive to conflict resolution, emphasizing stability and security as essential pillars. Through their diverse skills and expertise, they bring forth a multi-dimensional approach to address the complex challenges at hand. With boots on the ground, the peacekeeping forces transition into the implementation phase. Their mission is to actively carry out the objectives defined in the mandate. They engage in activities such as regular patrolling, closely monitoring and reporting on the ground situation, ensuring the safety of the local population, and providing support for the implementation of peace agreements.

By actively participating in these endeavors, the peacekeepers become the catalysts for change, working tirelessly to foster trust, reduce tensions, and create an environment that fosters lasting peace. Finally, the mission embarks on developing an exit strategy. This strategic plan ensures a responsible withdrawal from the conflict-affected area once the mission's objectives have been achieved. It involves a series of coordinated steps, such as transferring responsibilities to local authorities, supporting the establishment of democratic institutions, and setting up mechanisms to maintain peace and security in the end. By meticulously planning their departure, the peacekeeping mission aims to lay the foundation for sustainable peace, leaving behind a legacy of stability and progress.

The process of peacekeeping missions unfolds through a dynamic sequence of assessment, mandate establishment, deployment, implementation, and exit strategy development. This holistic approach, rooted in academia, brings together various elements to navigate the complex terrain of conflicts, aiming to restore harmony and build a future of enduring peace.

Peacekeeping missions are not always successful, but they can play an important role in resolving conflicts and preventing violence. Peacekeeping missions have been used successfully in a range of conflicts around the world, including in Bosnia and Herzegovina, Kosovo, and Sierra Leone. They have also been used to support peace processes in countries such as Colombia and Sudan. While peacekeeping missions can be effective in preventing violence and promoting peace, they can also be challenging and risky for the personnel involved, and may require significant resources and international cooperation to be successful. Peacekeeping missions are an important strategy for resolving regional conflicts that may lead to global security crises.

Here are a few examples of actual cases where peacekeeping missions have been used to resolve conflicts:

United Nations Mission in South Sudan (UNMISS): In 2013, South Sudan was plunged into a civil war following a power struggle between the president and his former deputy.[2] The conflict resulted in the displacement of over 2 million people and the loss of tens of thousands of lives. In response, the UN Security Council established UNMISS to protect civilians and support the implementation of a peace agreement.[3] The mission has been instrumental in facilitating negotiations between the warring parties and supporting the disarmament and demobilization of armed groups.

United Nations Interim Force in Lebanon (UNIFIL): UNIFIL was established in 1978 to monitor the ceasefire between Israel and Lebanon following the Lebanese Civil War. The mission has since been renewed several times and expanded to include activities such as humanitarian assistance and mine clearance. UNIFIL has played a crucial role in maintaining peace and stability in the region and preventing escalation of violence between the parties.[4]

United Nations Mission in Liberia (UNMIL): In 2003, Liberia was emerging from a long and brutal civil war that had destabilized the country and the wider region. The UN Security Council established UNMIL to support the implementation of a peace agreement and to provide security and stability in the country. The mission was successful in disarming and demobilizing armed groups, supporting the establishment of democratic institutions, and facilitating the return of refugees and internally displaced persons. United Nations Assistance Mission for Iraq (UNAMI): UNAMI was established in 2003 following the US-led invasion of Iraq to support the country's transition to democracy and the restoration of peace and security.[5] The mission has played a crucial role in promoting political dialogue and reconciliation between the different communities in Iraq and supporting the government in its efforts to combat terrorism and extremism. Peacekeeping missions are an effective strategy for resolving regional conflicts and preventing them from escalating into global security crises. These missions provide an important mechanism for promoting peace, stability, and reconciliation in conflict-affected areas, and for supporting the establishment of democratic institutions and the rule of law. Peacekeeping missions are military operations that are deployed to conflict zones to help maintain or restore peace. Peacekeeping missions are authorized by the United Nations Security Council and are typically composed of troops from a variety of countries. The goals of peacekeeping missions are to: Disarm and demobilize combatants, Monitor and enforce ceasefires, Protect civilians, Provide humanitarian assistance, Promote the rule of law, Support the development of democratic institutions.

CHAPTER 20

Economic Incentives

Economic incentives are a strategy used to resolve disputes by offering parties involved in conflict financial or economic benefits in exchange for their cooperation in resolving the dispute. Economic incentives can be used in a variety of contexts, from labor disputes to international conflicts, and can be a powerful tool for promoting cooperation and reducing tensions between parties. In fact, economic incentives can be used to resolve a wide variety of disputes, including disputes over trade, environmental protection, and labor rights. They are often used in conjunction with other strategies, such as diplomacy and peacekeeping.

Economic incentives can be an effective tool for resolving regional conflicts by addressing underlying issues that contribute to the conflict.[1] When incentives are offered to parties involved in a conflict, they can be used to address economic, social, and political grievances that may have contributed to the conflict. Additionally, economic incentives can provide an alternative to military or violent means of resolving disputes, which can help to reduce the risk of escalation and further conflict. One way in which economic incentives can be strategically important is by providing parties with an opportunity to improve their economic conditions.

This can include financial assistance, investment, or trade agreements that can help to create jobs, increase income, and stimulate economic growth. When parties have access to economic resources, they may be less likely to engage in violent or criminal activity, as they have more to gain by participating in peaceful activities. Another way in which economic incentives can be strategically important is by providing parties with a sense of security and stability. In many cases, conflicts arise due to a lack of access to basic resources such as food, water, and shelter.[2] By providing these resources through economic incentives, parties can feel more secure and less threatened, reducing the likelihood of conflict.

Economic incentives can also be used to address political grievances that may have contributed to the conflict. For example, a government may offer economic incentives to a group that has been marginalized or oppressed, providing them with a greater voice in decision-making and a greater stake in the economic well-being of the country. The effectiveness of economic incentives in resolving regional conflicts will depend on a number of factors, including the specific incentives offered, the parties involved, and the broader political and economic context. However, research has shown that economic incentives can be effective in reducing the likelihood of conflict and promoting peaceful resolution. For example, studies have found that economic incentives can be particularly effective in addressing conflicts related to access to resources, such as water or land.[3] Therefore, economic incentives can be an important tool for resolving regional conflicts by addressing underlying economic, social, and political issues that may have contributed to the conflict. While the effectiveness of economic incentives will depend on a number of factors, they have the potential to reduce the risk of escalation and promote peaceful resolution.

One example of economic incentives being used to resolve a dispute is the Northern Ireland peace process. During the 1990s, Northern Ireland was embroiled in a long-standing conflict between Catholic and Protestant communities, which had resulted in violence and instability in the region for decades.[4] As part of the peace process, economic incentives were used to encourage both communities to work towards a resolution of the conflict. One of the key economic incentives offered to the parties was increased investment in Northern Ireland's economy. This included the establishment of the International Fund for Ireland, which provided funding for economic development projects in Northern Ireland and the border counties of the Republic of Ireland. A range of international donors, including the European Union, the United States, and Canada, supported the fund.

The economic incentives offered as part of the peace process were instrumental in encouraging both communities to engage in negotiations and work towards a resolution of the conflict. The increased investment in the region's economy helped to create jobs and improve living standards, which in turn reduced tensions and created a more stable environment for peace negotiations. Economic incentives can also be used in other contexts, such as labor disputes. For example, in 2018, West Virginia teachers went on strike to demand higher wages and better benefits.[5] As part of the negotiations to end the strike, the state government offered the teachers a 5% pay increase and a freeze on health care premiums.

This economic incentive was enough to convince the teachers to end the strike and return to work. Therefore, economic incentives can be an effective strategy for resolving disputes by providing parties with tangible benefits in exchange for their cooperation in resolving the conflict. However, it is important to ensure that the incentives offered are fair and equitable and that they do not perpetuate existing inequalities or exacerbate tensions between parties.

Here are a few examples of economic incentives being used to resolve regional conflicts that could have led to global security crises:

Iran Nuclear Deal: In 2015, the United States, along with other world powers, negotiated the Iran Nuclear Deal with the goal of preventing Iran from developing nuclear weapons.[6] As part of the deal, economic sanctions on Iran were lifted in exchange for Iran agreeing to limit its nuclear program. The lifting of the sanctions allowed Iran to re-enter the global economy, opening up new markets for its oil exports and attracting foreign investment. The economic incentives provided by the lifting of sanctions were a key factor in convincing Iran to negotiate the deal and reduce tensions with the international community.

South Sudan Conflict: In 2018, the government of South Sudan reached a peace agreement with rebel groups after years of civil war. The peace agreement included provisions for economic incentives, such as the establishment of a $100 million fund for infrastructure development and the creation of a national oil company to manage the country's oil resources. The economic incentives provided by the peace agreement were intended to promote economic growth and development in the country and reduce the grievances that had fueled the conflict.[7]

Israel-Palestine Conflict: Economic incentives have been proposed as a strategy for resolving the long-standing conflict between Israel and Palestine. In 2019, the United States proposed an economic plan, known as the "Peace to Prosperity" plan, which would provide $50 billion in investment for Palestine and neighboring countries in the region.[8] The plan was met with criticism from Palestinians, who argued that economic incentives alone would not resolve the political issues at the heart of the conflict. Accordingly, economic incentives can be a powerful tool for resolving regional conflicts and reducing tensions between parties. However, they must be used in conjunction with other strategies, such as political negotiations and social development programs, to address the root causes of the conflict and build a lasting peace.

Therefore, economic incentives are a type of strategy that can be used to resolve disputes. They involve offering rewards or punishments to encourage or discourage certain behaviors. For example, a government might offer tax breaks to businesses that create jobs in a certain area, or it might impose tariffs on goods imported from a country that is engaging in unfair trade practices. As noted, economic incentives can be an effective way to resolve disputes because they can help to change the cost-benefit analysis of the parties involved. For example, if a business is considering polluting a river, the government could impose a fine for each unit of pollution that is emitted. This would make it more expensive for the business to pollute, and it might encourage the business to find a cleaner way to operate.

Here are some examples of actual cases of economic incentives being used to resolve regional conflicts:

The European Union (EU) has used economic incentives to help resolve conflicts in the Balkans. For example, the EU offered financial assistance to countries in the Balkans that met certain conditions, such as holding free elections and respecting human rights. This helped to promote peace and stability in the region.

The United States has used economic incentives to help resolve conflicts in the Middle East. For example, the US offered financial assistance to the Palestinian Authority in exchange for its cooperation in the peace process. This helped to create a more conducive environment for peace talks.

China has used economic incentives to help resolve conflicts in Africa. For example, China has invested heavily in infrastructure projects in Africa. This has helped to create jobs and boost economic growth, which has helped to reduce tensions in the region.

These are just a few examples of the many ways that economic incentives have been used to resolve regional conflicts. Economic incentives can be an effective way to promote peace and stability, and they can be used in conjunction with other strategies, such as diplomacy and peacekeeping. It is important to note that economic incentives are not a panacea. They can be difficult to design and implement effectively, and they can be unfair to some parties involved. However, when used effectively, economic incentives can be a valuable tool for resolving disputes and preventing violence.

In the realm of global affairs, when regional conflicts arise, there is a pressing need for international organizations, government policy makers, and stakeholders to employ certain principles and strategies to defuse tensions and prevent these conflicts from spiraling into full-blown global security crises. By implementing effective economic incentives, these entities can play a crucial role in resolving regional conflicts while promoting stability and preventing dire consequences.

First, international organizations must adopt a principle of impartiality and fairness. They should strive to facilitate dialogue between conflicting parties, acting as neutral mediators rather than favoring any particular side. The approach helps establish trust and encourages all parties to participate in negotiations, knowing their interests will be taken into account. By promoting a level playing field, international organizations can lay the groundwork for constructive dialogue and compromise. Moreover, government policy makers should recognize the significance of economic incentives as a potent tool for conflict resolution. These incentives can be employed in various ways, such as financial aid packages, investment opportunities, and trade agreements.

By offering economic benefits to regions affected by conflicts, policy makers can provide tangible incentives for cooperation and peace. This approach not only addresses the immediate economic needs of the affected regions but also fosters interdependence and mutual interests, making conflict less attractive and cooperation more enticing. Stakeholders, including local communities, businesses, and civil society organizations, should actively engage in the resolution process. Their involvement is crucial for sustainable and inclusive solutions.

By encouraging their participation, decision-makers can ensure that the proposed economic incentives align with the needs and aspirations of those directly affected by the conflicts. The stakeholders can also provide valuable insights into the underlying causes and dynamics of the conflicts, contributing to more informed and effective strategies. To effectively implement economic incentives, international organizations, policy makers, and stakeholders must prioritize long-term solutions over short-term gains. Conflict resolution is a complex process that requires a comprehensive approach. Merely addressing immediate economic concerns may not be sufficient to resolve deep-rooted conflicts. It is essential to consider underlying political, social, and historical factors, and work towards addressing them in tandem with economic incentives.

This integrated approach promotes sustainable peace and reduces the likelihood of conflicts resurfacing in the future. Furthermore, transparency and accountability are fundamental in providing economic incentives. International organizations and policy makers should ensure that the allocation of resources and benefits is fair and transparent. This transparency helps build trust and minimizes the potential for corruption, which can undermine the effectiveness of incentives. Additionally, accountability mechanisms should be put in place to monitor the implementation and impact of the incentives, ensuring that they deliver the intended outcomes and contribute to conflict resolution. Lastly, flexibility and adaptability are essential principles when employing economic incentives.

Conflicts are dynamic, and the underlying factors can evolve over time. Therefore, it is crucial for international organizations, policy makers, and stakeholders to continually reassess and adjust their strategies to address emerging challenges and opportunities. Regular evaluations and consultations with the parties involved allow for course corrections and improvements, enhancing the effectiveness of the economic incentives in resolving regional conflicts. By adhering to these principles and employing effective strategies, international organizations, government policy makers, and stakeholders can significantly contribute to conflict resolution and prevent regional conflicts from escalating into global security crises. The judicious use of economic incentives, coupled with a comprehensive approach and a genuine commitment to peace, can lay the foundation for a more stable and harmonious world.

CONCLUSION

One theory that can be applied to the situation where regional conflicts escalate into global security crises is the "Security Dilemma" theory. The Security Dilemma is a fundamental concept in international relations that explains how a state's actions taken to increase its own security can inadvertently lead to insecurity for other states, ultimately resulting in a spiral of arms races, mistrust, and conflict. In the context of regional conflicts escalating into global security crises, the Security Dilemma theory suggests that as tensions rise between neighboring states, each state may feel compelled to increase its military capabilities and territorial control in order to secure itself against potential threats. However, this behavior can be perceived as aggressive or threatening by other states in the region, leading them to respond in kind by also increasing their military capabilities and territorial control.[1]

This, in turn, can create a situation of heightened insecurity and potential conflict that could escalate into a global security crisis. Another theory that could be applied is the Balance of Power theory. This theory suggests that states seek to balance power in the international system in order to prevent any one state from becoming too dominant or threatening the security of other states. In the context of regional conflicts, neighboring states may seek to balance power in the region by forming alliances, building military capabilities, or engaging in diplomacy to prevent any one state from gaining too much influence or control over the region. However, if these efforts fail and one state does become too dominant or threatening, neighboring states may feel compelled to respond, potentially leading to a global security crisis.

There are many different types of disputes that can arise between states in the international political arena. These can range from relatively minor issues of trade or diplomacy to major conflicts over territory, resources, or ideology.[2] The occurrence of disputes between states encompasses various types that are frequently observed. Territorial disputes constitute one of the most prevalent forms, involving conflicting assertions over land or maritime territories. Such conflicts may arise from historical or cultural boundaries, as well as competition for valuable natural resources like oil, gas, or water.

Resolving territorial disputes often necessitates delving into intricate inquiries concerning sovereignty, international law, and the rights of indigenous populations. Another commonly encountered type of dispute is centered around the competition for finite natural resources, including oil, gas, water, or minerals. These disputes may emerge either between neighboring states or within different regions of a single state. The underlying contention often revolves around matters of resource access, pricing, distribution, and considerations related to environmental protection and sustainable development. Disputes stemming from ideological differences between states also contribute to the landscape of interstate conflicts. Disagreements pertaining to political ideology or values can manifest in various forms, such as conflicts surrounding human rights, democracy, religious freedom, or economic systems. If left unresolved through diplomatic means, these ideological disputes possess the potential to escalate into larger conflicts or even wars.

Moreover, economic competition plays a substantial role in instigating disputes between states. Trade disputes arise from conflicts over tariffs, trade barriers, or protectionist measures that restrict market access. While some trade disputes can be addressed through negotiation or mediation, failure to find resolution may exacerbate the conflict, leading to confrontations that are more substantial. Diplomatic disputes represent another dimension of interstate conflicts, wherein diplomatic relations between states may falter due to disagreements concerning foreign policies, human rights, or other contentious matters. These disputes can result in the expulsion of diplomats, suspension of diplomatic ties, or in extreme cases, military action if tensions escalate. Lastly, military factors can also precipitate conflicts between states. Military disputes may arise from issues such as border disputes, security threats, or disagreements pertaining to military alliances. Resolving military disputes poses considerable challenges due to their severity, potentially culminating in large-scale conflicts or even warfare.

Within the context of this book, various examples of regional conflicts have been presented. However, by employing the theoretical frameworks of security dilemma theory and balance of power theory.[3] We aim to gain insight into significant instances that may contribute to current global security crises. Furthermore, by shedding light on these conflict situations, our intention is to underscore the awareness of the inherent danger.

One such conflict that exemplifies the implications of the security dilemma is the ongoing turmoil in Ukraine. As tensions escalated between Ukraine and Russia, both nations took measures to enhance their military capacities and extend their territorial control. Russia, in particular, annexed Crimea and lent support to separatist movements in eastern Ukraine. These actions were perceived as aggressive by Ukraine and neighboring states, prompting increased militarization and an escalating cycle of conflict. The North Korean nuclear program presents another case that can be interpreted through the lens of the security dilemma. In response to perceived threats from the United States and regional powers, North Korea pursued the development of nuclear weapons and missile capabilities as a means to secure its safety. However, this endeavor has been viewed as a threat by other states in the region, resulting in heightened tensions and the potential for conflict. The ascent of China as a global power can be analyzed using the balance of power theory. As China's economic and military prowess has expanded, neighboring countries like Japan and South Korea have endeavored to counterbalance China's growing influence by bolstering their military capabilities and forging stronger alliances with the United States. Consequently, the theories of security dilemma and balance of power offer valuable frameworks for comprehending the intricate dynamics of global security crises. They underscore how actions taken by one state can lead to unintended consequences for others, consequently fostering a climate of conflict in an ever-evolving global landscape.

This book has highlighted the potential of regional conflicts to escalate and cause a crisis to global security. The cases of conflict in the Middle East, Africa, and Asia demonstrate that regional conflicts can have devastating consequences, including displacement of people, economic devastation, and political instability. It is therefore critical to address regional conflicts and establish preventative measures and effective conflict resolution strategies to prevent them from escalating. Preventative measures can include investment in regional stability and development, and the establishment of diplomatic channels for resolving conflicts. Effective conflict resolution strategies, such as mediation and negotiation, can be used to resolve regional conflicts before they become a crisis.

The role of international institutions, including the United Nations, and regional organizations such as the African Union and the European Union, is also crucial in preventing and resolving regional conflicts. Furthermore, global cooperation is necessary to address regional conflicts and their potential to escalate into a crisis. Sharing intelligence, resources, and technology can help resolve conflicts and prevent their escalation. It is important to recognize that preventing and resolving regional conflicts is not only necessary for global security but for regional stability and prosperity. Sharing information, resources and technologies is crucial in preventing and resolving regional conflicts that pose a threat to global security.[4] If so, specific measures can be presented to implement these methods.

Firstly, strengthening diplomatic efforts is crucial in preventing and resolving conflicts. Governments should actively engage in diplomatic dialogue, negotiations, and mediation to resolve disputes peacefully. Regional organizations and international bodies, such as the United Nations, can play a significant role in facilitating these discussions. Secondly, effective intelligence sharing between nations can help identify potential conflicts at an early stage, enabling proactive measures to prevent escalation. Countries should establish cooperative mechanisms to share intelligence on security threats, including terrorism, arms trafficking, and organized crime. Thirdly, conducting joint military exercises and training programs can build trust, enhance interoperability, and promote cooperation among nations. These exercises allow armed forces to work together, understand each other's capabilities, and develop joint strategies to address common security challenges. Fourthly, economic cooperation and development initiatives can contribute to regional stability by addressing the underlying causes of conflicts, such as poverty, inequality, and lack of resources.

Encouraging trade, investment, and development projects can foster economic interdependence, which often serves as a deterrent to conflicts. Fifthly, sharing technological advancements and building the capabilities of nations can help address security challenges. Developed countries can provide technical assistance, training, and resources to enhance the intelligence, surveillance, and reconnaissance capabilities of less developed nations, enabling them to effectively monitor and address security threats. Sixthly, supporting and participating in international peacekeeping operations can help resolve regional conflicts.

These operations provide a neutral and impartial force to stabilize conflict zones, facilitate negotiations, protect civilians, and monitor ceasefires. Seventhly, encouraging nations to engage in disarmament agreements and non-proliferation treaties can reduce the risk of conflicts stemming from the acquisition and use of weapons of mass destruction. International efforts, such as the Treaty on the Non-Proliferation of Nuclear Weapons, aim to prevent the spread of nuclear weapons and promote disarmament. Eighthly, proactive conflict prevention measures, such as early warning systems, diplomatic interventions, and peacebuilding initiatives, can help mitigate the root causes of conflicts before they escalate.

Engaging in preventive diplomacy and supporting mediation efforts can be effective in resolving disputes at an early stage. Ninthly, collaboration on information and cybersecurity is crucial in preventing and countering cyber threats that can destabilize regions. Countries can share best practices, exchange information on cyber threats, and develop joint strategies to protect critical infrastructure and combat cybercrime. Tenthly, promoting people-to-people interactions, cultural exchange programs, and educational initiatives can foster mutual understanding and reduce tensions between nations.

Building positive relationships at the grassroots level can contribute to long-term peace and stability.

It is important to note that the implementation of these measures requires strong political will, trust, and cooperation among nations. Additionally, the specific approach will vary depending on the context and nature of the regional conflicts being addressed. Even if we look at the current conflicts, they are not limited to domestic problems and they are expanding beyond their own territories, affecting other regions. The conflicts in Syria, Yemen, and Ukraine serve as examples of how regional conflicts can have far-reaching implications that extend beyond their borders.[5] The lessons learned from these conflicts underscore the need for preventative measures and effective conflict resolution strategies. Prevention is critical in addressing regional conflicts, and it should be the primary focus of international efforts. Investing in regional stability and development can help prevent conflicts from arising in the first place. Diplomatic channels should be established to resolve disputes between nations and to prevent conflicts from escalating. Preventative measures can also include early warning systems, economic incentives, and dialogue among stakeholders. Effective conflict resolution is equally important.

The international community should invest in mediation and negotiation to resolve regional conflicts before they become a crisis. The UN and other international institutions should play a leading role in this regard, with regional organizations playing a supportive role. Global cooperation is essential in addressing regional conflicts. The international community must work together to prevent regional conflicts and mitigate their impact. This can involve sharing intelligence, resources, and technology to resolve conflicts and prevent their escalation. Countries should be encouraged to work together to find common ground and to overcome differences. Therefore, it is essential to address regional conflicts and to prevent them from escalating into a crisis. Doing so will require continued research, collaboration, and the development of effective strategies that consider regional and global perspectives. By working together, we can create a safer, more stable, and more prosperous world.

It is clear that addressing regional conflicts is essential to prevent a global crisis from occurring. Preventative measures must be established, including investing in regional stability and development, and creating diplomatic channels for resolving conflicts before they escalate. Effective conflict resolution strategies such as mediation and negotiation must also be employed to resolve regional conflicts before they become a crisis. The importance of international institutions, including the United Nations and regional organizations, in preventing and resolving regional conflicts cannot be overstated. Furthermore, global cooperation is essential to address regional conflicts and prevent their escalation. Countries must be willing to share intelligence, resources, and technology to resolve conflicts and prevent them from spreading.

Accordingly, the development and implementation of effective strategies for addressing regional conflicts will require continued research and collaboration among international institutions, regional organizations, and governments. By working together, we can address regional conflicts and ensure a more stable, prosperous, and peaceful world.

"In short, an internal conflict is more likely to be seen as posing a threat to international peace and security if it is not contained within the territory of the state from whence it sprang,..."[6]

As Michael Edward Brown has pointed out in "The International Dimensions of Internal Conflict," preventing and resolving the spread within the context of regional conflict will not lead to a global security crisis

NOTES

INDEX

NOTES

PREFACE

[1] The Chinese Civil War was fought between the Kuomintang-led government of the Republic of China and forces of the Chinese Communist Party, armed conflict continuing intermittently from 1 August 1927 until 7 December 1949, and ending with Communist control of mainland China. The Communists gained control of mainland China and established the People's Republic of China in 1949, forcing the leadership of the Republic of China to retreat to the island of Taiwan. See Lew, Christopher R.; Leung, Pak-Wah, eds. (2013). Historical Dictionary of the Chinese Civil War. Lanham, Maryland: The Scarecrow Press, Inc: 3. and see also Lary, D. (2015). China's Civil War: A Social History, 1945-1949. United Kingdom: Cambridge University Press.

[2] See Routledge Handbook of State Recognition. (2019). United Kingdom: Taylor & Franci

[3] See The Rise of China. (2015). United Kingdom: Oxford University Press: 174.

[4] The security dangers of the 1990s and beyond are different and more complex than those of the Cold War, and strategic thinkers both in the academic and policy-making spheres must begin to understand the new environment lest they fall into the old trap of planning for the next conflict based on the conditions of the last conflict. See Congressional Record: Proceedings and Debates of the ... Congress. (1971). United States: U.S. Government Printing Office.

[5] Conflict in Syria. Global Conflict Tracker. (n.d.). Global Conflict Tracker. https://www.cfr.org/global-conflict-tracker/conflict/conflict-syria

[6] Contemporary Persian Gulf: Essays in Honour of Gulshan Dietl, Prakash Chandra Jain and Grijesh Pant. (2018). India: Taylor & Francis.

[7] How China's Silk Road Initiative is Changing the Global Economic Landscape. (2019). United Kingdom: Taylor & Francis.

8 In the past, arbitration, direct bargaining, the use of intermediaries, and deference to international institutions were relatively successful tools for managing interstate conflict. In the face of terrorism, intrastate wars, and the multitude of other threats in the post–Cold War era, however, the conflict resolution tool kit must include preventive diplomacy, humanitarian intervention, regional task-sharing, and truth commissions. See Bercovitch, J., Jackson, R. (2009). Conflict Resolution in the Twenty-first Century: Principles, Methods, and Approaches. United States: University of Michigan Press.

INTRODUCTION

1 For his prescient analysis of religious fundamentalism, politics, scientific progress, ethical codes, see Fukuyama, F. (2006). The End of History and the Last Man. United Kingdom: Free Press.

2 Engaging Geopolitics provides a comprehensive introduction to the influence of geography, demography and economics on politics and international relations in the world in which we live today. See Shelley, F. M., Braden, K. E. (2014). Engaging Geopolitics: Taylor & Francis.

3 Blumenthal, D. (2020). The China Nightmare: The Grand Ambitions of a Decaying State. United Kingdom: AEI Press.

4 I can suggest some reputable sources that may contain information related to these topics, such as the United Nations website, which provides information on a wide range of global security and cooperation issues, including peacekeeping, disarmament, and counterterrorism. The website of the North Atlantic Treaty Organization (NATO), which provides information on NATO's role in promoting global security and cooperation, including joint military operations and crisis management. The website of the International Institute for Strategic Studies (IISS), a leading think tank on global security issues, which provides analysis and commentary on a wide range of security issues, including nuclear proliferation, arms control, and counterterrorism. Also, books written by experts in the field, such as "Cooperative Security: The OSCE and Its Code of Conduct" by Wolfgang Zellner, "The New Politics of Global security" by Michael E. Brown, Sean M. Lynn-Jones, and Steven E. Miller, and "Global Security Cooperation:

Theory and Practice" by Emilian Kavalski. These sources may provide more specific information on the sources and origins of the words related to global security cooperation mentioned earlier.

5 Amid Strained Multilateral System, States Must Recommit to United Nations Charter Obligations, Prioritize Human Rights, Secretary-General Tells Security Council | UN Press. (2023, April 24). UN.org. https://press.un.org/

6 See Documents on Disarmament. (1974). United States: United States Arms Control and Disarmament Agency.

I. THE SOURCES OF GLOBAL SECURITY CRISIS

CHAPTER 1. THE UNINHABITABLE EARTH: CLIMATE CHANGE

1 There is a broad consensus that climate change presents the international community with a formidable challenge. Yet progress on all fronts-prevention, mitigation, and adaptation-has been slow. See Sayem, M. A. (2022). Religion and Ecological Crisis: Christian and Muslim Perspectives from John B. Cobb and Seyyed Hossein Nasr. United Kingdom: Taylor & Francis.

2 Environmental ethics necessitate virtues such as interconnection, responsible behavior, inclusive participation, and elaboration of the elements of cumulative obligations. Cultivating Sustainability in Language and Literature Pedagogy: Steps to an Educational Ecology. (2021). United Kingdom: Taylor & Francis.

3 See Climate Change - United Nations Sustainable Development. https://www.un.org/sustainabledevelopment/climate-change/.

4 The Paris Climate Agreement establishes a global goal on adaptation of enhancing adaptive capacity, strengthening resilience and reducing vulnerability to climate change. IPCC — Intergovernmental Panel on Climate Change. https://www.ipcc.ch/.

5 Climate change widespread, rapid, and intensifying. https://www.ipcc.ch.

[6] The global temperature has risen about 0.2 degrees Celsius per decade over the past 10 years. The global average temperature in 2010 was approximately 14.6 degrees Celsius (58.3 degrees Fahrenheit), and it is estimated to be around 14.9 degrees Celsius (58.8 degrees Fahrenheit) in 2020. See WMO Report. THE GLOBAL CLIMATE IN 2015–2019. WMO-No. 1249: 6-7

[7] A Human Health Perspective on Climate Change: A Report Outlining the Research Needs on the Human Health Effects of Climate Change. (2010): 57.

[8] United States: National Institute of Environmental Health S Torti, J. (2012). Floods in Southeast Asia: A health priority. Journal of Global Health, 2(2).https://doi.org/10.7189/jogh.02.020304ciences.

[9] Sub-Saharan Africa (SSA) is one of the regions where climate change is expected to push the most people into poverty (39.7 million) if no concrete climate and development action takes place by 2050. The impacts of climate change could be felt most immensely by those living in fragile and conflict-affected settings in SSA. See Conservation Agriculture in Africa: Climate Smart Agricultural Development. (2022). United Kingdom: CABI. P.23.

[10] Singer, A. J. (2021). Teaching Climate History: There is No Planet B. United Kingdom: Taylor & Francis.

CHAPTER 2. GHOST IN THE WIRES: CYBERSECURITY THREATS

[1] Cyber espionage is a form of cyberattack that steals classified, sensitive data or intellectual property to gain an advantage over a competitive company or government entity. Georgetown Journal of International Affairs: International Engagement on Cyber VI, Fall/Winter 2016, Volume 17, No. 3. United States: Georgetown University Press: 103

[2] See Van Der Staak, S., & Wolf, P. (2019). Cybersecurity in Elections Models of Interagency Collaboration. https://www.idea.int ; and see Defending Democracies: Combating Foreign Election Interference in a Digital Age. (2021). United States: Oxford University Press: 89

[3] Silent Wars: Espionage, Sabotage, and the Covert Battles in Cyberspace. (2023): Fortis Novum Mundum.

[4] Intelligence on the Frontier Between State and Civil Society. (2020). United Kingdom: Taylor & Francis.

5 The Sony Pictures hack resulted in the theft of confidential data and the release of sensitive information, as well as the destruction of thousands of computers. See Urbas, G., Smith, M. (2021). Technology Law: Australian and International Perspectives. India: Cambridge University Press.

6 See A Comprehensive Overview of Global Challenges - P. Kumar, C. IBS. (2023): 34.

7 Himeles, S., & Department of Homeland Security. (2011). Preventing and Defending Against Cyber Attacks. https://www.dhs.gov.

8 For the general state of National cybersecurity strategy of China. See China's Cyberattack Strategy Explained. (2022). Boozallen.com.

9 Human Rights Watch. (2022). China. Retrieved from https://www.hrw.org/asia/china-and-tibet

10 Freedom House. (2021). Freedom on the Net 2021: The Pandemic's Digital Shadow. Retrieved from https://freedomhouse.org/report/freedom-net/2021/pandemics-digital-shadow

11 Center for Strategic and International Studies. (2022). Chinese Cyberpower. Retrieved from https://www.csis.org/programs/technology-policy-program/chinese-cyberpower

12 United Nations. (2019). The United Nations Global Counter-Terrorism Strategy.

13 Council of Europe. (2020). Guide to human rights for internet users. Retrieved from https://rm.coe.int/guide-to-human-rights-for-internet-users-3rd-edition/1680998cbe

CHAPTER 3. GENERATION KILL: TERRORISM

1 This term was borrowed from the title of the book "Generation Kill" written by Evan Wright. "Generation Kill" is a non-fiction book published in 2004 by the American author and journalist Evan Wright. Originally published as a three-part article in Rolling Stone, the book tells of Wright's experiences as a reporter covering the U.S.'s 2003 invasion of Iraq while

embedded with the 1st Reconnaissance Battalion of the U.S. Marine Corps. The title "Generation Kill" refers to the military slang term for the act of killing civilians or non-combatants. See Analysis of Generation Kill by Evan Wright.

[2] Drastic advances in technology and communication have intensified the ever increasing pace of globalization. some views assert that terrorism is spreading not because of globalization but because some people are excluded from globalization. On the other hand, certain views claim that globalization may be one of the main causes of the spread of terrorism because it assists terrorist groups to distribute their literature and enforce their views on like-minded people in other parts of the globe. See Globalization and terrorism: an overview (ResearchGate).

[3] The terrorism threat in Southeast Asia is increasing because of links between local extremists and terrorist groups such as ISIL, with the situation in the southern Philippines of pressing concern. We must plan on the basis that a mass casualty attack against western targets in Southeast Asia will take place. See Global Terrorism Index. (2021). Global Terrorism Index 2021: Measuring the Impact of Terrorism. Retrieved from https://www.visionofhumanity.org/

[4] United Nations Security Council. (2020). Threats to International Peace and Security Caused by Terrorist Acts.

[5] United Nations Office on Drugs and Crime. (2021). Terrorism Prevention and Security Measures. Retrieved from https://www.unodc.org/unodc/en/terrorism/terrorism-prevention.html

[6] United Nations Development Programme. (2021). Preventing Terrorism and Countering Violent Extremism through Inclusive Development. Retrieved from https://www.undp.org/content/undp/en/home/librarypage/democratic-governance/preventing-terrorism-and-countering-violent-extremism-through-i.html

[7] See Algora-Weber, M. (2011). Madrid train bombings: what we have learnt from that sad event. ISBT Science Series, 6(1), 216–218. https://doi.org/10.1111/j.1751-2824.2011.01486.x

[8] See Strom, K., & Eyerman, J. (2008). Interagency Coordination: Lessons Learned From the 2005 London Train Bombings. https://www.ojp.gov.

9 Outlook Web Bureau. (2022, January 19). Mumbai Terror Attacks: What Happened On 26/11? https://www.outlookindia.com ; Wikipedia Contributors. (2023, May 4). 2008 Mumbai attacks. Wikipedia; Wikimedia Foundation. https://en.wikipedia.org/wiki/2008_Mumbai_attacks

10 See Liberty on Hold: France Responds to Terror Attacks. (2016). Opensocietyfoundations.org.

11 For more context on the terrorist incidents, see this book. See European Union Agency for Criminal Justice Cooperation. https://www.eurojust.europa.eu.

12 The Manchester Arena Inquiry is an independent public inquiry, established on 22 October 2019 by the Home Secretary. The purpose of the Manchester Arena Inquiry is to investigate the deaths of the victims of the 2017 Manchester Arena attack. The Attack – Manchester Arena Inquiry. https://manchesterarenainquiry.org.uk/report-volume-one/part-1-missed-opportunities/the-attack/.

13 See Wright, R. (2016). The Jihadi Threat ISIS Al Qaeda and Beyond. https://www.usip.org/sites/default/files/The-Jihadi-Threat-ISIS-Al-Qaeda-and-Beyond.pdf

14 See The Impact of 9/11 on Business. (2023). Investopedia.

15 For a comprehensive collection of cutting-edge essays that investigate the contribution of Critical Terrorism Studies to our understanding of contemporary terrorism and counterterrorism. See Routledge Handbook of Critical Terrorism Studies. (2016). United Kingdom: Taylor & Francis.

16 See US Security and Counterterrorism Legislation Handbook Volume 1 Strategic Information and Basic Laws. (2013). United States: International Business Publications, USA. P.74.

[1] See The Global Nuclear Nonproliferation Regime - Council on Foreign Relations. https://www.cfr.org/report/global-nuclear-nonproliferation-regime.

[2] Nuclear Non-Proliferation in International Law - Volume VI: Nuclear Disarmament and Security at Risk – Legal Challenges in a Shifting Nuclear World. (2021). Netherlands: T.M.C. Asser Press: 472-75.

[3] In the past, U.S. policymakers have avoided rectifying the contradiction by labeling disarmament as a long-term goal. However, this is increasingly unacceptable to non-nuclear weapon states. See Nuclear Scholars Initiative: A Collection of Papers from the 2013 Nuclear Scholars Initiative. (2014). United States: Center for Strategic & International Studies: 26-28.

[4] The numbers provided are approximate estimates based on various sources, including assessments by experts, intelligence agencies, and research organizations. It is important to note that due to the sensitive nature of nuclear arsenals, the exact numbers and details are often subject to uncertainty and speculation. To obtain the most accurate and up-to-date information on nuclear inventories, I recommend referring to reputable sources such as government reports, official statements, international organizations specializing in arms control and non-proliferation, and research institutions focused on nuclear studies. These sources may provide more detailed and precise data on nuclear warhead inventories of different countries.

[5] Source: Own work based on data from MIT. Lewis, D. (2022, December 10). Estimated Global Nuclear Warhead Inventories, 2022 - MIT Faculty Newsletter. MIT Faculty Newsletter.

[6] See Lewis, D. (2022, December 10). Estimated Global Nuclear Warhead Inventories, 2022 - MIT Faculty Newsletter. MIT Faculty Newsletter. https://fnl.mit.edu/november-december-2022/estimated-global-nuclear-warhead-inventories-2022/

[7] Hartle, A., Tian, X., Kizilkaya, Z., Apressyan, R., Kashnikov, B., Leunis, J., Damme, G. V. (2020). Moral Constraints on War: Principles and Cases. United States: Lexington Books.

[8] Against War: Building a Culture of Peace. (2022). United States: Orbis Books.

[9] See the bulletin. 1975: All in our time: A foul and awesome display - Bulletin of the Atomic Scientists. https://thebulletin.org/premium/2020-12/1975-all-in-our-time-a-foul-and-awesome-display/.

[10] The Treaty on the Prohibition of Nuclear Weapons was adopted at the UN Headquarters in New York in July 2017. The Treaty comprehensively prohibits the use, development, export, and possession of nuclear weapons. See Casey-Maslen, S. (2019). The Treaty on the Prohibition of Nuclear Weapons: A Commentary. United Kingdom: OUP Oxford: 4-6.

[11] The New York Times Almanac 2002. (2006). United States: Taylor & Francis: 1173-174.

[12] See SIPRI. We must strengthen multilateralism in a new era of risk

[13] See Khan, Z. (2014). Pakistan's Nuclear Policy: A Minimum Credible Deterrence. United Kingdom: Taylor & Francis.

[14] See Global nuclear arsenals are expected to grow as states continue to modernize–New SIPRI Yearbook out now. (2022, June 13). SIPRI. https://www.sipri.org/media/press-release/2022/global-nuclear-arsenals-are-expected-grow-states-continue-modernize-new-sipri-yearbook-out-now

CHAPTER 5. CATALYST FOR A GLOBAL SECURITY ARCHITECTURE: REGIONAL CONFLICTS

[1] For much of the last half century, the Middle East and North Africa (MENA) has seemed the outlier in global peace. Today Iraq, Libya, Israel/Palestine, Yemen, and Syria are not just countries, but synonyms for prolonged and brutal wars. Cultural Sociology of the Middle East, Asia, and Africa: An Encyclopedia. (2012). India: SAGE Publications: 270-74.

[2] Wittes, T. (2019). Syria's Conflict and the Implications for U.S. National Security. Testimony before the Committee on Armed Services, U.S. Senate. Retrieved from https://www.brookings.edu/testimonies/syrias-conflict-and-the-implications-for-u-s-national-security/

3 Bercovitch, J. (2014). Conflict Prevention. Oxford Research Encyclopedia of International Studies. doi: 10.1093/acrefore/9780190846626.013.26

4 Böhmelt, T., & Pilster, U. (2019). Regional Integration Organizations and Conflict Prevention: A Network Perspective. Conflict Management and Peace Science, 36(2), 119-140. doi: 10.1177/0738894216663197

5 World Bank. (2021). Conflict, Security, and Development. Retrieved from https://www.worldbank.org/en/topic/conflictsecurityanddevelopment

6 Regional mechanisms for the prevention of conflict and violence exist today in the Association of South-East Asian Nations (ASEAN), the African Union (AU), the Economic Community of West African States, the Southern African Development Community, the Organization of American States (OAS), OSCE, and other regional and sub-regional organizations." The AU Charter specifically supports AU action in the event of gross violations of human rights. In addition to these conflict and violence-prevention mechanisms, regional institutions for the promotion and protection of human rights exist in ASEAN, AU, the Council of Europe, OAS, See Bercovitch, J., Jackson, R. (2009). Conflict Resolution in the Twenty-first Century: Principles, Methods, and Approaches. United States: University of Michigan Press: 40-46.

7 Towards World Constitutionalism: Issues in the Legal Ordering of the World Community. (2005). Netherlands: Brill: 441-45

8 Recalibrating U.S. Strategy Toward Russia: A New Time for Choosing. (2017). United States: Center for Strategic & International Studies: 46-48.

9 The Case of Crimea's Annexation Under International Law. (2017). Poland: SCHOLAR Publishing House: 254-56

10 The Russia-Ukraine war is having an outsized impact on the global supply chain, impeding the flow of goods, fueling dramatic cost increases and product shortages, and creating catastrophic food shortages around the world. And Global supply chains continue to be disrupted by the ongoing conflict in Ukraine. However, this article shows that this is not the only influencing factor. Stackpole, B. (2022, July 5). Here's how and why the global supply chain is in crisis. World Economic Forum.

[11] Russia Today. (2022, March 2). Russian Foreign Minister Lavrov: Any crossing of Russia's "red lines" will be met with strong military response. Retrieved from https://www.rt.com/russia/518961-lavrov-russias-red-lines-military-response/

[12] Deutsche Welle. (2022, April 15). NATO-Russia relations plummet amid Ukraine conflict. Retrieved from https://www.dw.com/en/nato-russia-relations-ukraine-conflict/a-61402820

[13] The Washington Post. (2022, July 8). Russian cyberattacks: What you need to know. Retrieved from https://www.washingtonpost.com/politics/2022/07/08/russian-cyberattacks-what-you-need-know/

The Financial Times. (2022, May 23). Russia-Ukraine war escalates energy security fears. Retrieved from https://www.ft.com/content/ea21e88b-f88a-4e33-8e3a-480c4b201e6e

[14] The Financial Times. (2022, May 23). Russia-Ukraine war escalates energy security fears. Retrieved from https://www.ft.com/content/ea21e88b-f88a-4e33-8e3a-480c4b201e6e

II. THE CAUSES OF REGIONAL CONFLICTS

CHAPTER 6. RESOURCE SCARCITY

[1] Salgado, M., Farid, M., Fayad, D., Laurent Kemoe, Lanci, L. S., Mitra, P., Muehlschlegel, T. S., Okou, C., Spray, J. A., Tuitoek, K., & Unsal, F. D. (2022). Climate Change and Chronic Food Insecurity in Sub-Saharan Africa. Departmental Papers, 2022(016). https://doi.org.

[2] Kemp, G., VanDeveer, S. D., Bleischwitz, R., Andrews Speed, P., Johnson, C., Boersma, T. (2014). Want, Waste Or War? The Global Resource Nexus and the Struggle for Land, Energy, Food, Water and Minerals. United Kingdom: Taylor & Francis: 8-9.

[3] Kreye, M. E. Sustainable Operations and Supply Chain Management. United Kingdom: Taylor & Francis.

[4] To find more information and visual representations of water scarcity on the World Health Organization website: https://www.who.int/news-room/fact-sheets/detail/drinking-water

[5] To find more information and visual representations of food scarcity on the FAO website: http://www.fao.org/food-insecurity/en/

[6] See Energy scarcity on the International Energy Agency: https://www.iea.org/reports/world-energy-outlook-2020/access-to-electricity

[7] Metals and mineral resources are key raw materials in many industrial sectors, such as construction, energy, and transportation. Although recovery of many metals in being done through recycling, this still doesn't meet the demand so extraction of primary resources is needed. See this website for more information of mineral scarcity on the World Bank website: https://www.worldbank.org

[8] For more information of land scarcity on the FAO website:

[9] Civil War in Darfur, Sudan. (2003). Climate-Diplomacy. Routledge Handbook of Water and Health. (2015). United Kingdom: Taylor & Francis.

[10] Water Resources in Jordan: Evolving Policies for Development, the Environment, and Conflict Resolution. (2010). United States: Taylor & Francis.

[11] Brears, R. C. (2022). Financing Nature-Based Solutions: Exploring Public, Private, and Blended Finance Models and Case Studies. Switzerland: Springer International Publishing: 9-10.

CHAPTER 7. POLITICAL INSTABILITY

[1] This section is referenced from the following sources: See Smith, J. (2018). The impact of political instability and violence on terrorism in North Africa. Terrorism and Political Violence, 30(1), 125-150.; Ananian, D. (2019). The Syrian Crisis and the European Union's Quest for Political Stability. In The Syrian Conflict (pp. 101-125). Springer, Cham.; Kang, J. (2017). Assessing the Causes of Conflict in the Korean Peninsula: A Political Stability Perspective. Asian Journal of Peacebuilding, 5(1), 3-25.

[2] See The Impact of Global Terrorism on Economic and Political Development: Afro-Asian Perspectives. (2019). United Kingdom: Emerald Publishing Limited.

³ Natural resources are essential to sustaining people and peace in post-conflict countries, but governance failures often jeopardize such efforts. See Governance, Natural Resources and Post-Conflict Peacebuilding. (2016). United Kingdom: Taylor & Francis.

⁴ See Chaitram, S. S. S. (2020). American Foreign Policy in the English-speaking Caribbean: From the Eighteenth to the Twenty-first Century. Germany: Springer International Publishing: 127-29.

CHAPTER 8. ETHNIC AND RELIGIOUS TENSIONS

¹ Reuters. (2022, August 6). New Evidence Shows How Myanmar's Military Planned the Rohingya Purge. VOA; Voice of America (VOA News).

² See CFR. Conflict in Ethiopia. Global Conflict Tracker. https://www.cfr.org.

³ The Ethiopian Orthodox Church has been facing a crisis due to a split in the popular Orthodox Church. A group of rebel bishops declared their own assembly in the Oromia region². This has caused deadly violence and social media and messaging platforms have been restricted ahead of rival planned rallies. The Ethiopian Orthodox Tewahido Church (EOTC) has a version of Christianity that emerged in the fourth century and more than 40% of Ethiopia's population of about 100 million belongs to this church. See Ethiopia Orthodox Church split: Social media restricted - BBC. https://www.bbc.co.uk/news/world-africa-64597375.; See also How the Orthodox Church in Ethiopia can play a role in reconciliation - The Conversation. https://theconversation.com/how-the-orthodox-church-in-ethiopia-can-play-a-role-in-reconciliation-101273.

⁴ Gilead, D. Z. (2022). A World of Soma: A Utopic, Biopsychological, and Happy Science Fiction Novel : iUniverse; Sudan – Darfur «World Without Genocide - Making It Our Legacy. (2021). Worldwithoutgenocide.org. https://worldwithoutgenocide.org/genocides-and-conflicts/darfur-genocide

⁵ Responding to a diplomatic stalemate and a catastrophic humanitarian crisis, Yemen's civil actors work every day to build peace in fragmented local communities across the country. See Yemen: the Sectarianization of a

Political Conflict | ISPI. (2022, December 9). ISPI. https://www.ispionline.it/en/ publication/yemen-sectarianization-political-conflict-19933

[6] Religion and Extremism stresses that the ideological rejection of diversity underlies religious extremism resulting in violent behaviours and, increasingly, in hardening social and religious attitudes and responses. See Religion and Violence. (2016). Switzerland: MDPI AG.

[7] See New African. (1991). United Kingdom: IC Magazines Limited.

CHAPTER 9. THE ROLE OF FOREIGN POWERS

[1] Throughout the course of the Syrian Civil War, regularized military and political exchanges strengthened the Russia-Iran relationship while contributing to greater coherence between Moscow and Tehran on the limits and parameters of cooperation. Political Handbook of the World 2016-2017. (2017). United States: SAGE Publications.

[2] The democratic promise of the 2011 Arab Spring has unraveled in Yemen, triggering a disastrous crisis of civil war, famine, militarization, and governmental collapse with serious implications for the future of the region. See Lackner, H. (2019). Yemen in Crisis: Road to War. United Kingdom: Verso Books: 54-55.

[3] See Dienel, H. (2016). Linking Networks: The Formation of Common Standards and Visions for Infrastructure Development. United Kingdom: Taylor & Francis.

[4] In the 1960s and 1970s, the Chinese government supported African Independence Movements and gave aid to newly independent African nations. Among the most notable early projects were the 1,860 km TAZARA Railway, linking Zambia and Tanzania, which China helped to finance and build from 1970 to 1975. See Global Land Grabs: History, Theory and Method. (2016) : Taylor & Francis.

[5] See China in Africa | Council on Foreign Relations. https://www.cfr.org.

[6] China Global Investment Tracker (CGIT). (2022). American Enterprise Institute. Retrieved from https://www.aei.org/china-global-investment-tracker/

[7] United Nations Conference on Trade and Development (UNCTAD). (2020). World Investment Report 2020. United Nations.

[8] Kaplinsky, R. (2014). A new era in African manufacturing? International Journal of Technological Learning, Innovation and Development, 7(1), 9-23.

[9] Alden, C., Chen, L., & Soares de Oliveira, R. (2018). China's presence in Africa: Investments, infrastructure, and influence. Oxford Research Encyclopedia of International Studies.

[10] International Trade Administration. (2018). Africa: United States Department of Commerce. Retrieved from https://legacy.trade.gov/td/sectors/itafta/

[11] See Chinese Investment in Africa Rises as Project Values and Bilateral .... https://www.iisd.org/articles/chinese-investment-africa-bilateral-trade-decline ; See also Chinese Investment in Africa - China Africa Research Initiative.

[12] Oluwole, V. (2022, February 20). China ranks ahead of America as the largest investor in Africa since 2010. Business Insider Africa; Business Insider Africa. ; Africa: FDI flow from China by country | Statista ; Leading countries investing in Africa | Statista. https://www.statista.com/statistics/1122389/leading-countries-for-fdi-in-africa-by-investor-country/.

[13] There are several sources where you can find graphic data on China's investment statistics by African country. China Africa Research Initiative (CARI): CARI is a research program at Johns Hopkins University that tracks Chinese investment in Africa. They provide an online database that includes information on China's investments in each African country. You can access their data visualization tool here: https://www.sais-cari.org/data-china-africa-investment.AidData: They have a data visualization tool that allows you to explore Chinese investment in different countries, including in Africa.

See also "The United Nations Conference on Trade and Development (UNCTAD)": UNCTAD provides data on FDI flows to different countries and regions. Similar to the World Bank, their data may not specifically break down investment by China, but it can provide you with an overall picture of investment trends in each African country. You can access their data here: https://unctad.org/statistics.

[14] Angola enjoyed a remarkable oil bonanza from 2002 to 2014, as the end of a long-running civil war coincided with a rise in oil production, high world oil prices, and large reconstruction assistance from China. Angola: Where did

all the money go? Part 3, the China connection. https://www.theafricareport.com.

[15] The following articles can help you understand the implications of Chinese investment for African countries. See What China Wants From Africa? Everything – Forbes ; Chinese investment in Angola: The evolution of a profitable ; Why Is China Building Africa? - Forbes.

[16] The persistence of corruption, sectarian bias towards Alawites, nepotism and widespread bribery that existed in party, bureaucracy and military led to popular anger that resulted in the eruption of the 2011 Syrian Revolution. The country ranked 129th out of 183 countries as per the 2011 Corruption Perceptions Index. See Davis, J. (2016). The Arab Spring and Arab Thaw: Unfinished Revolutions and the Quest for Democracy. United Kingdom: Taylor & Francis.

III. THE IMPACT OF REGIONAL CONFLICTSON GLOBAL SECURITY.

CHAPTER 10. THE DISPLACEMENT OF MILLIONS OF PEOPLE

[1] United Nations High Commissioner for Refugees (UNHCR). (2022). Figures at a Glance. Retrieved from https://www.unhcr.org/figures-at-a-glance.html

[2] With refugee resettlement at a record low in 2020, UNHCR calls on States to offer places and save lives - UNHCR Nordic and Baltic Countries. (2020). UNHCR Nordic and Baltic Countries. **https://www.unhcr.org/neu/ 50329-**with-refugee-resettlement-at-a-record-low-in-2020-unhcr-calls-on-states-to-offer-places-and-save-lives.html

[3] At least 89.3 million people around the world have been forced to flee their homes. Among them are nearly 27.1 million refugees, around half of whom are under the age of 18. See Figures at a Glance - UNHCR Philippines. (2021). https://www.unhcr.org.

[4] See Federal Democracies. (2010). United Kingdom: Taylor & Francis.

[5] PIIE. Designing a National Strategy for Responding to Economic Dislocation. https://www.piie.com/. See Social Dislocation. (2020, April 9). Arthashastra; https://ecotalker.wordpress.com.

---

⁶ The European Union's Broader Neighborhood: Challenges and Opportunities for Cooperation Beyond the European Neighbourhood Policy. (2015). United Kingdom: Taylor & Francis.

⁷ International migration is at an all-time high. However, government officials, policy makers, NGO advocates, academic researchers and international agencies have only recently begun to consider the human rights dimension of migration. See The Human Rights of Migrants. (2001). Switzerland: IOM/OIM.

CHAPTER 11. THE SPREAD OF VIOLENCE AND EXTREMISM

¹ FitzGerald, D. S., Arar, R. (2022). The Refugee System: A Sociological Approach. United Kingdom: Polity Press.

² The seven years of continuous conflict have taken a heavy toll on the population at various levels. About 23.4 million Yemenis (73% of the population) have become dependent on humanitarian aid. The military operations had caused the internal displacement of 4.3 million Yemenis by March 2022. About 40% of them are living in unofficial displacement camps and do not have adequate access to basic services. See Displacement, humanitarian needs surging inside Afghanistan and across region. (2022, February 8). UN News.

³ According to the United Nations Develop Programme (UNDP), Insurgency-related conflicts claimed the lives of almost 350,000 lives in the North-eastern part of Nigeria up till the end 2020, Since 2009, the North-east has been the theatre of the violent campaigns of the Islamic extremist group, Boko Haram, its breakaway group, the Islamic State's West Africa Province (ISWAP), and counter-insurgency forces. See Boko Haram, including JAS, ISWAP and Ansaru. (2021). European Union Agency for Asylum.

⁴ See Topic in Focus: Countering Violent Extremism – Africa Center for Strategic Studies. (2022, April 4). Africa Center for Strategic Studies. https://africacenter.org/in-focus/countering-violent-extremism-in-africa/

⁵ Bhatia, K., & Ghanem, H. (2017: 10): unemployed or underemployed educated Arab youth are more likely to be radicalized is cause for serious concern, because unemployment in many Arab countries seems to rise with the level of education, and many new graduates are only able to find low-

paying jobs in the informal sector. This underlines the importance of education and labor market reforms for preventing violent extremism. See Basic Needs and the Urban Poor: The Provision of Communal Services. (2017). United Kingdom: Taylor & Francis.

CHAPTER 12. THE DISRUPTION OF GLOBAL TRADE AND COMMERCE

[1] See Global Communications: opportunities for trade and aid.. (1995). United States: Office of technology assessment Washington D.C.

[2] The conflict is a major blow to the global economy that will hurt growth and raise prices. Beyond the suffering and humanitarian crisis from Russia's invasion of Ukraine, the entire global economy will feel the effects of slower growth and faster inflation Impacts will flow through three main channels. One, higher prices for commodities like those that food and energy will push up inflation further, in turn eroding the value of incomes and weighing on demand. Two, neighboring economies in particular will grapple with disrupted trade, supply chains, and remittances as well as an historic surge in refugee flows. And three, reduced business confidence and higher investor uncertainty will weigh on asset prices, tightening financial conditions and potentially spurring capital outflows from emerging markets. See Cordner, L. (2017). Maritime Security Risks, Vulnerabilities and Cooperation: Uncertainty in the Indian Ocean. Germany: Springer International Publishing.

[3] See Alok Raj et al. (2022). Supply chain management during and post-COVID-19 pandemic: Mitigation strategies and practical lessons learned, Journal of Business Research, Volume 142.

[4] In 2019, the trade level between U.S. and China decreased significantly with an over 10 percentage point. In 2019, U.S. exports to China were $106.6 billion, an 11.3% ($13.5 billion) decrease from 2018; U.S. imports from China were $452.2 billion, a 16.2% ($87.4 billion) decrease; and the trade deficit was $345.6 billion, a 17.6% ($73.9 billion) decrease. See U.S. Department of Commerce, Office of Technology Evaluation. (2019). U.S. Trade with China.

[5] Consumers always pay the price for increasing tariffs as these costs are passed-through to customers by importers. Economists tell us that eventually, consumers will balk at increased prices and stop or limit buying your product.

Most companies simply cannot or will not absorb the additional cost of goods sold burdened with 25% tariffs, and instead will tack on the increased costs to the selling price of finished products. See Agricultural Economics Report. (1965). United States: Department of Agricultural Economics, Michigan State University.

[6] Robinson, A. (2017). Modern Approaches to Manufacturing Improvement: The Shingo System. United States: Taylor & Francis.

[7] Zdouc, W., Van den Bossche, P. (2017). The Law and Policy of the World Trade Organization: Text, Cases and Materials. United Kingdom: Cambridge University Press: 86-87.

[8] Harvard Business Review (2020) reported Global Supply Chains in a Post-Pandemic World: When the Covid-19 pandemic subsides, the world is going to look markedly different. The supply shock that started in China in February and the demand shock that followed as the global economy shut down exposed vulnerabilities in the production strategies and supply chains of firms just about everywhere. Temporary trade restrictions and shortages of pharmaceuticals, critical medical supplies, and other products highlighted their weaknesses.

[9] The world is getting richer, but fragile countries and territories are not. By 2015, most of the poor will live in these economies, most of which have been or still are affected by civil conflicts. Lukas Rüttinger et al. (2022).

[10] The statistics and status data in this section were compiled from a variety of sources, including: Peterson Institute for International Economics (PIIE). (2021). Trade Wars: The Costs of Trump's Trade Policies Revisited.; United States Trade Representative (USTR). (2018). Findings of the Investigation into China's Acts, Policies, and Practices Related to Technology Transfer, Intellectual Property, and Innovation under Section 301 of the Trade Act of 1974.; United States Trade Representative (USTR). (2019). Update Concerning China's Acts, Policies, and Practices Related to Technology Transfer, Intellectual Property, and Innovation.; United States Trade Representative (USTR). (2020). Report to Congress on China's WTO Compliance. ; World Trade Organization (WTO). (2021). Trade Forecast: Strong Rebound but Uneven Recovery.; International Monetary Fund (IMF). (2022). World Economic Outlook: Managing Divergent Recoveries.

CHAPTER 13. THE OUTBREAK OF WAR

[1] World Drug Report 2020. (2020). United Nations : World Drug Report 2020. https://wdr.unodc.org/wdr2020/en/index2020.html

[2] See Global security Management: New Solutions to Complexity. (2020). Germany: Springer International Publishing: 3-4.

[3] Christie M. Gardiner, Fernand de Varennes (2020) discusses human rights : While formal accession to core international human rights instruments is commonplace across the region, the realisation of human rights for many remains elusive as development pressure, violent conflict, limited political will and discrimination maintain human rights volatility.   ; Crock, M., Saul, B., McCallum, R. C., Smith-Khan, L. (2017). The Legal Protection of Refugees with Disabilities: Forgotten and Invisible?. United Kingdom: Edward Elgar Publishing Limited.

[4] See Wall, K., Cortright, D., Seyle, C. (2017). Governance for Peace: How Inclusive, Participatory and Accountable Institutions Promote Peace and Prosperity. United Kingdom: Cambridge University Press.

[5] Ericsson, F. (2023, March 9) reports an analysis in the article of "'"Changing the way they live": In 2014 the bestial jihadist Sunni-group ISIS popped up as a strong, armed force in Iraq. ISIS grew strong in the chaos and power vacuum that had occurred in Syria, and in 2014 it crossed the border to also include Iraq in its struggle to create an Islamic state. See Wayne, C., Mintz, A., Valentino, N. A.(2021). Beyond Rationality: Behavioral Political Science in the 21st Century. United Kingdom: Cambridge University Press.

[6] Yemen has faced continuing crises since 2010. The fighting and divisions have destroyed much of Yemen's physical, political and social infrastructure, undermining its tribal traditions and religious tolerance, and impoverishing the country. The outbreak of war in 2015 caused the world's worst humanitarian crisis. Building a New Yemen: Recovery, Transition and the International Community. (2021). United Kingdom: Bloomsbury Publishing.; See also Rethinking Peace Mediation: Challenges of Contemporary Peacemaking Practice. (2021). United Kingdom: Bristol University Press.

[7] See Russian Trade Policy: Achievements, Challenges and Prospects. (2019). United Kingdom: Taylor & Francis.

[8] Routledge International Handbook of Migration Studies. (2019). United Kingdom: Taylor & Francis. ; Salisbury, P., Hill, G., Kinninmont, J., Northedge, L. (2015). Yemen: Corruption, Capital Flight and Global Drivers of Conflict. United Kingdom: Royal Institute of International Affairs.

[9] The OAS and the AU have had an ongoing collaborative relationship since 2007, when a "Declaration of Intent to Cooperate" was signed by both organizations. Two years after this Declaration, a Memorandum of Understanding (MOU) was finalized between the OAS General Secretariat and the Commission of the African Union (2009). See Fretter, J., Bercovitch, J. (2004). Regional Guide to International Conflict and Management from 1945 to 2003. United States: SAGE Publications: 25.

[10] South China Sea | Council on Foreign Relations. (2020). Council on Foreign Relations. https://www.cfr.org/south-china-sea

[11] United Nations Office on Drugs and Crime. (2021). United Nations : Office on Drugs and Crime. https://www.unodc.org/

IV. THE CHALLENGES OF RESOVING REGIONAL CONDLICTS

CHAPTER 14. THE LACK OF INTERNATIONAL COOPERATION

[1] Steven Patton. (2019). "The Peace of Westphalia and it Affects on International Relations, Diplomacy and Foreign Policy": The Treaty of Westphalia is considered the beginning of modern international relations since it introduced the concepts of sovereignty, mediation, and diplomacy. The treaty ended the Thirty and Eighty Years Wars and created the framework for modern international relations. The concept of state sovereignty is one of the most important principles introduced by the treaty. It is intended to preserve the existing political situation and the distribution of forces. The treaty also introduced the principle of political balance. See Elliot, J. M., Reginald, R. (2007). The Arms Control, Disarmament, and Military Security Dictionary. United States: Wildside Press, LLC: 123-24.

[2] See Routledge Companion to Media and Humanitarian Action. (2017). United Kingdom: Taylor & Francis.

³ See Taylor, E. (2010). What Does That Mean? Exploring Mind, Meaning, and Mysteries. United States: Hay House: 123-24

⁴ The United Nations mattered only to the extent that it could make a useful contribution to solving the problems and accomplishing the tasks just outlined. Those were the problems and the tasks which affected the everyday lives of people. It was on how the Organization handled them that the utility of the United Nations would be judged. If that point was lost sight of, the United Nations would have little or no role to play at all in the twenty-first century. See "We the peoples: The role of the United Nations in the 21ˢᵗ Century" presented to GENERAL ASSEMBLY BY SECRETARY-GENERAL | UN Press. (2000, April 3). Un.org.

⁵ See Ferguson, R., Coleman, P. T. (2014). Making Conflict Work: Harnessing the Power of Disagreement. United States: Houghton Mifflin Harcourt: 14-16.

⁶ "The Future of Power" by Joseph S. Nye Jr. analyzes the international fault lines of the twenty-first century and shows how U.S. power and influence can best be deployed to resolve them. He addresses the evolving notion of power in a new world of non-state actors and emerging economies See Joseph S. Nye, Jr.(2011). The Future of Power. United Kingdom: Public Affairs.

⁷ Colombia's 2016 Peace Accord ended five decades of conflict with the Revolutionary Armed Forces of Colombia (FARC) and represents the path to lasting peace. The United States has a long history of supporting the Peace Accord, and we value its continuing implementation and achievements thus far. See Truth, Justice and Reconciliation in Colombia: Transitioning from Violence. (2018). United Kingdom: Taylor & Francis.

⁸ See Treaty on the Non-Proliferation of Nuclear Weapons (NPT) | IAEA. (2016, June 8). Iaea.org. https://www.iaea.org/topics/non-proliferation-treaty

⁹ The Coordination of Humanitarian Affairs (OCHA) is responsible for coordinating the global emergency response to save lives and protect people in humanitarian crises. OCHA advocates for effective and principled humanitarian action by all, for all. OCHA coordinates humanitarian response to expand the reach of humanitarian action, improve prioritization and reduce duplication, ensuring that assistance and protection reach the people who need it most.

[10] Crisis Group. (2019). Syria: Towards a new international order? International Crisis Group. https://www.crisisgroup.org/middle-east-north-africa/eastern-mediterranean/syria/227-syria-towards-new-international-order

[11] Mearsheimer, J. J. (2001). The tragedy of great power politics. W. W. Norton & Company.

[12] Ikenberry, G. J. (2018). The end of liberal international order? International Affairs, 94(1), 7-23.

[13] Barnett, M. (2011). Empire of humanity: A history of humanitarianism. Cornell University Press.

[14] Jentleson, B. W. (2014). American foreign policy: The dynamics of choice in the 21st century. W. W. Norton & Company.

CHAPTER 15. THE DIFFICULTY OF BUILDING TRUST BETWEEN WARRING PARTIES

[1] The United Nations Security Council adopted Resolution 242 on November 22, 1967, in an effort to secure a just and lasting peace in the wake of the Six-Day War. The resolution is considered one of the most important documents in the history of the Arab-Israeli conflict[1]. It calls for the withdrawal of Israeli armed forces from territories occupied in the recent conflict and for respect for the sovereignty, territorial integrity, and political independence of every state in the area and their right to live in peace within secure and recognized boundaries free from threats or acts of force. See CFR. What Is U.S. Policy on the Israeli-Palestinian Conflict? Council on Foreign Relations. https://www.cfr.org

[2] Israel and Palestinian Territories: the region is home to some two million Palestinians in the Gaza Strip and three million in the West Bank. Although most of Israel's 9.5 million residents are Jewish, there are around two million Arab citizens. International diplomatic efforts to broker a political settlement have made limited headway. More recent U.S.-led diplomacy has focused on resolving several core issues. .

[3] See Hauss, C. (2010). International Conflict Resolution 2nd Ed.. United Kingdom: Bloomsbury Academic: 102-103.

[4] See Doudou Sidibé. (2020). Negotiating peace agreements in internal conflicts: What Perspectives? Negotiations, 33(1), 41–56. Available at https://www.cairn.info/revue-negociations-2020-1-page-41.htm See also Which Side Are You On? Bias, Credibility, and Mediation. Andrew Kydd. American Journal of Political Science. Vol. 47, No. 4 (Oct., 2003): 597-611. Published By: Midwest Political Science Association

[5] Watch YouTube Providence College. (2011). The Underlying Causes of the Conflict in Northern Ireland between Catholics and Protestants. [Video] https://youtu.be/eW9TgEOPaLI. And see also InterTradeIreland helps SMEs across the island by offering practical cross-border business funding, intelligence and contacts. InterTradeIreland. Helping small businesses in Ireland and Northern Ireland. (2023).

CHAPTER 16. THE ROLE OF DIPLOMACY AND MEDIATION

[1] See Nations, U. (2016). A New Era of Conflict and Violence. United Nations. https://www.un.org/en/un75/new-era-conflict-and-violence

[2] What began as protests against President Assad's regime in 2011 quickly escalated into a full-scale war between the Syrian government—backed by Russia and Iran—and anti-government rebel groups—backed by the United States, Saudi Arabia, Turkey, and others in the region. Three campaigns drive the conflict: Conflict in Syria | Global Conflict Tracker. (2015). See also Syria's War and the Descent Into Horror. (2019). Council on Foreign Relations. https://www.cfr.org/article/syrias-civil-war

[3] The OSCE's origins go back to 1975, when the countries in the two opposing blocs in the Cold War signed the Helsinki Final Act, enshrining principles such as territorial integrity and respect for human rights. The act was followed by a series of follow-up meetings to monitor implementation, in a process known as the Conference on Security and Co-operation in Europe (CSCE). Following the adoption of the 1990 Paris Charter envisaging a new post-Cold War European order, in 1995 the CSCE was put on a more permanent, institutional basis and renamed the OSCE. See Global Community Will Be Judged by Way It Responds to "Horrors" in Ukraine, Intergovernmental Organization Chair Tells Security Council | UN Press. (2022, March 14). Un.org. https://press.un.org/en/2022/sc14828.doc.htm

[4] The UN Security Council has the primary responsibility for international peace and security. The General Assembly and the Secretary-General play major, important, and complementary roles, along with other UN offices and bodies. See Nations, U. (2018). Maintain International Peace and Security | United Nations. United Nations; United Nations. https://www.un.org/en/our-work/maintain-international-peace-and-security

[5] See Dolan, C. J. (2018). Obama and the Emergence of a Multipolar World Order: Redefining U.S. Foreign Policy. United States: Lexington Books: 74-76

[6] The trajectory and ultimate outcome of the war will, of course, be determined largely by the policies of Ukraine and Russia. But Kyiv and Moscow are not the only capitals with a stake in what happens. This war is the most significant interstate conflict in decades, and its evolution will have major consequences for the United States. See Charap, S., & Priebe, M. (2023, January 25). Avoiding a Long War: U.S. Policy and the Trajectory of the Russia-Ukraine Conflict. Rand.org; RAND Corporation. https://www.rand.org.

[7] French President Emmanuel Macron has pointed to the 2015 Minsk Agreement between Kyiv and Moscow as the blueprint for a breakthrough in the Ukraine crisis. Following talks with his Russian and Ukrainian counterparts, Macron said on Tuesday that the Minsk II agreement – which was aimed at ending the war in eastern Ukraine – is the "only path on which peace can be built". See Jazeera, A. (2022, February 9). Ukraine-Russia crisis: What is the Minsk agreement? Al Jazeera. https://www.aljazeera.com

[8] See Annan, Kofi. "Intervention to the General Assembly of the United Nations." United Nations. September 24, 1999. [https://www.un.org/press]; United Nations Guidance for Effective Mediation. United Nations. 2012. [https://peacemaker.un.org/sites/peacemaker.un.org/files/Guidance%20for%20Effective%20Mediation.pdf]

CHAPTER 17. PRINCIPLE OF CONFLICT RESOLUTION

[1] Creative problem solving is less structured than other innovation processes and encourages exploring open-ended solutions. It also focuses on developing new perspectives and fostering creativity in solving any regional conflicts. See Encyclopedia of Giftedness, Creativity, and Talent. (2009). United States: SAGE Publications: 354.

[2] See Rothman, J. (2017). Re-Envisioning Conflict Resolution: Vision, Action and Evaluation in Creative Conflict Engagement. United Kingdom: Taylor & Francis.

[3] See Kingston, A. (2023). Cold War: America vs. Soviet Union. (n.p.): A.J.Kingston. See also Haass, R. N. (2014). Foreign Policy Begins at Home: The Case for Putting America's House in Order. United States: Basic Books.

[4] The Eritrean–Ethiopian War, also known as the Badme War, was a major armed conflict between Ethiopia and Eritrea that took place from May 1998 to June 2000. After Eritrea gained independence from Ethiopia, relations were initially friendly. However, disagreements about where the newly created international border should be caused relations to deteriorate significantly, eventually leading to full scale war. See Janssen, S. (2020). The World Almanac and Book of Facts 2021. United Kingdom: Skyhorse Publishing.

[5] The conflict ended after the two countries signed a peace deal in Algiers in December 2000. The fundamental reason for the Ethiopia-Eritrea war is the competing economic interest and personal animosity between Eritrea's ruling party, Eritrean People's Liberation Front [EPLF], and the formerly dominant member party of EPRDF [Ethiopian People's Revolutionary Democratic Front], Tigray People's Liberation Front [TPLF] – and their leadership.

See Gebreselassie, E. (2019, July 9). Between peace and uncertainty after Ethiopia-Eritrea deal. Al Jazeera. https://www.aljazeera.com/features/ 2019/7/9/between-peace-and-uncertainty-after-ethiopia-eritrea-deal

[6] The immediate cause of the eruption of conflict was a dispute over their 1000-km border, which was never fully demarcated when Eritrea peacefully

seceded from Ethiopia in 1993. The underlying causes are believed to have been divergent economic policies, within national economies that were heavily dependent on one another, and personal antagonism between the two leaders who had been allies in a rebellion against the former Ethiopian regime of Mengistu. The three main fronts in the war were at Badme in the west, Zela Ambessa-Egala in the central area and Burrie in the east. See UCDP - Uppsala Conflict Data Program. (2023). Ucdp.uu.se.

CHAPTER 18. DIPLOMATIC EFFORTS

[1] public diplomacy offers a mechanism for achieving foreign policy breakthroughs and conflict resolution but one that has not yet been either theoretically articulated or empirically tested. See Academic. (n.d.). Public Diplomacy and International Conflict Resolution: A Cautionary Case from Cold War South America | Foreign Policy Analysis | Oxford Academic. https://academic.oup.com/fpa/article/16/1/1/5380601. See also Svetlana Radtchenko-Draillard. Psychology and Diplomacy in the Analysis of Negotiation: the Unavoidable Links and the Inevitable Interdependencies. 2021.

[2] By integrating the realms of soft power diplomacy and conflict resolution, this proposal puts forth a comprehensive framework for a distinctive form of peace diplomacy found in Scandinavia. The diverse approaches, policies, and mediation tactics employed by the three Scandinavian nations underscore the significance of diplomatic endeavors and the cultivation of conflict resolution through a gradual process that fosters trust and comprehension among the conflicting parties. See Levitan, N. (2023). Scandinavian Diplomacy and the Israeli-Palestinian Conflict: Official and Unofficial Soft Power. (n.p.): Taylor & Francis.

[3] Shuttle diplomacy, or mediated communication, can be useful in these types of situations, at least in the early stages when direct communication is likely to be counterproductive. The essence of shuttle diplomacy is the use of a third party to convey information back and forth between the parties, serving as a reliable means of communication less susceptible to the grandstanding of face-to-face or media-based communication. See corissajoy. (2016, July 12). Shuttle   Diplomacy.   Beyond   Intractability.

https://www.beyondintractability.org/; Princen, T. (2014). Intermediaries in International Conflict. United States: Princeton University Press: 173.

[4] See LIFE John F. Kennedy: The Legacy. (2017). United Kingdom: TI Incorporated Books. And "The Cold War: The Definitive Encyclopedia and Document Collection" [5 Volumes]. (2020). United States: ABC-CLIO.

[5] The Iran-Iraq War ended in August 1990 when Iraq agreed to Iranian terms for the settlement of the war. The terms included the withdrawal of Iraqi troops from occupied Iranian territory, division of sovereignty over the Shaṭṭ Al-Arab waterway, and a prisoner-of-war exchange. See Iran-Iraq War: Causes, Summary, Casualties, & Facts. And "Iran-Iraq War - Summary, Timeline & Legacy - HISTORY." https://www.history.com/topics/middle-east/iran-iraq-war. **See also T**ucker, S. C. (2008). The Encyclopedia of the Arab-Israeli Conflict: A Political, Social, and Military History. United Kingdom: ABC-CLIO.

[6] To access the content of the Oslo Accords (officially referred to as the Declaration of Principles on Provisional Self-Government), a bilateral agreement signed by Israel and the Palestine Liberation Organization (PLO) on September 13, 1993, following extensive covert deliberations held in Washington, DC, please refer to the Nations, U. (2023). Refworld | Declaration of Principles on Interim Self-Government Arrangements ("Oslo Agreement"). And also Milestones: 1993–2000 - Office of the Historian. (2023). State.gov. https://history.state.gov/milestones/1993-2000/oslo

[7] See PA-X: Peace Agreements Database. (2023). Peaceagreements.org. https://www.peaceagreements.org/ and Szewczyk, B. M. J. (2010). The EU in Bosnia and Herzegovina: Powers, Decisions and Legitimacy. France: European Union Institute for Security Studies.

CHAPTER 19. PEACEKEEPING MISSIONS

[1] The first UN peacekeeping mission was established in May 1948, when the UN Security Council authorized the deployment of a small number of UN military observers to the Middle East to form the United Nations Truce Supervision Organization (UNTSO) to monitor the Armistice Agreement between Israel and its Arab neighbours. Over the past 70 years, more than 1 million men and women have served under the UN flag in more than 70 UN

peacekeeping operations. More than 100,000 military, police and civilian personnel from 125 countries currently serve in 14 peacekeeping operations. See UN Peacekeeping: 70 Years of Service & Sacrifice. (2020). United Nations Peacekeeping. https://peacekeeping.un.org/en/un-peacekeeping-70-years-of-service-sacrifice

[2] Bangladesh Army in Overseas Operations. (2017). Bangladesh: Overseas Operations Directorate, Bangladesh Army Headquarters.

[3] South Sudan is one of the world's most divided and unstable countries. Since achieving statehood in 2011, the country has plunged into civil war (2013-15) and become the scene of some of the worst human rights abuses on the African continent. Despite ongoing political turmoil, states and international institutions have pledged enormous resources to stabilize the country and shore up the current peace process, but have had limited influence in dealing with the effects of rampant corruption and factionalism. See The Challenge of Governance in South Sudan: Corruption, Peacebuilding, and Foreign Intervention. (2018). United Kingdom: Taylor & Francis.

[4] The United Nations Interim Force in Lebanon (UNIFIL) was created by the Security Council in March 1978 to confirm Israeli withdrawal from Lebanon, restore international peace and security and assist the Lebanese Government in restoring its effective authority in the area. According to the UNIFIL website, its mandate is to monitor the cessation of hostilities, accompany and support the Lebanese armed forces as they deploy throughout the south of Lebanon, and assist the Government of Lebanon in ensuring the return of its effective authority in the area. It is difficult to say whether UNIFIL has successfully carried out its mission. While there have been no major conflicts between Israel and Lebanon since 2006, there have been several incidents that have threatened to escalate into full-scale conflict. The situation remains tense, and UNIFIL continues to play an important role in maintaining stability in the region. See The Oxford Handbook of the Use of Force in International Law. (2015). United Kingdom: OUP Oxford and UNIFIL | United Nations Peacekeeping. And also See Debating UN peacekeeping in Lebanon - Brookings. https://www.brookings.edu.

[5] See The United Nations in Iraq. (2020). The United Nations in Iraq | the United Nations in Iraq. https://iraq.un.org/en/about/about-the-un

[1] See Gorbachev's New Thinking and Third World Conflicts. (1990). United States: Transaction Publishers.

[2] See Disaster Upon Disaster: Exploring the Gap Between Knowledge, Policy and Practice. (2019). Germany: Berghahn Books. And also see Oxford Textbook of Social Psychiatry. (2022). United Kingdom: OUP Oxford.

[3] Natural resources such as land, water, timber, minerals, metals and oil are vitally important sources of livelihoods, income and influence for countries and communities around the globe. When natural resources are poorly managed or inequitably shared, however, or when business operations are implemented without due consideration for context and communities, they can contribute to tensions that can escalate into violent conflict, or feed into and exacerbate pre-existing conflict dynamics. See Sustainable Development: Critical Issues. (2001). Ukraine: OECD Publishing.

[4] See Ali, M., Kollmann et al. "School for Advanced International Studies Northern Ireland": Understanding Conflict 2008 Student Field Trip to Northern Ireland. Retrieved May 15, 2023, from https://sais.jhu.edu.

[5] Guardian staff reporter. (2018, March 6). West Virginia teachers' strike ends as lawmakers accept pay demands. https://www.theguardian.com.

[6] The United States was one of the countries that signed the agreement. However, there were some disagreements between the United States and Iran over the terms of the agreement. Some members of Congress were also opposed to the agreement. However, President Obama was able to secure enough support to prevent Congress from blocking the agreement. See Quarterly Current Affairs - October to December 2018 for Competitive Exams Vol 4. (n.d.). (n.p.): Disha Publications.

[7] As one example of economic incentives to resolve disputes, Khartoum and Juba agreed earlier in June to repair oil infrastructure facilities destroyed by the war within three months to boost production and said a joint force would be established to protect the oilfields from attacks by rebel forces on either side of the conflict. See Abdelaziz, K. (2018, June 27). South Sudan rivals sign peace agreement in Khartoum. U.S. https://www.reuters.com/Article/us-southsudan-unrest-idUSKBN1JN1I9

[8] In 2019, the "peace to prosperity" plan, set to be presented by White House senior adviser Jared Kushner at an international conference in Bahrain, includes 179 infrastructure and business projects. The ambitious economic revival plan, the product of two years of work by Kushner and other aides, would take place only if a political solution to the region's long-running problems is reached. More than half of the $50 billion would be spent in the economically troubled Palestinian territories over 10 years while the rest would be split between Egypt, Lebanon and Jordan. See Spetalnick, M. (2019, June 22). Exclusive: White House's Kushner unveils economic portion of

Middle East peace plan. And also see Bakkour, S. (2022). The End of the Middle East Peace Process: The Failure of US Diplomacy. (n.p.): Taylor & Francis.

CONCLUSION

[1] See Booth, K., Wheeler, N. (2008). The security dilemma : fear, cooperation and trust in world politics. United Kingdom: Macmillan Education UK.

[2] We can gain insight, however, by studying various types of conflicts to understand better what states fight about. The following six types of international conflict: ethnic, religious, ideological, territorial, governmental, and economic.

[3] security dilemma, in political science, a situation in which actions taken by a state to increase its own security cause reactions from other states, which in turn lead to a decrease rather than an increase in the original state's security. balance of power, in international relations, the posture and policy of a nation or group of nations protecting itself against another nation or group of nations by matching its power against the power of the other side. See Booty, H. (2011, January 31). The Balance of Power: a Cause of War, a Condition of Peace, or Both? E-International Relations. https://www.e-ir.info.

[4] See Nations, U. (2018). Maintain International Peace and Security | United Nations. United Nations; United Nations. https://www.un.org/en/our-work/maintain-international-peace-and-security

[5] See North Korea Crisis. Global Conflict Tracker. https://www.cfr.org/global-conflict-tracker/conflict/north-korea-crisis.

[6] This point is made by Michael Edward Brown. (1996). The International Dimensions of Internal Conflict. MIT Press: 518.

INDEX

EYES OF A TYPHOON

FROM REGIONAL CONFLICTS TO GLPBAL SECURITY CRISIS

Author: JAYSON PARK

Jayson Park is a distinguished scholar and expert in the field of international relations, renowned for his comprehensive understanding of global affairs, diplomatic strategies, and policies. With a Ph.D. in International and Area Studies, his academic journey has been dedicated to unraveling the complexities of international dynamics and fostering insights into the ever-evolving world of diplomacy.

Currently serving as a senior fellow and director at the Strategic & Regional Relations Institute, Park continues to shape the discourse on international relations and provide invaluable guidance to policymakers and researchers alike. Drawing from his vast experience and profound expertise, he offers unique perspectives on critical issues that shape our global landscape. Park's dedication to his field is evident through his previous role as a research fellow at the East-West Center. There, he delved deep into the cultural dimensions of international relations, uncovering the intricate connections between societies and their impact on diplomatic interactions.

His contributions have been recognized and sought after by both academia and governmental institutions. Throughout his career, Park has been actively involved in a wide array of international relations affairs and research activities in the central government. This hands-on experience has enriched his knowledge and further solidified his expertise, allowing him to navigate complex geopolitical landscapes with insight and finesse.